"FUMBLE FOUR BARS IN"

Bill Worland

MINERVA PRESS
MONTREUX LONDON WASHINGTON

ISBN 1 85863 973 5

First Published 1996 by
MINERVA PRESS
195 Knightsbridge
London SW7 1RE

Printed in Great Britain by
Antony Rowe Ltd, Chippenham, Wiltshire

Impressions of America: Leadville.
Oscar Wilde.

Over the piano was printed a notice:

"Please do not shoot the pianist. He

is doing his best."

My contribution-

Musical quotes and anecdotes:
Fame, acclaim, rejection.
As the theme is imperfection,
Oscar Wilde is my selection.

.....and advice-

Piano plonkers in that dive,
Don't risk your life and limb.
Take my advice, and stay alive,
Don't fumble four bars in!

*From Bill, to Dee, Con amore
Con giocoso.*

April 1999

Impressions of America: Leadville.
Oscar Wilde.

Over the piano was printed a notice:

"Please do not shoot the pianist. He

is doing his best."

My contribution-

Musical quotes and anecdotes;
Fame, acclaim, rejection.
As the theme is imperfection,
Oscar Wilde is my selection.

.....and advice-

Piano plonkers in that dive,
Don't risk your life and limb.
Take my advice, and stay alive,
Don't fumble four bars in!

April 1999

"FUMBLE FOUR BARS IN"

CONTENTS

INDEX TO SONG LYRICS

PRINCIPAL LIGHT MUSIC COMPOSITIONS BY BILL WORLAND

Intermezzo '45
Shopping Spree
Pavilion Waltz
Rhapsodie Tristesse
Latin Lover
A Minor Affair
Light of Heart
Gaucho
Pepita
Paths of Peace
Bossa Romantica

Suite: Twenty Fingers, comprising:	1. Punchinello
(Four hands at the piano)	2. Going Dutch
	3. Sandman Serenade
Spanish Suite: Tres Señoritas, comprising:	1. Miguela
	2. Carlotta
	3. Conchita

Midnight in Manhattan
Brighton Belle
Neapolitan Suite: In The Shadow Of Vesuvius
It's Spring Again
Happy Hacienda

Petite Suite: comprising	1. Leeds Castle (descriptive)
	2. To Eleanor (Romance – Queen Eleanor of Castile and King Edward I)

Sombrero
Honky-Tonk Town

ACKNOWLEDGEMENTS

The Performing Rights Society Ltd
The Performing Rights Journal
The British Academy of Songwriters, Composers and Authors
The Light Music Society
Melody Maker
The Daily Mail
The Evening News
The Daily Telegraph
'The Power and the Glory'
  Words and music by Bill Worland and Ronnie Bridges, c. 1968.
  Reproduced by kind permission of B. Feldman & Co. Ltd, London,
  W1V 5TZ.
'Candlelight' (Groves)
  Copyright c.1970, Hye Fye Music Ltd, 8/9 Frith Street, London,
  W1V 5TZ. Permission granted. All Rights Reserved.
'Something to Sing About' (Groves)
  Copyright c.1972, Hye Fye Music Ltd, 8/9 Frith Street, London,
  W1V 5TZ. Permission granted. All Rights Reserved.
Campbell Connelly Music Co. Ltd.

All other lyrics contained in this book are the copyright
of the author.

CHAPTER ONE

AUTOBIOGRAPHIES

My original intention, yonks ago, was to compile a booklet of anecdotes gathered during lengthy activity as a pianist in the music world, but it soon became apparent that it would be like a painting without a frame: a stage devoid of a backdrop. So I decided to provide a background of personal thoughts, opinions and experiences, and to introduce the many personalities with whom I have been associated and their influence in a musical lifetime. Another facet is the involvement in the sphere of song-writing, composition and orchestration. When it came to the crunch, however, back in 1980, I heard an inner voice saying, 'Who do you think you are? Who wants to read about a nonentity?' The seed of doubt having been implanted, realism took over and, reluctantly, I abandoned the idea.

Then, browsing around the local bookshop several weeks later, I eventually reached a section which literally (pun not intended!) abounded with life stories. Admittedly, many related to well-known personalities, particularly those in showbiz. But it did not escape my notice that there were a few written by some who did not possess a household name. Indeed, some were by hitherto unknown writers who had since achieved some measure of recognition simply through publication of their first literary effort, an autobiography.

As if reading my thoughts, a young West Indian standing next to me exclaimed, "Ev'rybody's writing autobiographies, man!"

Seizing on his observation, I compiled some humorous verses in pseudo-calypso idiom. But the idea of writing a book stayed on ice. The verses referring to Margaret Powell, Eamonn Andrews and Ernie Wise have now lost their topicality, but I include them here not only because they are appropriate but to demonstrate how a chance remark, given a little thought and imagination, can be used creatively.

10

AUTOBIOGRAPHIES

Chorus: Ev'rybody's writing autobiographies, autobiographies,
What's in a name?
Ev'rybody's writing autobiographies,
Autobiographies, the name of the game.

Verse 1:   Some write it cool, some write it hot.
Some play the fool, some tell the lot.
There's room service, 'below stairs',
Making public private affairs.

REPEAT CHORUS

Verse 2:   You may never be surprised,
By you-know-who in disguise,
But you can make it, by yourself.
'This is your life' – up on the shelf.

REPEAT CHORUS

Verse 3:   Your grammar makes them choke a bit,
And people make a joke of it.
Like-Wise, make money, be a hit,
Funny, innit? Like wot you writ!

REPEAT CHORUS

Verse 4:   Paperback humanity, the glossy face of vanity,
To entertain, or simply bore,
Room for one more – all about me!

REPEAT CHORUS

Well, I hope there *is* room for one more because I am at long last taking the plunge. As I write, I can hear from my garden a pair of wood pigeons incessantly cooing the first three notes of 'Chicago, Chicago' occasionally interrupted by staccato chatter from neighbouring magpies and that most mournful of sounds, the cry of rooftop seagulls.

Yes, 'Chicago, Chicago, that toddl'ing town', copyright 1922. Toddl'ing? No, I don't think I would have quite reached that stage in 1922, yet appropriate I guess for someone who made his debut in life in June 1921. And now, nearly seventy-two years on, I *am* toddling again – the first cautious and uncertain steps in this egotistical literary endeavour. But better toddling than be reduced to doddering!

At various times, people from all walks of life have expressed their interest, either in terms of admiration or envy (or both!): 'It must be wonderful being endowed with such a gift. To communicate through playing music, writing words and music.' On the other hand, musicians, generally speaking, are not ones given to throwing around complimentary remarks. My soft tinkering on the keyboard in between numbers when on a gig would, at best, provoke an amused mutter: 'He's at it again. Still got writer's itch.'

I would be the last to deny the lasting spiritual and emotional mental benefit which springs from the use of creative talent of any kind. But the very first germ of an idea has to be nurtured and fed all along the way, helped to grow, given shape and form, to hopefully emerge as something worthwhile and satisfying to its maker. That which evolves may be still-born, mediocre, successful, yet short-lived; it may even become immortal. Whatever the outcome, every act of creativity is not without its birth-pangs. A good deal of mental anguish and tension is generated right from the start, relieved only by spasms of joy and elation as the work takes shape with perhaps a really original line or twist in the story – an inspired melodic line which suddenly comes from out of the blue.

One constantly strove after a professional attitude and standard, especially with respect to writing, for I was often competing with well-known and established writers. Nevertheless, I made my mark with published works, some recorded material and successful participation in a number of song festivals, including some on TV. Additionally, my works received many broadcasts, mainly in the sixties and seventies, with music used in TV ads, an Enid Blyton 'Famous Five' cassette and, more recently, in two British films. So generally I can express a great deal of satisfaction in my role as pianist, often on a freelance basis, but, where composing is concerned, it's a much tougher world. In terms of sheer effort and concentration, there are some items which have gained little or no compensation. Not necessarily in a financial sense – recognition of one's craft is just as important and rewarding. So composition has sometimes been a labour of love.

When, in 1966, I turned to writing seriously, I had no illusions or high-flying fancies that I would make the big-time scene overnight. There were the usual peaks and troughs of joy and despondency which all new writers experience, and one soon discovers that the striving for perfection endured in creative processes pales into insignificance when compared to the immensely difficult task of marketing the finished product single-handed, so often meeting with rejection.

The artist, the sculptor needs a gallery for exhibition purposes. The poet, novelist and playwright – a publisher, a theatre. Without such media the work, regardless of its merits, will never be seen or heard by those who matter in a world of massive exploitation, ruled largely by commercial interests. Similarly with music; a new score needs an orchestra to bring it to life. But the prohibitive cost of recording is well beyond the average composer's means, just as reading a simple manuscript is beyond the competence of many employed in today's recording and publishing circles. The demos rule, OK? So the destiny of a new-born work has a parallel with human entry into this world. Stars whose brilliance dims only when departing this life; others belong to a much lesser galaxy. Many destined to depart as they arrived – nonentities still. It is the immortal few who cast their glow for ever. So one attempts to write selectively, while aware that the music jungle is largely dominated by mediocre, here-today-gone-tomorrow tunes, refusing to give up the ghost. It matters not whether we stay in the longest running show, 'Life', for a few years, three score years and ten, or maybe more. What does matter is the performance. As far back as 1971 this philosophy found its expression in words and music. Cue for song –

LIFE

One: Do you give out, or just give in?
      Just play about, or play to win?
      Laugh at the strife in Life,
      The greatest show on earth.
      Will you try hard, or hardly try?

Give up the ghost, or make the most
Of every part in Life you have to play on earth.
Shakespeare wrote, and I quote: "All the world's a stage,"
Big revolving stage – never still.
Though today you may be a nonentity,
Tomorrow you could be top of the bill.
What matter if sometimes you flop,
If you've worked hard to reach the top,
You've played your part in life,
The greatest show on earth.

Two: There'll be those who applaud, those who criticise,
From it all you'll learn, if you're wise.
At the end, it's so sad, if you've had to spend
A lifetime finding out what Life's about.
Some have the luck to make the grade before the final act is
played
While others never seem to make the hit parade.
So you may take your exit still without success.
But then that's Life, I guess, yes, that Life, I guess.
Yes, that's life, that's life,
The greatest show on earth.

(Spoken, resignedly) That's life!

"Make him [the reader] laugh and he will think you are a trivial fellow, but bore him in the right way and your reputation is assured." W. Somerset Maugham.

If, in compromising, I fall between two stools, it will be due to keeping with that line in 'Autobiographies' I am endeavouring 'to entertain, not simply bore' And recalling the expressed opinions of other learned men:

Voltaire: "The only reward to be expected for the cultivation of literature is contempt if one fails, and hatred if one succeeds."[1]

Doctor Samuel Johnson: "No man but a blockhead ever wrote, except for money."[2]

---

[1] 1694–1778 Letter to Mlle Quinoult
[2] 1709–1784 Boswell's *Life of Johnson*, 5th April 1776

Logan Pearsall Smith: "A best-seller is the gilded tomb of a mediocre talent."[3]

It would appear that I just can't win!

---

[3] 1864–1946 *Afterthoughts*, 1931

CHAPTER TWO

THE GOOD OLD DAYS

A subject which can be boring to those who have not lived through such times, yet nostalgia plays a large part in all our lives. So often it is the music of the day which evokes memories – even a wistful yearning for the good old days to return. Of course they never do, and never will. Generally, such times are associated with carefree, youthful days and, inevitably, vary a great deal. Exceptionally, they may link with material success, wealth; an era of personal achievement; stability. Much depends on the individual's make-up. Frequently, popular music accurately mirrors the mood of any particular era, be it misery or happiness.

Noel Coward's 'Twentieth Century Blues' painted a pretty desperate and gloomy picture: "What is there to strive for, to live, to keep alive for?" Fortunately, there was the other side of the coin. The fast and hectic razzmatazz and boop-boop-ado tunes; the flappers; the bright young things as they were known, dancing the night away to the Black Bottom and the Charleston, attired in long swinging lengths of pearls and shapeless, short dresses, or shifts (the Twiggies of the Twenties, one might say), determined to keep alive – even if the pace killed them!

In retrospect, the succeeding decades have gone by with alarming speed until here, in the 1990s, Coward's words and music (sadly) must spell out a chilling and haunting reprise for many. There is little I can recollect from my earliest years compared with that since gleaned from the experience of older folk, parents, films, books and music. Until the autumn of 1929 I grew up (in the company of two younger brothers, Albert and Arthur) in that part of London Town in which I was born – the Old Kent Road, the inspiration for so many comical cockney songs. Long before I had left school I knew many of them by heart, thanks to my folk's 78 rpm collection of music hall recordings. When evacuated in November 1940 to Llandudno, my folks took with them a portable wind-up gramophone. At a later date they asked Uncle Henry (still in East Ham) to send the records. Sadly, Henry was the world's worst packer – a record breaker in the most literal sense, for not one record survived the wartime journey!

Outsiders would hardly rate it a desirable or salubrious area, but such shortcomings were more than adequately compensated for by the humour and camaraderie of its people – all the more apparent in hard times. And from what I have learned – make no mistake about it – they *were* hard times – bloody hard times. My father suffered the fate which befell so many other patriots: ex-servicemen in the immediate post-war years suffered long periods of soul-destroying unemployment. But my father eventually clinched a job in the civil service which was described as 'temporary' but turned out to be lifelong. Nevertheless, there were always three good meals a day thanks to my mother's housekeeping and culinary skills. The challenge of extreme adversity in fact made her more stoical than ever and served to bring out all that was best in her. I am thankful that so much of that admirable trait rubbed off on to me, for it proved invaluable. Without it, I feel sure that many future problems, especially long-term ones, would have floored me.

The really vivid memories of that eight year period are few. Uppermost in my mind are the countless occasions, in the wee small hours, when my parents would rush me round to Guy's Hospital, and the many out-patient visits that entailed waiting in a huge, draughty hall. It had a tiled floor and the hall would echo loudly to the footsteps of busy nursing staff, visitors and, most of all, children running riot despite the efforts of mothers to control them. The canteen which served hot sweet tea in heavy mugs; the smell of spicy buns, mingling with all those other antiseptic odours, characteristic of hospitals; the huge, thick, dark glass jars of cod liver oil and malt – an evil-smelling concoction which my brothers and I were constantly assured was 'good for us'!

The threatened mastoiditis never materialised; my health taking a decided turn for the better soon after beginning school and after a tonsils and adenoids operation – commonplace in those days.

It was at my first school – Pages Walk it was called – I absorbed a piece of music never to be forgotten, no doubt due to its repetition. There, in the centre of the great, high assembly hall, was the invention of the age – a gramophone, the type which for decades has been associated with the HMV label, except that in this instance there wasn't a dog listening attentively to the green-coloured horn, but a school monitor whose task it was the keep the spring wound up and thus maintain the required 78 rpm. Truly, until the coming of the radiogram, our music for years hence was mostly by Handel!

The tune was as corny as my pun – 'The Parade of the Tin Soldiers' – and to the tinny, blaring accompaniment we would shuffle, rather than march, to our respective classrooms each morning. There were no school-organised trips to foreign countries in those days. I have vague recollections of only one outing – a day at the then famous Crystal Palace.

Wireless, as it was popularly called then, made its debut in 1922, in the embryonic form of 2LO from Savoy Hill, as did the crystal set from which trailed a pair of earphones. (Cans, to you young 'uns!) Next came the year of the flickering silver screen and scratchy soundtrack – the talking motion picture – which, in spite of its tendency to frequently break down, was acclaimed by the public with the same degree of wonderment which greeted television about a decade or so later. I don't think I would have seen the very first movie; my memory is confined to two songs: 'I'm A Dreamer' and 'If I Had A Talking Picture Of You', from an early twenties musical. Even today, my wife insists that I pay more attention to the songs in the film or the background music than to the film itself. I have to confess that she is right. So often the composer seems to have reached an inspired passage in the score which has me anticipating more when, due to the dictates of the film, it suddenly stops, or is replaced by something more in keeping with the dialogue or action.

My dad's father died in 1929, at the ripe old age of eighty-eight. In our share of the estate was an upright piano – an enormously heavy instrument, its mechanism clad in walnut. Two features in the design and construction gave clues to its probable age. The front panels, top and bottom, had a delicate fretwork motif backed with a dark green, silk-like material. Very faded, it was later replaced by new, solid walnut panels – a perfect match with the existing woodwork, a tribute to the immaculate, caring workmanship of a bygone age. A reminder too, when recalling the ridiculously low cost, of the grossly inadequate rewards for skill and craftsmanship. Yes, they were the good old days all right... but not for everyone.

Whereas metal candlestick holders were the ubiquitous and useless accessory on the majority of pianos built in the twenties and thirties, our piano had, quite simply, a repeat of the fretwork motif in the form of small decorative shelves either side of the lid to the keyboard. That old piano was to be the focal point of many future parties when other pianists, much older and more advanced than I, decided that the shelves should be put to practical use – accommodating the beer! Another clue was the printed label on the action: 'This action was invented and patented by Robert Wornum in 1828.' Whatever its age, it had obviously been in the family for a long, long time.

Reference to Groves *Dictionary of Musicians* told me a little more. Robert Wornum (1780-1852) was the inventor of the 'diagonally and upright-strung low upright pianofortes'. The family business was well known in eighteenth- and nineteenth-century London.

The impact of the Wall Street Crash reverberated around the globe, but in our own little corner an inheritance, albeit modest, was to bring about pleasant and desirable changes. The family fortunes were on the up.

So it was soon to be farewell to the locality which had bred so many pubs with curious names: The Dun Cow, The World Turned Upside Down, The Bricklayers' Arms, and, without a shadow of doubt, that most famous landmark of London, The Elephant and Castle. Goodbye too Tower Bridge Road, lined either side on market days with stalls, the accumulating debris of boxes, cartons, waste paper and rotting fruit, all caught in the light of hissing paraffin lamps. There were no nine-to-five days for those traders. And a fond farewell, although temporarily, to two other pleasures. One was the sarsaparilla I would enjoy at a stall in Petticoat Lane on fine Sunday mornings; the other, my acquired taste, even at that early age, for jellied eels! I was hooked on the dish just as much as my mother, also a native of Bermondsey. I can still remember my parents' amusement when assuring me that it wasn't the end of the world – one could get jellied eels in other parts of London too.

The decade nearing its end foreshadowed the changes in style and presentation of popular dance music. Bigger bands with a more logical line-up – the banjo, with its high-ringing snap was being ousted by the Spanish guitar (often played by the band's vocalist or 'crooner') and the euphonium was replaced by the string bass. Many string players were turning to reed instruments – saxophones and clarinets – with the result that violins became relegated to a minor role, doubled occasionally by reed players, mostly effective in waltzes. Second fiddle, in fact, to the reed section. Nevertheless, the best of the twenties tunes were still very much in demand during the next decade, establishing themselves as standards which I would be learning and playing for many years to come.

My good old days, musically and otherwise, were about to begin.

THE GOOD OLD DAYS

Chorus: I love that do-wacka-do-wacka-do-wacka music
Like they played in the good old days,
The kind of beat that was all the craze,
Way back, way back in the good old days.
The tunes that people were hummin'
Banjos a-strummin' –
You can still hear them being played,
So many survive, still they're alive,
From yesterday's hit parade.
Give me a trumpet, a clarinet, trombone, sousaphone,
Piano and old banjo,
Beat the drums and away we'll go,
With all those toe-tapping tunes you know.
This sound is not just a has-been,
It's round on the jazz scene,
So while the band still plays,
You can lose your blues, dance out of your shoes,
Like they did in the good old days.

Interlude: Roaring Twenties, you're a legend now,
But no one has forgotten Charleston, Black Bottom.
Fashion changes, pop may come and go.
But an evergreen can steal the scene,
And even stop the show.
Repeat chorus… I love that etc.

Early on a beautiful Sunday morning in the summer of '29 I journeyed with my father to the pre-war terrace house he had bought in East Ham - situated north of the Thames and a short distance from the borders of Essex. As luck would have it, the open-top bus in which we were travelling was halted amidst other traffic at Tower Bridge. I don't suppose I was alone in my childish wonderment as I watched the vast span gradually come apart in the centre, the two parts eventually becoming almost vertically balanced at extreme ends of the bridge.

At Aldgate we were joined by Uncle Bill, his limp and dependence on a walking stick grim reminders of a limb lost in the ravages of World War One. I was to see much of him in the ensuing years and, as I grew older, came to appreciate more and more his love of life, easy-going manner and, most of all, marvelled at his agility in the face of such a severe physical handicap. But then I guess I have never been indifferent to those denied the right and joy of living a normal life because of a cruel disability, be it from birth or sustained later in life. And nothing but outright admiration and encouragement for the fighter, refusing to be laid low by his or her plight, sheer guts, determination and tenacity winning the day.

The object of the journey, as you may well have guessed, was to prepare for moving day, primarily to cut and lay floor coverings. No wall-to-wall carpets in those days but wall-to-wall cork linoleum. My father would often get very impatient when something went wrong with household tasks. He was far from being the expert do-it-yourselfer. But with some expertise from Uncle Bill, not to mention a generous supply of best ale from the local off-licence, all went well!

Although only a five minute stroll from the main road bus stop to the house, it truly seemed like another world. The Sunday stillness was broken only by church bells and occasional passing cars. And from the front parlours of neat little houses in plane tree-lined streets came the tinkling of pianos. 'Stumbling' was a syncopated tune of the times, and the title just about summed up the variety and style of performance. Childish endeavours, Zez Confrey addicts tying their fingers in knots, and the more ambitious wrestling with the popular classics! The air seemed cleaner, the sun brighter and, glimpsing taller trees of the local parks in the distance, all was right in my world. I was going to enjoy living here. Way back, I penned an instrumental piece of music in the Latin idiom and called it by a bilingual title, 'Happy Hacienda', a bright happy-sounding piece and I guess it was appropriate to our new abode. In any language the word 'home' should conjure up happy childhood days, growing up in an environment of love, laughter, security, compassion and understanding, with (inevitably) a few tears. Our new abode was not lacking in these basic ingredients, and with my interest in music destined to grow and deepen through constant encouragement over the years, it was, quite simply, a Happy Hacienda.

Here, I am unable to resist making a comparison. Time; the see-saw of fashion; the influx of immigrants has changed the countenance of the locality. So many houses have undergone face-lifts and been painted in an immense variety of colours. Some tasteful, many of them downright gaudy and dreadful. Neat hedges, brick walls and whole front gardens sacrificed to the demands made by the car for parking space – more often than not, a rusty old banger, also making its contribution to the ever-rising level of decibels and pollution to the area.

Nothing is forever I know, but it is sad to have to record that, on balance, the changes do not add up to progress.

CHAPTER THREE

DAISY

Shortly after the move in September '29 my parents decided to end my aimless tinkering on the keyboard of the newly-acquired piano, putting my apparent interest to the test by sending me to two half-hourly lessons per week. The cost was the princely sum of one shilling and sixpence (seven and a half pence to the decimal doters).

I went along for my introductory lesson straight from school. The house was much larger than ours, being the first in an adjoining road, barely one minute away. Huge bay windows with a southerly aspect overlooked a fairly large front garden in which grew the fashionable evergreen hedge, its colour almost a match for the green-painted iron- and woodwork of the house. Cream paint covered the stone pillars and sills whilst the front door, with the then popular varnished grain, was covered with a striped rail-hung canopy to protect against blistering in the sun. On the wall between front door and bay window, the inscription on a highly polished brass plate indicated that my tutor-to-be was a maiden lady – a Miss M.D. Dixon who had gained qualifications such as LRAM, ARCM, and was a gold and silver medallist to boot.

To the left of the square hall was a long corridor with a red-tiled floor running the length of the house, terminating at doors leading to the rear garden. Centre of the hall was a steep flight of stairs and, standing impassively on the other side, was the main feature – a solid, beautiful old grandfather clock, its steady unhurried mechanism reminiscent of more leisurely, graceful days. 'Take your time, take your time' seemed to be its repetitive message. Once inside, my somewhat nervous and awestruck feelings vanished. I was soon at ease, chatting to a charming lady in her late forties or perhaps early fifties, her fair complexion accentuating the vivid blueness of her eyes twinkling behind rimless pince-nez spectacles.

The front parlour – about three times the size of ours, despite containing some bulky Victorian furniture – still conveyed an air of spaciousness, probably due to the delicate, pale blue distempered walls and a high, elaborate, corniced white ceiling. I later learned that Daisy – as she was popularly known – lived there with her elderly mother, to whom I was introduced as she entered carrying a tray. She served us with tea and Madeira cake. Apparently, this was the custom when pupils had to sometimes attend straight from school, as I had done that day – a thoughtful custom indeed.

The preliminaries over, Daisy produced several brand-new books from a drawer in the capacious sideboard. I exchanged my comfortable seat on the chaise longue for a much harder and solid one – the music stool. There were four books in all, comprising my introduction to what was to be a happy and lifelong association with music. The initial lesson was abruptly interrupted by the sudden appearance of a huge black cat. With the graceful agility of the feline species, it leapt from a high-backed chair to the top of the piano, threaded its way through the various trinkets and photographs, miraculously leaving them intact and landed on my lap to the accompaniment of loud discord as its back legs hit the keyboard.

"There's a lucky omen!" exclaimed Daisy. "She doesn't make a fuss of everyone like that!"

From subsequent visits however, it became evident that Daisy's cat roamed at will, its favourite spot being the large, square, cloth-covered table in the centre of the room which, in effect, was Daisy's 'office'.

Her handwriting was most unusual: individualistic in style, rarely joined, upright printed characters throughout. She used a black fountain pen, constantly dipping it in and out of a big inkpot. Whether the ink chamber had broken or whether it was just a habit, I never did find out. Cast as she was in the strict Victorian mould, I am certain that much of today's world would be abhorrent and totally unacceptable to her. Not that a sense of humour was lacking; nor was she a musical snob, dismissing anything other than classical music as rubbish. "A good teacher is always learning," she would declare, and the foundation of her teaching methods was, to quote her own words: "It's fun to learn." That's how it always seemed to me, but perhaps I am biased as there is a world of difference between *having* to play and *wanting* to play.

To illustrate such a statement, I have to point out that it was an era in which the piano took pride of place in the home. There were, of course, always those people who bought an instrument which was hardly ever played – often non-musical families. Music was unimportant to them; it was merely an exercise in keeping up with the

Joneses! Much worse than that in my view was the oft-encountered parental obsession, forcing thousands of unwilling and unfortunate children, some of whom they believed to be child prodigies, to take piano lessons. Later in life, I met many who were still resentful about it, not to mention others who, obviously having a fair degree of feeling for music, had made some progress only to give up completely upon leaving school. The common lament was: "I wish I'd kept it up."

Daisy was a native of Tyneside, but her speech belied the fact save for an occasional word such as 'film' which lapsed into the Geordie 'fillum'. Her father had been a very skilled man in the ship-building world and she had travelled abroad with him sometimes. An essential part of his job was to sail with a new vessel when it was handed over to foreign buyers to undergo its trials. Nevertheless, there was a quaint, but charming naivety in her make-up where more material and mundane matters were concerned, perhaps due in part to her heavy involvement with music, the working week being from Tuesday until Saturday. On Monday evenings she would treat herself to a visit to a local cinema accompanied by a friend or a neighbour.

About six months later my parents received a letter, penned in Daisy's neat, printed style, waxing enthusiastic about my progress.

Until I began piano lessons I was known by everyone – relatives and friends alike – as 'Bill' and that suited me, just as it still does today. But Daisy proved to be the exception, insisting on 'Billy' right from the start. I didn't like it, but I never protested – just a tacit acceptance – so it stuck, as my parents saw from the letter. Another year rolled by – a year in which I had become increasingly interested in the school orchestra. It was not an orchestra in the accepted sense, essential sections like brass, woodwind and percussion being absent. It consisted entirely of some twenty violins, urged along by the German-born music master (who had a filthy temper!) at the piano. It did not even possess the lower-pitched strings such as violas, cellos and basses. There were no peripatetic teachers as of today, with schools providing tuition, instruments and great opportunities for the child of musical promise, and tours abroad, plus the chance even for those not so gifted to participate in some real music-making. Generally, our music lessons were confined to learning to sing in unison by the tonic sol-fa method (doh, ray, me, etc.,) and that was that.

So, albeit violins only, I suppose it was no mean feat for a junior elementary school to possess such a luxury. The music master also did group teaching privately at home. This was brought to the attention of parents in a typed promotional letter given to pupils to take home. I rushed out of school that day, brimming with enthusiasm. My mother's response, "We'll have to see what your father thinks about it. I think you've more than enough to get on with, just learning piano," left me rather crestfallen. The letter was folded and placed behind the chiming clock on the sitting room mantelshelf. (Somehow, *every* letter and bill seemed to find a home there!)

My father agreed with my mother's sentiments and it was many years later before I realised that although they regretted having to disappoint me, there was another reason – a financial one. They just couldn't afford it. I recall that I rid myself of disappointment and frustration that evening by engaging in the rough and tumble of a game of football in a nearby park. Next to music I had a keen interest in most sporting activities – mainly football and cricket, never being exceptionally good at either, my rating always in the reserves. But a valuable safety valve, I suppose, although I was then too young to appreciate it.

Returning to music: I guess there will always be musicians who become attracted to another instrument just as there are comedians who want to play Shakespeare and straight actors who would like to have a crack at comedy. Even today, the yen for the violin, the most noble yet probably the most difficult of instruments to master, often comes surging back when I hear the huge string sections of today's orchestras, be it symphonic or a special arrangement of popular music. To my ears it is a thrilling and enthralling sound. The fiddle, as a doubling instrument, would also have given me an opportunity to join string sections of local orchestras. Plenty of room for fiddle players, of course, whereas a piano is employed only when a soloist is engaged to play the main work at a concert, such as a well-known concerto.

CHAPTER FOUR

LOVE AND MARRIAGE

The vast number of marriages which survive 'until death us do part' despite considerable and often challenging differences in personalities must surely be a tribute to human tolerance and understanding. Or is it just human endurance?

My mother had no illusions about life. She rarely looked beyond the basic necessities and anything over and above was gratefully accepted as a bonus. The expression, in troubled times, "So long as you can keep a roof over your head and some grub inside you, mate, you've got to be grateful," put her philosophy in a nutshell. One of the younger members of a family of ten and with a self-confessed dislike of learning the three Rs (which was about all that was taught in her childhood days,) she would have us in stitches with her numerous comical mispronunciations: "evacuated milk"; "condemnation on the windows"; buying "Rembrandts" at the market, and reference to her favourite singing group, the "Inkpots", are some that spring to mind with the least prompting.

But what she lacked educationally she made up for in so many other ways. Not least was her instinctive nose for a bargain, and a built-in radar as protection against those who sought to take advantage of her educational shortcomings. As Mr Irving Berlin wrote in that gorgeous down-to-earth line: 'He signs his cheques with exes, but they cash them just the same.'

Social occasions were few while we were growing up, and she was at her happiest devoting her time unstintingly to our upbringing and extending hospitality to friends and visitors alike. Nothing was ever too much trouble, hard work was the cure for all ills. A house kept as clean as a whistle – another great source of contentment. If you are thinking it was a home where one dared not move a cushion out of place, leave things lying around or put one's feet up at the table, then how wrong you are! It was meant to be lived in, and with kids always bringing in friends, there was inevitably, in such a small dwelling, an aftermath of debris. No moaning or griping about it – simply a swift restoration by Mum in next to no time at all. Extremely conscientious workers, I have perceived, often get put upon. No wonder my mother would sometimes fall asleep beside the fire in the evening, utterly exhausted, having cut herself into a dozen parts as if there were to be no tomorrow. That same streak in her would produce a great deal of worry when not able to pay bills on the due date, which was often the case during one period of nearly two years when, with the best will in the world, it was impossible to balance the family budget. When discussing, even arguing about, such matters, my father would say, in sharp contrast, "What are you worrying about? We won't be the only ones late in paying up." And referring to whoever the bill was from, he usually added, "They've got more money than us – they can afford to wait."

He lived for the day. Tomorrow would take care of itself. He loved parties, gregarious social occasions, pomp and pageantry. Life was to be enjoyed; the extrovert, with an expansive view of the world and generous to a fault, money burning a hole in his pocket often getting him in a tight corner. Whereas a prolonged restrictive money situation meant a worrying time for my mother, it was no more than an unhappy phase for my father. Money was made round to go round, to circulate. And with his positive way of thinking, always optimistic, bad times couldn't last for ever. Like Mr Micawber, his philosophy was that something would turn up somewhere, somehow to save the day.

As usual, it did. Eventually, in the shape of a transfer from the Ministry of Labour to the Inland Revenue on a permanent basis with a resultant pay increase.

It was in 1933 when we were all looking forward eagerly to two weeks holiday by the sea – the first long break the family could afford since moving house. But it was not to be. My father became very ill and, as his condition rapidly deteriorated, I could not help overhearing the anxious conversations between my mother and neighbours who were offering help and sympathy. There was one person in particular who gloomily cast doubts on his chances of survival. Drawing attention to the fact that my father was some nineteen years my mother's senior, she shook her head knowingly and muttered darkly, "Fifty-six is a funny age." I was old enough to know that the adjective was commonly misused in situations far removed from comedy. (At least today, there is a bit more definition in 'Funny, ha ha' and 'Funny peculiar'.)

Dad languished all through a hot summer and I was afraid that he would die, try as I might to push the terrible thought from my mind. Mother soldiered on in her stolid fashion, throughout a testing and exhausting period, not helped, I would imagine, by the coincidence of the school holidays. Mercifully, a turning point was reached in the early autumn and my father slowly recovered his strength. But the illness had taken its toll, reducing his normally well-built and rotund stature considerably.

After a period of convalescence, he returned to work, and in fact continued in his job until aged seventy-five. I am convinced that having something to do, being usefully employed and maintaining an interest in many things contributed greatly to his reaching the ripe old age of eighty-two before departing this life.

The loss of earnings for such a long time left its mark too. Another adverse period, destined to last until I left school and took up employment, more than two years later, was just beginning.

CHAPTER FIVE

...GIVE ME YOUR ANSWER, DO

At one critical stage, I thought my music studies would come to an abrupt end. It had become increasingly difficult to pay for lessons, let alone the new music books required if I was to maintain a satisfactory rate of progress. Mere mention of such a possibility produced a horrified "Good gracious, no!" from Daisy. "It would be a crime to give up now."

Then in a much calmer voice, removing and polishing her spectacles (as she so often did when mulling over a problem) she would add, "I quite understand. Tell your people to pay me as and when they can."

It was not long after that kindly reprieve that I began earning some spare cash by assisting our roundsman with his bread deliveries. Saturdays were the hardest – eight-thirty until about five-thirty, with a break for lunch, even later if we ran out of bread and I had to go back to the bakery and cycle back with a few more loaves to finish off deliveries. I also did some weekdays during school holidays, these being much easier, with little or no monies to collect. No matter what time of day it was, the tantalising aroma of newly-baked bread hung around the perpetually warm bakehouse and, returning there on dark evenings, one could hear the non-stop chirruping of crickets long before entering.

I was soon to be given my own leather sling bag with pockets for copper and silver and a wallet for notes. Being responsible for so much money and giving correct change was, I suppose, somewhat risky, though the thought never crossed my mind at that time. Fortunately, I had a good head for figures, especially mental arithmetic, but I was also being provided with early lessons in salesmanship, human relations and the capable handling of other people's money. Les, the roundsman, had a basic wage, which wasn't much to write home about, enhanced only by commission earned on sales of flour, tea and a huge variety of cakes and other confectionery. True, I didn't share the commission, but I was more than satisfied with my rate of pay, often more than doubled by the addition of regular tips from many generous customers. Characteristically, my mother declined to take any part of such monies, being content with a treat of sweets, chocolates or flowers. But the debt for lessons and books, thanks to bread – as we would say in today's slang – was rapidly cleared.

I was well into my last school year when, without any warning, there came an attempt by local authorities to stop part-time employment of school children. An official was ushered into our classroom by the headmaster who sternly requested, "Stand up any boy here who is engaged in part-time work of any kind."

Sensing the implication behind the request, I sat tight. A couple of classmates looked in my direction whispering, "Go on! You do a baker's round!"

Staring steadfastly ahead, I did my best to ignore their urging, hoping the kerfuffle they'd started would go unnoticed. Fortunately, attention was quickly diverted elsewhere as two boys shuffled rather unwillingly to their feet and had their names and addresses taken. That was the end of their pocket money.

I told my folks of the incident in case there were any repercussions from not coming clean. Surprisingly, they were more amused than worried. Les shared their amusement and added admiringly, "Blimey! You were quick on the uptake!"

Okay, so as kids we were, in some cases, perhaps, being unfairly exploited. But I don't think I came into that category. I had no intention of giving up something which I thoroughly enjoyed doing with subsequent loss of income – money which I was putting to good use – earned through my own enterprise. Why should I give it up? And fifty-eight years on, you can call me mercenary if you wish. I prefer to describe such a situation as the belief in the encouragement of individual initiative, enterprise and resourcefulness.

Having got out of the red, I was shortly afterwards presented with two large parcels of music, which I received upon arriving home from school one afternoon. My mother had purchased them from a door-to-door salesman for just sixpence each. (Shades of the TV serial, *Pennies From Heaven*!) They comprised a mixture of selections and albums, mostly from the Twenties, and some pre-war ballads. Publishers offered these bumper bundles apparently in an effort to dispose of items – some were bestsellers in their heyday, others just flops from the word go. I took the music along with me hoping to gain Daisy's interest, although I was anything but optimistic. For nearly six years I had received formal and legitimate classical training, far removed, as I thought, from popular dance music and 'syncopation', as it was then described.

Daisy looked through some of the pieces, then up at me, her eyebrows arched in surprise, and remarked, "But this is jazz – and dance music. Do you *really* want to learn how to play it?"

My doubts about getting her assent had made me a little apprehensive. All I could do was to muster a nod of the head, and a meek, "Yes, please."

Off came the specs for the polishing ritual and, having pondered for a few moments, Daisy, to my delight, came up with an acceptable proposition. "This is what we'll do. I'll help you as far as I can and see how you get on. But there must be no neglect of the classics."

I was more than happy to go along with the deal. Big-headed though it may sound, I took to syncopation like a duck to water. Progress was indeed rapid and, thanks again to 'bread', I began buying my own piano copies of currently popular songs, then usually about sixpence each, but sometimes twice that much for a big hit or a piano album.

It is perhaps worth mentioning here that the commercial piano copy for sale to the public was kept as simple as possible, bearing in mind the obvious limitations of the many rather than the few. But with banjo/ukulele chords and fingering and words included, all within a specially designed and often coloured cover, it was pretty good value. Sheet music today is even more simply arranged. Frankly, much of it is hardly worth printing because so many pop songs are useless for piano only without supporting instrumentation, having been written initially with the modern pop group sound in mind, which, with its vast range of sophisticated sounds and gimmicks, can turn an extremely trite and banal song into a top-selling record.

Returning to the thirties, however, I had quickly reached the stage where I could 'fill'; that is greatly elaborate and extemporise the average copy, mainly because I listened intently to radio programmes. I must admit to experiencing some embarrassment (but inwardly a secret pleasure) on numerous occasions when Daisy would enthuse and bubble after listening to my interpretation of each new number. She expressed surprise and pleasure that my classics had not suffered one bit from my leaning toward 'modern' music – as she put it.

New music was also coming in from another source. My Dad's niece, Millie, a nurse at a Greenwich hospital, frequently visited us, sometimes staying over at weekends. She was a well-built, good-looking woman of thirty-odd years, her most striking feature being a crown of beautiful auburn hair. Millie and her two surviving sisters had sadly lost both parents at an early age. (Her father was the youngest of my Dad's three brothers) She was happy to be within easy travelling distance of close relatives and her appreciation of hospitality was more than adequately expressed in the small gifts she would bring on each and every visit. For me, it was always music. She would hardly get inside the living room before she handed me the latest bundle, saying, "Come on, let's hear what you can do with these."

Dad's father was a hard-headed businessman from Cambridgeshire. His Suffolk-born mother was quite the opposite, being meek and sweet-mannered. Through the ownership of quite a few properties – a retail shop, and a timber wharf by the old Iron Bridge in Canning Town – all four sons had worked spasmodically for him, the years being peppered with disagreements and reconciliations. Family history seemed to indicate a large measure of influence and affluence around the turn of the century. One relative, whose full-size portrait hung over the staircase in the Town Hall, was twice mayor of ~~Stratford~~ West Ham, and there is an insignificant little turning in the borough called Worland Road. The foundation stone at the Public Hall, Canning Town, bears his name, and the year, if I recall correctly, was 1892. More recently there is a modern-day centre named The Worland Centre, built in Vicarage Lane, Stratford.

In the early fifties I received a letter from a Mrs Thomas residing in Iowa, USA, whose maiden name was Worland. She had tracked me down through the London telephone directory, after her son looked up the name when travelling home on leave from the USAAF in Germany. She had traced family roots back to seventeen-hundred and something and, being Catholic, there was some belief that they were associated with the historical Pilgrim Fathers. I kept in touch for a while, but just hadn't the time to do any serious investigation into the family's origins. But just by coincidence I did find a link back to the seventeenth century – a stone which marks the site of The Magpie Inn, Magpie Hill, at Ware in Hertfordshire, landlord, Henry Worland...

Returning to my grandfather however... There was a gentler side to his character revealed to me during those times when families tend to reminisce. It was his practical sympathy and generosity which ensured that the future would not be bleak for Millie and her sisters. His gifts had not been wasted or abused. Millie was well-spoken, well-educated, radiating a quiet, but attractive charisma. Again, I have to note the stark contrast to my mother's rough-and-ready Cockney upbringing, and yet they got on famously. A couple of years later my favourite cousin had a boyfriend in tow, Jim, and, shortly before the war, married him. Oh, lucky Jim!

Time to leave school; but not time to leave music behind. On the contrary, my interest continued to broaden. I bought ragtime piano solos, albums of tunes destined to become 'standards', selections from musical comedy and films, the *Billy Mayerl School of Syncopation* plus, of course, the composer's piano solos.

They were incomparable to the average pop song, which one could play competently at sight. They posed a challenge, even to the advanced pianist, and a fair amount of practice and concentration was needed to effect a creditable performance. I now attended for my lesson only once a week and, in order to give sufficient coverage to both classics and dance music, it was arranged that I would be the last pupil of the day so that the normal one hour was often exceeded – sometimes doubled. Extra payment, however, would not be accepted. Daisy was pleased that I had continued after leaving school. How could anyone fail to respond to such generosity and encouragement?

It was around this time that I raised the likelihood of taking examinations.

"I would only recommend such a course if you were seriously considering a career of teaching, or that of a soloist," was Daisy's reply.

The former had never appealed to me, confirmed in the ensuing years when I firmly declined many requests to teach. Apart from my lack of enthusiasm, I always had more than enough on my plate. As for becoming a soloist...

The musician who can commit to memory, without a fault, a lengthy concerto, sonata or similar work in which he or she must be at one with the accompanying orchestra is indeed a gifted and talented person for whom my admiration has no bounds. I did not possess the powers of concentration and dedication to ever attain such perfection.

34

As if reading my mind, Daisy continued, "You should soon be able to play quite competently dance music, or light music together with other instruments. Auditions determine one's ability, therefore all the qualifications in the world don't matter. You are either good enough or not good enough."

The wisdom of her statement, coupled with the awareness of the kind of music with which I had instinctive rapport, became steadily apparent as the years rolled on. And many, many more years rolled on – into the 1980s – before I came across further confirmation of Daisy's statement.

Brilliant concert pianist, Denis Matthews, in his book, *In Pursuit of Music*, wrote that, contrary to popular belief, having LRAM, ARCM after one's name was no guarantee of rosy prospects. They might have some value as status symbols for potential teachers, but cut very little ice in the sphere of performance. The book also contains an amusing but acutely perceptive remark made by his young daughter. Having been away for a week, Denis returned at breakfast time, shut himself in the music room and was still practising the Brahms's B flat concerto when it was his daughter's bedtime. Witnessing this, she vowed, "If ever I do music when I grow up, I'm going to do it for FUN!"

And *I* was finding it great fun. My forte, fast developing through a love of variety in music, was versatility – an important basic requirement for the freelance musician. And Daisy had given me the right answer. I didn't need a carriage, a bicycle made for two. Simply wings of song.

CHAPTER SIX

CARRY ON BUSKING!

It was around this time that I began cultivating the art of busking, adding a new dimension to my studies, in a skill which is essential to the building of one's repertoire. This entailed picking up tunes from the past. Tunes of which I had never seen the printed copy, but knew well enough to make an attempt at learning them. To the general public, playing without music is popularly known as 'playing by ear'. But it goes much deeper than that. The trained musician is using his knowledge of harmony, melodic progression and chord sequences.

And to the layman, the term 'busker' probably relates only to the street musician, but it has been used for countless years in the profession. No doubt it stemmed from those distant days when the theatre-going public was entertained by street buskers whilst queueing for the next performance, particularly in the West End. When playing for dancing, it was common practice for example for the band to have the music up for, say, two current quicksteps. Should the MC decide that the dance was going well enough to continue with a third, at short notice, you don't lose your audience of dancers by fiddling around setting up more music. The leader, usually the pianist, would bang out a four bar introduction to a well-known standard, at the same time telling the nearest soloist the title, or sometimes perhaps just the key.

A large proportion of the commercial orchestrations in those days emanated from the giant publishing company Chappells, and were affectionately known as the 'Lallys'. Jimmy Lally was the top staff arranger who must have turned out a fantastic number of arrangements until his retirement some years after the war. Then the new climate of pop music spelt the end for hundreds of dance bands and orchestras, professional and semi-pro alike and the market for the printed commercial arrangement died too.

I became actively involved in such music a few years later while working in the business, and I learned to appreciate the wonderful scope of the commercial, with so many cued-in parts, enabling it to be used by any combination from a duo to a twelve piece (or in the case of full orchestra twenty-odd parts). Whenever busking is mentioned, I am reminded of my wartime association with a Leeds musician.

There was an expression he always used when some idiot (usually the worse for drink) wanted to sing some obscure (or obscene!) ditty and hadn't got a clue as to the tune or the key, even sometimes being tone-deaf. Also, when we got a request for a number which none of us knew terribly well, but would do our best to oblige, referring to the introduction, he would turn to me and say with a sickly grin, "Fumble four bars in, kid!"

I cannot leave the subject of busking without correcting the misconception that drummers do nothing else but busk. They have been the butt of a host of jibes and jokes in the profession, sometimes unkind and disparaging. A band leader asked to supply a five-piece band replied, "I can send you four musicians and a drummer!" Perhaps he nursed a personal hatred of skin beaters. Another anecdote, based on fact, presents the other side of the coin. A fellow pianist was with a band busking a string of choruses – all different tunes – and all went well until they suddenly *segued* into a tune unfamiliar to my friend. To get some idea of the harmonies, he called out to the drummer-leader, "What are the chords?"

"Never mind the chords," he snapped, "play the bloody rhythm!"

Surely, *the* drummer story, *par excellence*. To be candid and fair, I have known and played alongside many drummers whose music-reading capacity was poor, but they were good drummers, even if limited to gigs for dancing mostly with small outfits. Obviously, where light music is concerned, such as special orchestrations or the band required to back cabaret acts, one would naturally book a musically literate drummer. Possibly because people's vision and thinking is limited to kit drums in a dance band or pop group, they tend to completely overlook the genuine percussionist's range of gear, embracing instruments classed as tuned percussion-vibes, tympani, xylophones, celestes, glockenspiels and so on.

My frequent travels from coast to town, inevitably using the Underground service for at least part of the way, was the catalyst for a song about London's buskers in the subways, early in the seventies. Some of them could hardly be classed as musical, but I can recall the more talented few, including a flautist, and a fiddle player treating us to Mozart melodies. But even busking has become respectable – how about that talented twosome, the Cambridge Buskers? It is also international. In Bad Ischll, Austria, this year, I photographed a group of Chilean and Colombian buskers as I listened, fascinated by their Latin rhythms and haunting panpipes. Imagine my great surprise (and pleasure) on hearing and seeing them again some two months later in Canterbury.

The GLC did its damnedest to get rid of the buskers, but they proved to be as immovable as the Rock of Gibraltar. There are still some around. The GLC isn't.

UNDERGROUND MOVEMENT

Chorus: Underground movement, Underground movement,
This way to the trains, to melodic refrains,
London's on the move.
Underground movement, Underground movement,
A shame, GLC, you ain't in the same key,
Can't get in the groove.
Down in the subway, push-and-shove way,
Morning, evening, matinee.
We play the West End, feather-our-nest end,
See how they pay to get carried away:
By the sound of the music,
'Cos they've found an improvement
Since the Underground movement
Got stuck in the Tube.

Bridge: Urban, suburban, bowler and turban,
Cloth cap, sari, faded jeans.
Multi-coloured waves of commuters,
Slaves to computers – jaded machines.
Like us, loathe us, they feed and clothe us,
And there's one thing that's for sure,
Day in day out, way in, way out,
Ev'ryone comes back for more:

Repeat chorus as above.

CHAPTER SEVEN

'IF YOU CAN PLAY PIANO...'

I made some new contacts by picking up a few gigs with other freelance musicians also in their teens, but it seemed that the new year had ushered in a flat, uninteresting phase so I spent quite a lot of time concentrating on my accordion playing. I had purchased a brand-new instrument the previous year, on the 'never-never'. Contrary to that popular reference to hire-purchase, I had just made the final payment. It was now mine, all mine.

Accordions, and indeed accordion bands, reached a peak of great popularity in the mid- to late thirties, many acts using the Continental instrument – button-type right-hand keyboard instead of the familiar black-and-white piano keys.   It became the obvious 'doubling' instrument for pianists, but on most gigs it was used sparingly, principally in tango and rumba tunes. However, it could prove to be a life-saver when, arriving at a totally strange venue, it was impossible for other instruments to get in tune with an out-of-tune piano. Fortunately, such occasions were very few. Today, of course, such problems don't arise, thanks to the electronic keyboard.

'If you can play piano, you can play anything' – so runs the old saw. Not entirely true of course but, certainly, the piano is a firm foundation, putting one streets ahead when it comes to learning other instruments, especially if they are also of the keyboard family. When I had mastered a couple of numbers, one of them, I recall, was 'Temptation Rag', I took the accordion along to music lessons. I had taught myself, since the only strange feature to me were the small buttons operated with the left hand, which produced either a single note (bass) or an entire chord. Daisy was interested and pleased, and made a prophetic remark to the effect that I would soon return to my first love the piano, once the novelty wore off. It was a peculiar situation in which pupil temporarily became teacher, as I explained the pattern and fingering of the bass buttons and the way in which couplers produced a variety of tone colours, an early forerunner of electronics.

To draw a parallel, we move on to the mid-seventies when I used an electric piano exclusively during a long summer season. Exclusively only because of short-sighted criminal neglect by the management (mis-management would be more accurate) of a once-proud and beautiful German-built grand. The cost of restoration to former glory would run into hundreds of pounds, yet regular tuning and care would have kept it in trim for a fraction of the cost.

The modern musician and arranger must make full use of anything new and, in the small outfit, electric piano was ideal to fill and sustain – for example, in a slow number, as a backing to a vocal, and was occasionally effective in adding tone colour. So I saw it more as a doubling instrument, to be used sparingly. The extreme ends of its range produced sounds nothing like conventional piano. And it was certainly no match for the crisp, clean rhythmic beat, percussion-wise, of a piano in faster numbers.

Significant, that following years of constant use of electronic keyboard and organs, we saw a shift to conventional piano by many pop singers and groups in the late seventies. The prime reason, I would guess, analogous to acoustic guitar versus its electric counterpart, is the more sympathetic response which can be coaxed from the former. Just like a violin; when in the hands of a capable artist it is controlled by the performer and his technique rather than simulated through the medium of electronics. But the relentless march of technology inevitably brought about an electronic keyboard which I found more acceptable – one which is 'touch responsive'. Prior to this advance, all I had ever learned about touch had to go out of the window – it was like playing a chunk of wood! And if you think that touch isn't important to a pianist, then let me put you right; there are books galore on the subject! Although I use electronics in the recording studios, I am still biased in favour of 'steam piano' and toward natural music, not electronics. "It'll never die out" (meaning the piano) was the oft-expressed opinion of my parents and those of their generation. A cliché? Yes, and sneer if you must, but so many age-old expressions have become clichés simply because they are as true today as they were when first uttered.

The 'Big Brother' box, records, cassettes and CDs have since taken over for those who have succumbed to the press-button age, as opposed to the more individualistic beings preferring sometimes to make their own music. Dare I venture to say 'home-made' rather

than 'ohm-made'? And if that isn't enough, you will have to put up
with my odd ode to sum up my 'steam piano' bias.

> I'm reading 'dots' – not mega watts,
> Don't need cathode assistance.
> No leads, no reeds, just things like strings –
> Response without resistance.
> I orchestrate, not oscillate,
> Through dominant and tonic.
> No draw-bars out, but four bars in,
> (Not fumbled!)
> And score – sans electronics.

Les Brown had vacancies for pupils. He was a professional pianist
who also played the accordion and organ and worked in many of the
West End nightclubs, plus doing the occasional broadcast, and had
some connection with Charlie Kunz and the Casani Club. But the
vacancies were limited to those who could prove that they had already
made substantial headway – advanced, in other words. Les resided
locally, in a large double-fronted house pleasantly situated close to
Plashet Park and the library. I had expected to meet an elderly man
but, to my surprise, he was about thirty-five, and an amiable, talkative
person.

We went into a rectangular-shaped room to the left of the hall. It
was sparsely furnished, dominated by a rosewood boudoir piano near
the bay window. In a few sentences, I gave Les the sum total of my
activities, emphasising the immediate need to learn more about dance
band work and cabaret accompaniment.

He made a gesture toward the piano.

"Play me something – anything you like."

I chose the first tune that came into my head. On a par with
'Alone' (which figures later in the story), it was another milestone in a
musical sojourn. Little wonder therefore that 'The Night Is Young
And You're So Beautiful' became indelibly imprinted in my memory.

"Very good," commented Les. "But all those flowery
embellishments and fancy arpeggios aren't conducive to good dance
band playing. Piano is essentially part of the rhythm section –
percussive. Keep to the centre of the keyboard as much as possible."

That advice was free. Les accepted me as a pupil and a date for the first lesson was fixed. It suddenly occurred to me that, in my intense desire to gain acceptance, the cost of tuition had been furthest from my mind. The fee turned out to be three shillings and sixpence or I could book six in advance for one guinea. The latter booked, having decided it would be well worth it, I took smug pleasure at being able to pay in advance! A guinea? A mere bagatelle! Two well-paid gigs would take care of that.

Memorable at this point are the only two gigs I did with a three-piece band at the Working Men's Club in the Barking Road. Memorable because of the star potential of one Vera Welch who lived a few minutes away in Ladysmith Avenue. It must have been shortly before she began singing professionally with the famous Ambrose Orchestra. Dame Vera Lynn, of course, East Ham's own Sweetheart of the Forces. I next saw her in 1946 when she called at the music publishers' office where I was working.

It was also the time when I borrowed a great deal of music from the public library, to help polish-up my sight-reading. I also borrowed the full piano solo of Gershwin's 'Rhapsody in Blue' from Les Brown, I devoted many hours, grappling with the more difficult parts. I was fortunate in that my cousin Grace worked in the library – another music-lover, especially of ballet music – so there was no limit to the amount of music I could borrow.

I told Daisy as tactfully as possible about the extra lessons from Les, for I had no wish to hurt the feelings of someone who had unstintingly helped me tremendously for more than eight years. I need not have worried about her reaction. She accepted it calmly and gracefully after having listened to my reasons for adopting such a course.

She appreciated my desire to move on, and said, "Quite frankly, there is little more I can teach you about current trends in modern music."

The ritual of removing spectacles and polishing already spick and span lenses followed, as she continued, "I'm so glad you still have an interest in the classics. You will find it a helpful influence in playing other forms of music."

As if to reinforce her understanding, she produced from the huge sideboard some old, well-worn books. One contained the Bach forty-eight preludes and fugues; the other was a complementary primer, which, I was soon to discover actually dissected each of Bach's masterpieces. It was essential to read and understand the contents, little by little, before embarking – 'or should it be emBaching? – upon an attempt to play any of the works. Whilst not overlooking or wishing to belittle the prolific and magnificent output of a genius like dear old JS, much of his music gives me the impression of creation dominated by precise, exacting background. Mental rather than emotional creation.

A mere eight or sixteen bars of a prelude would often occupy a complete lesson. Such concentration, with little to show for it at the end of the day, was alien to my nature and probably the principal reason for never being a skilful exponent of the forty-eight – a specialist field, anyway. I had not got beyond about a third of the works when I volunteered for the RAF. No doubt, however, that the main benefit derived from them was the concentration and discipline they imposed.

Daisy's assertion about the classics being helpful had puzzled me, until one evening when I attended for a lesson from Les, to be followed half an hour later with one at Daisy's place – of necessity as it was the only way in a crowded week that I could fit them both in. As I was leaving, he enquired, "What else have you got in your music case?"

"Some Bach and Chopin," I replied.

"Good. Keep it up, even though your interpretation may leave something to be desired."

Then, almost duplicating Daisy's words, he added, "The straight stuff will teach you more about jazz than jazz itself."

'Straight' was the term then used to describe classical and serious music. The reverse of today's fashion. The jazz and dance band boys had short hair; 'straight' musicians, long hair.

My lack of comprehension must have showed clearly. He went over to the piano and played the chopped, syncopated, off-the-beat passage from the overture, 'Poet and Peasant'.

"See what I mean?" asked Les. "You can't get much more syncopated than that, and Von Suppe was around long before you and me."

Swivelling around on the music stool, he went on to suggest that I listen to contemporary works, particularly those by Duke Ellington, elaborating thus: "Many modern composers and arrangers are influenced to some degree by the works of the masters. Not deliberately pinching complete melodies or anything like that, but the association with truly great music in their formative years – what they played, heard and studied - had a lasting effect, which unconsciously becomes embodied in the music of today. It's a natural process, much of it occurring unwittingly."

Had the next pupil not arrived, I do believe that Les would have continued to expound *ad infinitum*! My curiosity more than satisfied, I hurried off to Daisy's place where I had to erase from my mind, temporarily, the dance band scene and prepare it for the more exacting demands of Messrs Bach and Chopin. It was a musical Jekyll and Hyde era which endured for nearly two years. Immensely enjoyable, mentally and spiritually stimulating and uplifting.

An example of influences rubbing off came along when Les set me an exercise – to do a 'hot' chorus, that is, extemporise on the tune. I played my arrangement the following week and Les reckoned that I had 'cribbed' it from a Fats Waller recording, although he was unable to say exactly which record. This I hotly denied. I had spent a lot of time on the chorus of the American number, 'Bob White, What You Goin' To Swing Tonight'? (The only recording I can ever recollect hearing was by Bing Crosby). But most of my spare cash went on music, not records. I was anything but an avid record collector, nor am I today.

Les had, however, provided me with a clue which served to confirm that it really was 'all my own work'. He was a staunch Waller devotee, as I well knew, and I put it to him, "It seems that your liking for Fats has rubbed off on me!"

Smiling, and shrugging his shoulders, Les admitted, "Maybe it has. I certainly can't think of a better reason for turning out a good effort. Seems I'll have to eat my own words about this composer influence."

We both chuckled over the incident, which ended on a happy note and an encore of 'Bob White'.

The era of swing music was upon us yet a new and novel dance reigned supreme in British dance halls - 'The Lambeth Walk'. At the height of its popularity, we were obliged to play many, many weary encores. And so it became an addition to the other mostly corny, but understandably popular novelty dances like the 'Palais Glide', the 'Conga', the 'Paul Jones', the 'Spreading Chestnut Tree', 'Boomps-a daisy'. And in post-war years there came the 'March of the Mods' 'Aga-doo' and the terrible 'Hokey Cokey', not to mention the 'Birdie Song' and so on *ad nauseum*.

It is important to be able to divine what appeals to people – the customers who pay the piper and are therefore entitled to call the tune. Nevertheless, the majority of musicians, while aware of their prime responsibility, are at their best when uninhibited, given free rein, to play, for want of a better expression, musicians' music. The better-class and often unfamiliar tunes stand much neglected because of public demand and preference for that which is familiar, popular to its ears. But to the thinking and discriminating, so often that thus chosen has little musical (or lyrical) merit.

There have been many occasions when the band, or soloist, has given an immaculate interpretation of a lesser-known but beautiful song, yet it has attracted nothing in the way of dancers or applause, and is simply wasted on an unappreciative and tin-eared public. The deafening wave of apathy is then broken only *by sotto voce* mutterings of musicians.

"Cretins! Philistines! Oh, well. Back to rubbish and reality!"

Give them the nursery rhyme banalities of 'Brown Girl In The Ring' or something equally simple and they will think you're the greatest!

And so we return aptly to Mr Waller, who was once asked by a society dame as to his favourite music. He replied, "Bach, lady. But the public likes swing, so I play swing."

And his swift riposte to another who enquired, "Please, Mr Waller, what *is* swing?"

"Lady, if you don't know what it is, then you ain't got it!"

One could equate this comment with one made thirty years later when musical fashion was again in a period of change. A well-known composer, who shall remain nameless, asked whilst at an important meeting, "What is reggae?"

CHAPTER EIGHT

FIDDLERS THREE

Among my schoolmates were members of the junior orchestra with whom friendship continued, over varying periods of time. Sonny (the nickname had stuck) was the first of the fiddlers, but, compared musically with the remainder of the trio, I am sure that he would admit to being definitely last! He was with a band formed and led by accordionist Terry Blake, and I was asked to join. What a curious line-up we had!

Two accordions, alto sax doubling clarinet, piano, drums and violin. Mobile amplification was then in its infancy, so one fiddle was entirely out of place, superfluous, and incapable of balancing and being heard. Sonny was, however, a mate of Terry's who was displaying more than a passing interest in Sonny's sister (they later married so need I say more?). As it was the coronation year of King George VI, Terry decreed that we would be known as the Corona Band. Just as the thought of our curious line-up still raises a chuckle, so too does the stage attire. We were bedecked in white shirts and flannels, bright red ties with matching silk-like sashes! It was only the absence of frilly, ruched sleeves ('poofy' or 'queer', we called it; in today's parlance 'gay') that set us apart from a gypsy, gaucho outfit!

Terry's parents' boot and shoe repair shop had a spacious flat above it, and the main room was ideal for our weekly rehearsals. Terry's father always made sure that the neighbours did not have to endure our sometimes painful efforts after ten-thirty, so at this point in the evening it became more of a social affair than a rehearsal. In the next room, we would consume numerous cups of tea or cocoa and demolish mountains of cakes and sandwiches. Conversation, debate, argument, and light-hearted banter would flow incessantly until we got our marching orders – usually close on midnight.

In *Melody Maker* – the profession's weekly journal – argument raged for several months as a result of an article by a feature writer known as 'Mike', the editor eventually exerting his authority to wind up the controversy, putting an end to further correspondence. Coloured jazz singer Maxine Sullivan had recorded some swing versions of Scottish traditional songs, such as 'Annie Laurie' and

'Loch Lomond'. To the patriotic Scot, this was unquestionably a sacrilege! Patriotism apart, the battle was fought between the progressives and the purists. And our little band was just about divided on the subject. Terry's folks, of course, were on the side of the purists.

Compared to the ear-splitting, nerve-jangling, musically defunct up-dated versions of many classical and other standard works we have since had to endure, a jazzed-up 'Annie Laurie' now seems pretty innocuous to me. I admit to being neither progressive nor purist, preferring rightly, or wrongly, in common with all musical form, to judge each individual item on merit only. For example, I went along with the Tommy Dorsey treatment of 'Song of India', the adaptation of the Chopin étude 'So Deep Is The Night' and a little-known arrangement by Ray Noble of Lizst's 'Liebestraume' made in the late thirties. No disfigurement; simply and sensitively scored with just a rumba rhythm background. Similarly, there's Mozart's Opus 40 in G minor and, the use of Grieg's 'Morning' to advertise a well-known brand of instant coffee. Many people at that time asked me, "What's the tune used in that coffee ad?" A tastefully-produced commercial had unwittingly become a little gem of musical education. And Ravel's 'Bolero' made a come-back when used to accompany the unforgettable sheer grace and beauty of ice-skaters Torvill and Dean.

But I can recall some instant repellent reworkings: the jangling rock version of 'Nutcracker'; the butchery of both words and music by a singer, his name best forgotten (as it deservedly has been), in a recording of 'These Foolish Things', and the terrible boom-tiddy-boom version of 'Blue Moon' and many, many more, best consigned to the dustbin.

Truly, *Melody Maker* was the musical journal of repute, as was its sister publication, *Rhythm*, which was issued monthly. It contained many useful and informative articles, even special transcriptions of piano and guitar solos.

Shortly after my return to civvy street after the war, all the copies which had gathered dust between the years 1935-1940 and lots of old song copies were thrown out in a massive post-war spring-cleaning operation. What fascinating reading they would make today! With the advent of rock and roll, the goal of *Melody Maker* was obviously to boost circulation figures, its contents aiming on an ever-increasing scale to capture the teenage market. It now abounds with ads, with many columns devoted to studio and demo services; the charts; the multitude of discos and clubs; and advertises a bewildering (to me) array of electronic gear, much of which costs a small fortune – all reflecting the shifting sounds of pop, a vast scene, nothing very stable, songs and groups as ephemeral as the technology of the hardware and software. New sounds; bigger and louder sounds; a jargon all of its own.

'The old order changeth' – as indeed it must. Nothing is for ever. In the name of progress, music has become a multi-mega pound industry, undreamed of in my day. Such a far cry from the late thirties (from which I fear I have digressed somewhat), when it cost very little to form a band, requiring a minimum of equipment and transport. In a far less commercial environment, completely devoid of technological demands and pressures, we made music not just for our own kind – teenagers – but for *everyone*. And we thoroughly enjoyed every minute of it.

The Corona Band was doing well with local engagements. However, for the Coronation celebrations, we split up, because of the huge demand for entertainment. There was probably not a street in the country that had not organised a party. I had been asked to provide music for ours. As I recall, it was an overcast, showery day, but the main sporting events for the children, the fancy dress parade and so forth, all got underway, as did the consumption of sandwiches, tea, cakes, blancmange and jelly and custard before we had to admit defeat at the hands of the unreliable British climate. Rain-soaked festoons were rapidly becoming anything but festive in appearance and a hurried, concerted effort was made to clear the decks; the same half-dozen strong men who had laboriously shifted the piano outside now panted and grunted once more, making most uncomplimentary remarks about its weight while hauling it back into the house! Never mind the weather! Several impromptu parties got underway. People drifted in and out of each other's houses during the evening in a determined bid to see off the ample supplies of beer and refreshments. As a token of their appreciation of my efforts to entertain, the neighbours contributed to a whip-round.

A popular Bing Crosby hit of the day was 'Pennies From Heaven' and, as a result of making sure that *my* umbrella was upside-down, the pennies amounted to several pounds.

Later that year the Corona Band folded, but, before moving on, I think it worthwhile to relate the amusing incident which helped speed its demise, far-fetched as it may seem.

We had been playing at St George's Hall for several months, having hired it to run our own dances each Saturday evening. Girlfriends, mums and other relatives pitched in to undertake the catering chores, the raffle, cloakrooms, door duties etc., and on Sunday mornings the band would meet to share out the spoils. The average gig rate was then seven-and-sixpence; a well-paid gig ten bob. Since we always picked up something between these two amounts, we got a fair return after meeting all expenses.

The posters gave the time as seven thirty until eleven. The chap who supervised the hall and its lettings pointed out that, as it was a church hall, we should advertise the function not as a dance, but a dance and social. Furthermore, it should finish at ten thirty. Reluctant to spend more money on reprinting, we ignored him. We were all aware that the supervisor (or whatever his title was), a slightly-built man in his forties, with black curly hair, deep-set dark eyes and an immaculate waxed black moustache, had a passion for indulging in conversation on his favourite subject – believe it or not, the Russian secret police!

Strangely, there was something about his appearance which gave the impression of Russian descent. We hit upon a scheme whereby five of us would corner the unfortunate man by the refreshment bar during the interval and engage him in his pet subject. The remaining member of the band was assigned the task of standing on a chair and putting the clock back half-an-hour! To our delight (and surprise), the scheme went like clockwork for several weeks. Eventually, Mr Supervisor's suspicions were aroused, when the putter-back-of-clocks was caught red-handed. Time had run out for us. It was definitely the last waltz at St George's! Changes were due anyway. Johnny our sax player, who had improved greatly, left to join another band, the others lost interest, and a few gigs thence it was all over. It had been great fun though. I was left with the thought: 'Where do I go from here?'

Well, I went, in fact, into a talent competition – for pianists only. I decided to play an arrangement of 'Alone', the principal song in the Marx Brothers film, *A Night At The Opera*, which also featured singer, Alan Jones. The very mention of the song reminds me of an incident which was both terrifying and yet immensely rewarding. The competition was at our local Carlton cinema, which also featured a popular organ intermission, the huge Wurlitzer rising from the floor. There were also variety acts. What super value for a tanner! On the night I was booked to appear the show was compèred by Leon Cortez who, in the thirties, led a corny, Cockney-flavoured, knees-up kind of band, dressed in pearly king and queen garb, with the accent on comedy. He was joined by his wife, singer Doreen Harris and others on the adjudicating panel.

I stood in the wings clutching my music. To say that I was nervous – well, that would be putting it mildly! Leon was making some introductory spiel across the footlights, when suddenly a musician emerged from the orchestra pit.

"Your music, please, ladies and gentlemen," he requested.

"What for?" queried an elderly contestant.

"The MD wants it. We will come in on the last eight or sixteen bars and build up each act," he explained.

He took my copy, along with all the others. I was too stunned, petrified to argue. It was something entirely unexpected; something I had not bargained for. A serious flaw had been revealed. In all my years of playing, I had never made any real attempt to completely memorise anything. Odd snatches of tunes, yes, but to play confidently a complete piece without the dots in front of me... I tried to conceal the panic that grabbed me. Would I make a fool of myself? Would I be like the guy in the advertisement which always began, "They laughed when I sat down to play?" I was due on stage, last of the eight contestants, but was overwhelmed with a fear of failure, totally oblivious of who was playing what, whether good, bad or indifferent.

"You've played the piece dozens of times to get it right, you *must* be able to remember it," I told myself inwardly, in an attempt to combat nerves. No time now for reasoning – I had been announced.

White spotlights stabbed through the darkness and the curling tobacco smoke as I made my way to the grand piano positioned stage centre, their colour changing to blue as I began playing. Purely by coincidence, but obviously in my favour, *A Night At The Opera* was the feature all that week. 'Alone' too, I certainly had been only a few traumatic moments ago. Not now. I had got through the first chorus in a flowing rubato style just as if the music had been before me, and, as I set the tempo for a more rhythmic second chorus, I was joined by strings and rhythm sections of the pit orchestra. With brass and woodwind added, the last eight bars swelled with a grandiose treatment, a ripple of applause building up before I had reached the final arpeggio. I knew that I was home and dry.

Although up against stiffer opposition, second place in the next round was good enough to qualify for the final. The last act that evening featured *two* pianos, the duettists romping home with a sparkling version of 'The Blue Danube'. Several contestants later complained, "It's not fair, those two are professionals." But the competition was open to all-comers, regardless of status so their grouse was not valid.

I went off home, treading air, overjoyed at having attained third place – and five pounds in prize money. More important, the 'sink-or-swim' incident had boosted my confidence. If I could memorise one dance number, why not one hundred and one, a thousand and one? There really was no limit. The harmonies and melodic patterns of run-of-the-mill tunes were fairly predictable, and even the classier, less stereotyped numbers, with perhaps unusual construction, given a little more concentration, could be mastered. With the hundreds of tunes now stored in the memory, I sometimes wonder how long I could play non-stop without repetition.

I had not told Daisy about the competition. Reticence was not due to a fear of failure. Indeed, I don't think it had ever crossed my mind, youthful enthusiasm and exuberance overriding all other considerations. Had I known what was going to happen, I would no doubt have chickened out at the very thought of it! Little wonder then that I had not remembered about Daisy: Monday night is cinema night...

My parents were naturally pleased as punch about it but, as always, showed their pleasure briefly and unemotionally. What a contrast to the reception accorded me by Daisy when going along for my next lesson! She literally purred with delight.

"...such courage, competing against much older and experienced pianists... playing for the first time before such a huge audience, and having to move with the orchestra... and you knew the piece by heart."

I was truly embarrassed, totally unprepared for such torrential praise, having intended to tell her in simple terms and without any fuss. Mention of my dilemma in the wings only served to set her bubbling all over again! Eventually we got around to the lesson. I wasn't assuming an air of false modesty; I was happy about my success, but equally it was not my nature to brag about it. And as several days had elapsed, the excitement of the moment was a past, but pleasant memory, a nightmare transformed into a dream, an invaluable experience, a stepping-stone in a wide, musical stream.

Amongst the new contacts made was a lively young drummer, Joe. And harking back to the 'Fiddlers Three' theme, the second of the trio, Harry, makes his bow. Probably one of the best violinists in the school orchestra, Harry could really make a fiddle sing in a slow number, and make it sound exciting in a hot chorus without chopping note values – a corny and most irritating habit of the vast majority of string players of that era. Harry worked with his father in the confectionery business so, being a fairly prosperous family, it was no hardship for his folks to buy him a brand-new tenor sax. But the new outfit we hoped to form never got off the ground. Harry became seriously ill. It was impossible not to notice his rapid decrease in vitality: he would tire very quickly and lose interest. He was suffering from the scourge of those times – tuberculosis – and had to go into a TB sanatorium. Happily, he made a complete recovery, but his musical days were over, and the family moved away to the coast.

Somewhat discouraged by this setback, Joe and I soldiered on with other bands, and in a roundabout way – I can't recall with any degree of certainty how it happened – found ourselves playing in some larger bands comprised of musicians aged anything up to twenty years older than either of us. We were really and truly thrown in at the deep end. The musicianship of our elders bordered on, if not equalled, professional standards. Not surprising then, that we were sometimes painfully feeling our way in some numbers. Fortunately, the leader, a brilliant alto sax and clarinet player, took a balanced and kindly view of our youthful limitations, declaring that we all had to gain experience somehow, somewhere and continued to put work our way.

* * * * *

We had not been in touch since leaving school, but I recognised him as he strolled into the hall towards the stage, where I was chatting to the drummer – another new face in my circle, who had apparently booked Frank (who completes the fiddlers' trio) for the gig. Like me, Frank was of slim build, but much fairer, with hair and eyebrows the colour of straw. He removed a belted camel-hair coat, clearly a recent acquisition, for drummer Johnny was prompted to yell, "Where the heck did you get that from, Frank?"

"Do you like it?" Frank asked. "I bought it from so-and-so in Archer Street. He's a pro y'know. *All* the pros wear these kind of coats nowadays."

Under his coat was a flamboyantly coloured silk scarf which clashed loudly with the sombre black and white dress wear. In the years that followed Frank's way out mode of dress and colour generated a good deal of humour amongst the gig boys. Arriving for a jam session one Sunday morning, he took full advantage of its informality, attired in the most outrageous splashes of colour yet.

As if sensing the volley of good-natured jibes about to be unleashed, he cast a critical eye at our conventional white shirts and flannels, and with mock severity asked, "Why do you blokes all dress so funny?"

Yes, that was Frank's individualistic streak. He always had to be in the swim, having ventured to Archer Street. This was the musicians' haunt near the Windmill Theatre, which one could liken to an employment agency. It was where one picked up the work, the casual gigs, a resident hotel job, a summer season at Somewhere-on-Sea, and generally talked shop, mostly in pubs (and, very often, more than eight to a bar!).

The span of more than three years was bridged in between numbers, and during the interval. Frank had traded in his violin for an alto sax some two years previously, abandoning it when realising that he would never get beyond a mean scraping of Heyken's 'Serenade' and Dvorak's 'Humoresque'. And the lack of work for solo fiddle in the dance band sphere had forced the change. The conversation switched to bygone schooldays... "Remember old so-and-so? Have you seen anything of so-and-so? What's he doing now?" And inevitably, "What about old Lehmann?" (referring to the music master and his filthy temper). "I wonder if he's still as bad."

Together with Frank and Joe, the threesome became known as the 'Swing Trio' which initially established itself at the Oddfellows Club (memories of warm beer and stale cheese rolls during the interval!). The engagements there in turn provided other gigs through those who heard and liked us – purely on recommendation. The circle of contacts began to expand. We spread our wings a little, travelling to other parts of the capital, often earning more than the average rate. Although playing the occasional gig, individually or collectively with other bands, the bulk of gigs was fulfilled by the trio, the name largely displayed in red and silver on a disc, cut to fit the front of Joe's bass drum, nearly twice the size of its modern counterpart.

Frank's father had a Morris Minor, at best described as a box on four wheels, with two doors and a metal luggage carrier at the rear. Its capacity was just sufficient to accommodate the trio and all its gear, provided the bass drum travelled outside. Strapped to the rear carrier, it never looked really secure, but somehow survived each and every journey. They were, without a shadow of doubt, halcyon days. When not playing out somewhere, there was a choice of half-a-dozen modern cinemas within a square mile radius, variety shows at the Regal Palace or Stratford Empire, jaunts to the West End or to Petticoat Lane on a fine Sunday morning. Football at the West Ham ground Saturday afternoon, or, if the first team was playing away, our own organised kick-and-rush game in a local park or on Wanstead Flats. Maybe a spin out to Epping or to neighbouring Hertfordshire on bikes. What a pleasure to be able to belt along unhindered, on the tracks laid exclusively for bicycles!

Sundays, between twelve and two, one could join in a jam session at a local pub – especially the old Boleyn Tavern – enjoying at the same time a jar or two in convivial company. Or if one preferred, or the vagaries of our climate so dictated, there was always a welcome at Home Sweet Home for the lads, just to play music, cards, or darts. The Saturday night gigs over, we would congregate at the coffee stall situated at the centre of a five-road junction by the Boleyn corner, gossiping into the early hours about all and sundry. But as the summer days lengthened, so the odds against World War Two breaking out dramatically shortened. Yet such a possibility rated hardly more than a passing reference by the coffee stall gang.

Back to the 'good-old-days-but-not-for-everyone' theme. There was a huge army of unemployed and an unfair and even cruel exploitation of labour, especially of the miners. Poor housing conditions and many other forms of misery were inflicted on the poorer section of the community. 'Things haven't changed much, have they?' the cynics would rightly comment.

But the pound was worth a pound, the cost of living one of the lowest in the world – and stable. One could go with confidence to sporting events, not have them spoiled by gangs of hooligans. Interest and exchange rates weren't on a yo-yo string. In steady employment, with pleasant and rewarding hobbies, good homes and a circle of close friends, our youthful exuberance focused on the good things in life. Many others were not so fortunate.

And because of the overriding stability of those years – a foundation on which to build – I can look back on them with true gratitude and affection.

CHAPTER NINE

PRELUDE

The wailing of air raid sirens within minutes of the fateful announcement on the Sunday morning of September the 3rd 1939 was a hideous fanfare, a frightening prelude to the Second World War. For many, the wounds inflicted by the First had still not healed.

The closure of many large places of entertainment in the interests of public safety dealt a devastating blow to all and sundry in showbiz. In common with many other outfits, the Swing Trio found a niche for itself at weekends, playing in the lounge bar of a fairly respectable nearby pub. There was no alternative, until a few weeks later, when the powers that be, realising that the suppression of entertainment was anything but good for public morale, reversed the well-intentioned, but obviously hasty and ill-considered decision. So we were able to ditch the lounge job and return to playing for dancing.

Before moving on, however, I must put an record the funny incident which arose when the guv'nor of the house said, "I don't mind if you want to take the hat round."

This was in addition to our fee and although we thought it a bit of a come-down, we swallowed our pride and gave it a whirl. The very first night Joe went around with the lid of a biscuit tin and was almost back to the stage with a bumper collection when a joker in the crowd (there's *always* one!) clouted the lid from underneath with his hand. We couldn't do otherwise than join in the laughter which erupted, then tried to retrieve the proceeds with as much dignity as possible.

On the way home, Joe came up with a cracking notion to prevent such a fiasco happening again. The trap tray positioned on top of the bass drum held four ornate Chinese temple blocks.

"What about using the biggest one for collecting," Joe suggested. "It's just like a large money-box and that should do the trick."

Full marks, Joe! It did!

Christmas festivities in recent years had been held alternately at our house and at the home of my mother's relatives, at Barking in Essex.

It was the latter's turn that first wartime Christmas. The parties were always marvellous fun and the wartime one was no exception.

Furniture not required would be moved out, and up would come the carpets to make for easier dancing and the inevitable knees-up. It was incredible how the tiny rooms of those cosy terrace houses managed to accommodate so many extra people without the walls bulging. For me, it was to be the last Christmas on home ground for six years.

Some of my friends were among those who had joined the Territorial Army not long before hostilities began, and were now with the BEF in France.

'Sign on now and avoid conscription at the age of twenty' was the dubious incentive of the recruitment campaign. A classic heads I win tails you lose offer if ever there was one! Jim Gillman next door was one of many who, having been unemployed for so long, signed on for the army before September the 3rd. We were all in the garden and I vividly recall his mother rushing back indoors hysterically crying, "Oh, Jim! My Jim!"

I'm happy to record that Jim survived both Dunkirk and (having transferred to the paratroopers later on) the slaughter of Arnhem.

Recalling the 1914-1918 holocaust, my father predicted, "The minimum call-up age won't stay at twenty for long. It'll be down to eighteen in next-to-no-time."

It was now early 1940. I would be nineteen in the summer, Frank twenty, only two months after me. We decided to enlist together in order to at least have a choice of service rather than be conscripted with no choice at all. Joe's lack of interest was understandable on several counts. A year younger than I, with a widowed mother and sister at home, he was also swotting hard for his matriculation. But it was not going to be easy giving up the freedom and the apparent safety of civvy street. In that tumultuous year, the first large-scale action, culminating in the Dunkirk evacuation, motivated the decision to enlist. One could have been forgiven for thinking selfishly, 'Bugger that for a game of soldiers. I'll stay out till I *have* to go.'

Yet we *did* go. The backs-to-the-wall situation seemed to be the motivating force – a force that compelled many thousands of previously reluctant youngsters to volunteer.

The young, with an as yet short-lived appreciation of life, precious life, had suddenly grown old overnight. After all, if life is short, then youth is even shorter.

All the apprehension, the thoughts of danger became submerged, replaced by the acceptance that we were *all* in it. The unpalatable, inescapable consequences of total war.

CHAPTER TEN

OVERTURE AND BEGINNERS

It was an evening in late July. I sat on the edge of my bed, scribbling a few lines home. We were billeted in terraced Victorian houses in Wolesley Road, at the South Shore end of that premier resort of the north-west, Blackpool. There had been just enough time to speak to my mother through the medium of a neighbour's telephone prior to my departure from a bustling, crowded Euston Station. It was only my first day in the RAF and I already had a fed-up, you-know-what and far-from-home feeling!

But I made sure that my letter revealed nothing of my true inner feelings. It was cheerful and light-hearted. No use telling myself now, in the jibe I would use and hear hundreds of times in the next few years, "You shouldn't have joined!" It had been my decision, and I vowed to myself that under no circumstances would I ever send home a miserable, feeling-sorry-for-myself letter. I hadn't even asked my folks about enlisting. They had been pleased that Frank and I were going in together, accepting the situation as inevitable but sensible.

It was decision which I believe took many neighbours and friends completely by surprise, so many of them making it very plain that they thought I just wasn't the type suited to service life. Strangely, they also overlooked the fact that there were many, many others who fitted in the same category, but they had joined just the same. And from occasional snippets of conversation which I overheard, I had been sensitive, privately, to mother's thinly-veiled hopes that when it came to the crunch I would get cold feet. I knew that when the time came to depart, if there were any tears to be shed, they would he in private, sparing us both any last-minute agonies.

It had been a long day and after standing nearly all the way in a jam-packed train, the left-right, left-right, pick 'em-up-there exhortations from NCOs were unnecessary. We were glad to stretch our legs and, as the rain began to fall, the pace quickened and a long column of tired and hungry bods snaked its way through the town. Whatever my failings, lack of adaptability was not one of them for I soon settled down. The kitting-out parade was an illuminating revelation of the pathetic short supply situation. Few of us gathered complete kit or, come to that, complete uniforms. (In fact, it was November before I had my own rifle, tin hat and respirator!)

We were divided into groups of thirty bods each. On parade, men in ill-fitting uniforms, alongside some attired in a mixture of RAF blue and civvies, mingled with some without forage caps, some still wearing brown shoes, and presented a tragic-comic picture, a body of men that Fred Karno would have been proud of! A pathetic-looking assembly, we laughed at ourselves; we laughed at each other. And fifty-three years on, those who shared similar experiences will have a lingering amazement at how the hell Britain ever survived.

Drilling and rifle drill; a few pot-shots on the rifle range and, most of all, spit and polish kept us occupied. Three times round for inoculations and vaccination jabs, the needles becoming blunter and blunter, and a couple of visits to the Derby baths.

The normal populace was grossly swollen by the influx of holiday-makers and service personnel, which included some Polish airmen. As if that was not enough, the advent of Wakes Week, when t'mills closed, added several thousands more, all determined to make the most of it, war or no bloody war!

On days when it became physically impossible to drill on the promenade, the NCO would tell us to get lost (or words to that effect!) but to split up into small groups around the town. It was an order which we obeyed with the greatest of pleasure. Since our arrival in the rain, the sun had hardly taken a moment off, so we made the most of it too. After all, we would be here only a few weeks, then...?

Funny how events tend to become more significant with time, making them unforgettable. It was the tenth of August, Frank's birthday, and that morning at the wholly uncivilized hour of six o'clock we were assembled, ready to move off. Our exit, in common with our entrance, was made in heavy rain and a blustering westerly gale. The day before, the initial announcement, much to the glee of Scots in the group, was that we would be bound for Invergordon, Inverness. Glee quickly turned to consternation following discussion and intent study of official posting papers by the NCOs.

"That's cancelled," the corporal in charge said, abruptly. "This group is now posted to St Athan, Glamorgan."

The penny dropped. Of course! Was he not a Taffy from the Bridgend area? A spot of unofficial leave eh, boyo?

RAF St Athan occupied a vast, sprawling area of the Welsh countryside, about eighteen miles from Cardiff. In population and size it far outstripped the tiny village from which it had derived its name. Our beds that first night were a DIY job, damp-smelling palliasses which we stuffed with straw. The non-stop influx of recruits was creating accommodation problems but, after a few days, beds, mattresses and small lockers became available. One of the largest buildings housed a cinema, theatre, gymnasium, swimming pool, chapel and, a roller-skating rink of gigantic proportions. Hundreds of us were herded together in the latter. Fortunately, we got into huts before the winter set in.

Early in September I was lucky in the draw for weekend passes. The train reached the outskirts of Reading as the dusk rapidly deepened into total darkness. Piercing searchlights roved the skies, heralding yet one more murderous dusk-to-dawn aerial assault on dear old London Town. I got my first glimpse of the appalling and deeply distressing scenes in the Underground at Paddington. The train was hours adrift, and, unable to travel to East Ham (only trains below ground were running), I managed to get to Liverpool Street, scrambling on the last train, knowing only that it was heading in the right direction – east. I alighted at the nearest station to home (Forest Gate), planning to walk the two or three miles, despite the lack of a tin hat. Determined to get home, I spent the next hour running, walking and constantly throwing myself against the nearest wall each time a stick of bombs screamed its warning of impending death and destruction. There wasn't only flak from the skies, but plenty of the verbal variety from air raid wardens urging me, in the fruitiest of East End language, to take cover!

I had to climb over a neighbour's rear fence and drop on top of the Anderson shelter. It was the only way in, for no one could hear the doorbell when they were in the shelter at the bottom of the garden. I gave them a brief scare, but it was immediately forgotten, overshadowed by the happiness and surprise of the moment. My mother having recovered from my literally dropping in (I had not been able to let them know about the pass) said, typically, "I'll go and put the kettle on," adding, *en route* to the house, "and get some grub. You must be starving." Sweet music to my ears!

There was not much respite on Saturday. In between warnings and all clears, accompanied by a girlfriend, I looked up as many relatives and pals as possible, including, of course, a call on Daisy, where we were greeted in her usual ebullient fashion. The few hours left to us on Sunday seemed reduced to mere minutes. I took the opportunity to cram some selected music into a case and then set off on the return journey – another dreary, stop-start, crawling affair.

In the train, I reflected on the irony of it all. My enlistment had landed me in the comparative quiet of the Welsh countryside, but all the action was concentrated on my home town. My family and so many friends were in the thick of it. I would have been of much more use had I stayed and joined the Civil Defence Volunteers! When not training, we were engaged, one in every three days, on guard duties: boring, time-wasting and soul-destroying. The hastily thrown together pill boxes had no form of communication with each other or with SHQ. Water seeped up through the clay, ammo boxes floated around inside. With nothing more than three rookies with just rifles at each post, it was hardly surprising that a mock invasion exercise, which included the Home Guard, resulted in the conquest of St Athan in a matter of hours! And no wonder the forerunner of the Home Guard, the Local Defence Volunteers (LDV) came to stand for 'Look, Duck and Vanish!'

On off-duty days during the remainder of that beautiful summer, we foraged around the villages, and soon after my return from London, a gang of us went along to the sixpenny local hop at the village hall. As the band went off for a drink across the road during the interval, the cry to which I had already become accustomed went up. "Come on, Bill! Give us a tune!"

Bill duly obliged, the musicians came back and in talking to them it transpired that they often had more than one gig on Saturdays and it was becoming increasingly difficult to cover them all because the call-up had plucked more and more music men out of civvy street.

Frank joined in the conversation, and upon learning that he played saxophone, the leader of the trio asked, "How would you like to do this gig every Saturday?"

"We'd need a drummer," I replied, adding, "what about drum kit?"

"That's soon solved. We've got a spare kit – we'll leave this lot here for you."

RAF pay was two bob a day. Half of that most of us had allotted to our mothers, to use as they wished, or put into a savings account (there's optimism for you!). The gig would pay ten bob every Saturday. By comparison, this was a small fortune that we could ill afford to turn down and, frankly, I hadn't dreamed there would be any opportunities to use my talent outside thumping NAAFI pianos.

We decided to try and rake up a drummer from somewhere, and Frank, now equally enthusiastic, chipped in, "I'll write home for my sax tonight!"

Luck was with us in our quest, the very next day, in the shape of one Sid Broadbent, a likeable character from Leeds, aged about thirty.

"Aye, lad. I used t'play drums in local palais, town hall and such-like," Sid confirmed when we approached him. "'Appen I'm a bit rusty now," he said, somewhat ruefully, "but I'll have a go. I could do wi' brass."

Frank's alto duly arrived. Sid proved to be anything but rusty; in fact, he positively shone, and the next Saturday it was like being back in the old routine. By now, many friendships had been formed. There was always someone willing to stand in for us when necessary. We used to make our exit and entrance via a gap in the perimeter fence and bushes conveniently near a pill box. Those manning the post were made aware of the time we would be back to ensure that none of the group came to grief at the hands of a trigger-happy sentry!

Later came the rapid evacuation of government departments, on a massive scale, from the capital as the Blitz grew in intensity. My father's branch of the Inland Revenue was moved lock, stock and barrel from Waterloo to the Hydro Hotel, Llandudno, which was converted into offices shortly after September 15th, when the Magnificent Few inflicted the heaviest body-blows on the Luftwaffe to date. Unforgettable, the roar that threatened to lift the roof off the jam-packed canteen when the news came over the radio that evening. In November, my mother and two younger brothers joined Dad in Llandudno, having found furnished accommodation in a large house about halfway up the Great Orme. A breezy spot, but it had its compensations: a perfect view, taking in the town and the wide sweep of an almost perfectly semicircular sandy bay. To avoid time-consuming travel between three points, it was agreed that I would spend the first seven days' leave, early in December, in London, at a girlfriend's place and the next seven in North Wales.

The bulk of my civilian clobber had gone with other essentials to Llandudno. In the face of tight rationing regulations it became useful as hand-me-downs for my brothers. Remembering that the very last suit I had bought was a made-to-measure one left behind to wear when on leave, I went across the road and got the key from the next-door neighbour. The suit hung in a wardrobe alongside my evening dress garb and shirts. In a drawer were some ties and socks, all smelling strongly of mothballs. Mum might just as well have taken the lot. I struggled into the suit. It was like a strait jacket! I should have guessed it would be of no use. Prior to coming on leave, I had had to exchange my uniform for a larger size. I was still a growing lad!

I showed neighbours a picture postcard my mother had sent me of Haulfre Gardens, Invalid's Walk. On the back she wrote: 'Come up here, this is where we are.' I've still got that card, a constant reminder of my amusement at wondering how the hell an invalid's health could be improved by the uphill approach to the Walk, assuming, of course, one ever got that far!

The stillness of the house was so unnatural, almost eerie. I wanted to break it by playing something really loud and stirring on the piano. Chopin's 'Polonaise Militaire', I thought, that would be ideal. Then, in the very next moment I was overcome with a heavy feeling of sadness and I just couldn't do it. It was no use wondering how many years would pass before we all returned, assuming, of course, that we, or some of us, and the Happy Hacienda, survived the uncertainties that lay ahead.

Get out! Get rid of such morbid thoughts! That was the next reaction. I selected some favourite music. Pieces by Grieg, Debussy and Chopin. Coleridge Taylor's 'Petite Suite de Concert'. Some albums of ballet music by Delibes and Tchaikovsky, and, for good measure, something more contemporary, Frederic Curzon's 'Robin Hood Suite' and 'London Again' by Eric Coates. In my haste to depart, I almost forgot to return the key next door.

Somehow, I would find space for the music, even if I had to ditch some less essential items of kit. The opportunity we had seized at St Athan had whetted my appetite. I was more optimistic. Whether intuition or simply luck, such optimism was to be justified within a matter of weeks, in a manner no one could have possibly foreseen. I was soon to be 'back in the old routine' – but even more so than at St Athan.

Once again, all these years afterwards, there is a parallel with Denis Matthews's wartime experiences. Like me, he had enjoyed congenial company and the unexpected opportunity of making music, which made roughing it easier no matter what the conditions. Referring to permission to play at the Academy, Queens Hall shortly before the Dunkirk evacuation, James Agate wrote in *The Daily Express*, "There are those who hold that there is no room for the arts in a world at war. Against this is the argument that the arts are the one thing which survives war."

I certainly do not put myself on the same plane of the entertainment scene as Denis Matthews, but I soon found James Agate's opinion realised in the encouragement given by commanding officers and others. The same applied to those with sporting talent. Contrary to expectations, the certain privileges that musicians and sportsmen acquired created very little resentment in the RAF.

CHAPTER ELEVEN

BACK IN THE OLD ROUTINE

The new year brought a parting of the ways, the ex-Blackpool gang being posted to three different locations in Wales. Frank to Pembrokeshire, and me to Cardiff, where the RAF had taken over the civilian airport at Tremorfa. What a jammy posting! Again, there was a shortage of accommodation on camp. I was billeted in a private house near Splott Park, not ten minutes' walk away. A room of my own, home cooking, the centre of Cardiff within easy reach... it was all too good to be true!

It was bitterly cold when we assembled on the square next morning for church parade. Inspection over, the officer-in-charge barked, "Can any man here play the piano?"[4]

I was no longer a sprog. 'Oh, no. You don't catch me on that one. I'm not moving any bloody piano,' I thought to myself. 'That's the oldest one in the book.'

The question was repeated. I felt a dig in the back from a chum behind me.

"Go on, Bill," he urged, and as he was joined by other mutterings in the ranks and heads turned in my direction, I had no option. I fell out, saluted and was ordered to report to the padre in the drill hall.

The padre welcomed me with an invitation – a cuppa, which I gladly accepted. It was freezing out there on the wind-swept square. It turned out that the usual pianist was in the sick bay and the padre wanted to know if I could possibly play piano for the service: "An accompaniment is so helpful to the congregation."

We went into the hall. The stage curtains were open, revealing a walnut-encased boudoir grand piano. I had never before played for a church service but, despite feeling a trifle nervous, all went well and I enjoyed it. I enquired about using the piano when off duty and got the okay from the padre. Great! In the quiet, behind drawn curtains, I could get away for a while from having to 'play to the gallery'.

Immediately after lunch (not being on duty until Monday), I collected all my music and made for the drill hall. I had been convinced that war service would spell the end of musical aspirations.

---

[4] Rookie, newly enlisted recruit

Even as I lost myself as the music flowed and became more and more immersed, I felt it was all a dream – there must surely be a sudden awakening to the harsh realities, a sad ending to it all.

But there wasn't a sad ending – quite the reverse. Unexpectedly, my concentration was abruptly broken by the noisy entrance of several erks who emerged from the wings.

"You played for the church service this morning, didn't you?" one of them ventured.

I nodded a reply and stopped playing.

"I'm the bass player with the band, Joe Evans," he continued, and introduced the others. "You can play dance music as well, can't you?"

"Of course," was my eager reply. "Let's get started."

A rehearsal got underway, and in between numbers I learned that the CO was keen for RAF Cardiff to establish its own entertainment unit on a voluntary basis, to present shows, concerts and dances.

Despite his Welsh-sounding name, Joe was in fact, from the 'Smoke' – Lambeth – so we had plenty in common to talk about. The following week I was given official permission to join the band. It was all so utterly incredible! So much had happened in a mere twenty-four hours! One Sunday in each month we put on a show, to which the public were admitted. These were devised and produced by George Carter, a Geordie with a lot of imagination, coupled with a lot of experience gained from involvement in local operatic and musical comedy productions. He was also a very good 'quick sketch' artist.

Much of our scenery and props were scrounged or improvised. We would invade the big stores in the city, persuading management to part with obsolete window displays and dressings – anything which was useful to us. I recall a female shop window dummy used in a comedy sketch, which on the first night lost a leg when it shouldn't have, but such incidents only served to increase the fun. For the shows, the band was augmented by the addition of some civvy musicians, and the acts too were a mixture of RAF personnel and civvies, including our own 'Tiller' girls from the principal dancing school. Later, we gained permission to undertake suitable paid engagements, a small proportion of the fees going into RAF funds.

Generally, our efforts, entirely voluntary, to entertain were appreciated for we still had to carry out normal duties and bouts of training and a lot of off-duty time was devoted to preparations and rehearsals. Yet we soon became aware of an ill-founded, hostile resentment festering in the minds of a tiny minority (which included several NCOs) who were constantly seeking to make life uncomfortable and to destroy the 'minstrels' as we were collectively known. Fortunately, with the CO's enthusiasm, and the whole scene under the watchful eye of another enthusiast, the Accounts Officer, we were able to treat ignorant and incident-provoking remarks with the ice-cold contempt they deserved. We survived. That minority proved to be the sole dissonance in an eight-month cavalcade of music, song and laughter. There was now more music in my life than ever before.

Joe and I would spend some Sunday evenings at the huge Tabernacle where, apart from a short blessing, the accent was on choral singing. The majority of hymns were in Welsh, but that didn't spoil our enjoyment. The choir was large and well-experienced, so the singing was not in total unison like so many other services. Add a magnificent organ to the congregation and, aided by superb acoustics, you had a thrilling and spiritually uplifting sound that was second to none.

Returning from leave in Llandudno in late February, the final touch of good fortune presented itself. A civvy musician in the show asked me to join his four-piece band which played two or three times a week at a nearby dance club. With night duties few and far between, I was able to fulfil most of the dates offered. But unexpected happiness was soon to be countered by sadness. A letter from Frank told me that the airfield at Carew Cheriton, Tenby, had been bombed and our mutual friend Ron Miller, from Ilford, had been killed while in the camp hospital, which had taken a direct hit. I felt an acute sense of guilt at having been so happy, while all along we at Cardiff, untouched by the Luftwaffe. But our turn was soon to come...

There was another reaction. My mind switched back to St Athan, just after Christmas. I'd had my tea at the dining hall and returned to take over from Ron at the pill box. Rifle in hand, he stood transfixed, profuse tears running down his cheeks.

"What on earth's the matter, Ron?" I asked.

He babbled incoherently for a moment, then regaining composure, said slowly, "D'you see those huts over there? I just saw them all blow up and catch fire. It was terrible!"

A premonition?

Even more uncanny (and accurate) was the gut feeling, as we call it today, of one of the erks with me at an ops room briefing in the Middle East. As the aircrews filed out, he turned to me saying, "That rear-gunner – the one with the B for Baker crew..."

"What about him?" I asked.

"I've got the strangest feeling that he's not coming back."

I felt uneasy, but soon forgot the incident, attending to ops room duties.

The kites returned from their mission – over the Aegean – including B for Baker. But poor tail-end Charlie, as rear gunners were known, had bought it. Riddled with cannon-shells. I can recall other experiences of a similar nature which are beyond our ken, but not appropriate to this chapter.

There were two nights when the Luftwaffe selected Cardiff for long and heavy onslaughts. The first was well underway when Joe and I, with girlfriends, left the New Theatre where Sid Millward and his Nitwits were topping the bill. Having seen the girls home safely, there was only one way to get back to camp – walk. Arriving well after midnight, we spent the wee small hours extinguishing a seemingly endless rain of incendiaries.

When I next had leave, in May, my mother joined me in London. She busied herself around the house, dusting and cleaning, and letting in fresh air – a kind of mini spring-clean, although it appeared to be quite clean and tidy in my eyes, and even though the place would be vacated the next weekend and remain empty until Lord knows when! A combination of home-sickness and the diminished Luftwaffe activity no doubt motivated her decision to travel. That night, however, London came in for one of its heaviest bashings. Once again, no Anderson shelter for me. Not stupid bravado: I just couldn't stay for hours on end in such cramped conditions. Come what may, I got my head down on the sitting room bed-chair and slept through it all until awakened by the all clear at six in the morning.

All good things and, logically, all bad things too have to come to an end. My run of incredible good fortune was broken on the morning of September 8th. The drill hall doors were flung open wide, and a bunch of my friends made their way up to the stage shouting, "You're posted overseas, Bill. They've caught up with you at last! Go and look at PORs."

I did and in a matter of hours I was on my way. Eight days' embarkation leave, nearly three of them to be absorbed in travel. Cardiff-London. London-Llandudno and so back to Cardiff.

(In 1988, I made a sentimental journey with my wife, Olive, to Llandudno. It had retained its wide streets, especially Mostyn Street, and the charming Victorian shopping arcades. And the Hydro, along with other hotels, had undergone a face-lift, and was looking very swish indeed. We made our way up Invalid's Walk – that postcard still raising, inwardly, a chuckle – to the Sunshine Cafe, where my mother had worked part-time. Outside were colourful tables, chairs and parasols. It was now known as the Haulfre Restaurant, the change having been made about a year previously, one of the staff told me.

And the damp and draughty cottage in which my folks had lived had been taken over by the council gardeners and was full of tools, mowers etc. A brief wave of nostalgia swept over me as I was transported back to 1941, standing on the same spot where I'd been photographed just before journeying back to Cardiff, embarkation leave over.)

At West Kirby, the kitting-out parade suggested that we would be heading for much hotter climes. As a 'reserve' on the draft – a precaution should someone go sick, desert, or go AWOL, I would only sail if used to replace the absent airman. So not being required, I remained, along with many others, in limbo, being given two more periods of leave. Musically, I was back to pub and NAAFI piano-bashing.

I thought, 'You *have* had it now, until this lot's over.'

New friendships were formed, and those who tagged along quickly became perceptive of my value as a 'puller-of-pints'! Southport and New Brighton were out of bounds. Nevertheless, we used to make it – a great nosh of fish and chips, then to a pub with a piano where, after the initial round, generous dockers and factory workers would maintain a free supply of beer during the rest of the evening!

There was little else to do. We were kicking our heels, impatient to be on the move. Mail forwarded told me that Frank was also headed overseas. When would we meet again? Then, after a couple of weeks at Wilmslow, it was off to the docks at last to board, of all things, a converted cattle ship, on December 4th, the *MV Orestes* of a mere 4700 tons displacement.

CHAPTER TWELVE

FOR ALL WE KNOW

The convoy, some seventy strong, streamed out of Liverpool dock the morning of December 8th, the rank and file unaware of the Japanese attack on Pearl Harbour, bringing the Yanks into the conflict the day before we sailed. There were about three hundred troops crammed into the *Orestes* – the smallest vessel in the convoy. A merchant seaman told me, prior to sailing, "The small craft always travel on the outside of the convoy to give protection to the larger and more important ships inside."

'What a cheering prospect,' I thought. 'First in the line of fire!'

RAF personnel with machine-gun experience were detailed to man the gun-pits. I was one of them, stationed amidships on the port side. Day after dreary day, we ploughed through mountainous seas, heading west all the time, lashed by Atlantic gales, rain, sleet and snow. I would clamber down after each spell of duty, the weight of heavy protective clothing – greatcoat with a hood, heavy-duty black rubber mackintosh and Mae West – compelling me to make slow, ponderous movements, the spray freezing on my face, clinging to a balaclava helmet under a tin hat which seemed to weigh about ten tons! Several hours in these conditions made me ravenous.

Down below, I would consume several meals, indifferent to the quality of the food – food was rejected left, right and centre by hordes of violently seasick bods, many of them sprawling in pathetic heaps on the floor. Not one member of the gun crews was ever sick. I suspected that, in common with myself, they had never been afloat in anything more than a row boat on a calm lake or river. So it seemed that the old maxim of fresh air and plenty of food had proved its worth. Manning the gun-pits had proved to be a blessing in disguise.

The *Orestes* was one of the earliest twin-screw vessels to be built. In 1917, to be exact, the life-span of such craft being about twenty-five years. With 1941 nearly gone, it didn't need a mathematical genius to deduce that the old lady was very ancient – almost time for a trip to the breaker's yard! Would we make it to wherever we were supposed to be going? My ears had become accustomed to a cacophony of creaks, groans and shudders as the *Orestes* laboured bravely, each rise and fall accompanied by clanking and rattling rhythm of chains, securing, hopefully, the many vehicles stowed on the upper deck. The cry of sea birds, the ship's alarm bells and pounding engines, all intermingling with the unceasing roar of an awesome, endless expanse of restless, huge waves. I was made to realise the truth of an extract from a book I had read some time, somewhere which stated that if you want to learn to pray go to sea.

Gradually we became used to the alarms, dubbed as 'panic stations', sometimes practice, sometimes for real, the latter usually associated with intense activity by corvettes and destroyers fussing around like hens protecting their chicks. Shutter signals would flash from ship to ship and depth charges would be released. But any completely strange situation, sound or movement seemed to be greatly heightened, even appearing sinister, especially at night, when the release of parachute flares cast an eerie glow that gave vessels a ghost-like appearance.

The worst over, we changed course. Calmer, warmer weather made a further exploration of the ship much easier. I hadn't expected to find a piano on board such an old tub, but there it was – an old upright, and, surprisingly, not only did every note function, but it was reasonably in tune. Till then, music had been confined to playing over and over again the same half-dozen records, using needles much the worse for wear. One dominating title has erased the others from my mind – an Al Bowlly recording of 'For All We Know' – all the apprehension and foreboding of the voyage emphasised in the lyrics. "For all we know, we may never meet again" and, "Tomorrow was made for some, tomorrow may never come, for all we know." As one can easily imagine, such words initially evoked many a grim-humoured response!

Freetown was reached on Christmas Eve. We were joined by another convoy of similar size inside the wide, sweeping boom. It was to be an incident-prone voyage from now on, the first occurring just after dusk with the cry, "Man overboard!" One idiot had decided to have a swim, only to find the swift-flowing undercurrent too much for him. Fortunately, there were others present who promptly threw over a life-buoy, the type with battery-operated illumination. He was subsequently picked up by a French destroyer, having narrowly escaped being swept outside the boom.

I fetched my hammock and blankets from below and for the remainder of the voyage, bar one tropical rainy night, slept on deck near the gun-pit. During the early hours of the next morning there was a noisy fracas in the detention cell, which contained several bods on jankers – mostly for returning late from leave. One had gone berserk in the heat and was so violent that he had to be restrained by the use of a straitjacket. The poor chap, visibly heavily sedated, was taken ashore to hospital. Christmas was anything but merry for him.

The heavy 'ack-ack' group also disembarked. One chap in particular couldn't get off the *Orestes* quickly enough – one with whom many of us sympathised. He was a survivor of a torpedo attack – and it showed. One could see how he relived the horrific experience every time the alarm bells jangled. In place of the 'ack-ack- group came a unit of the Royal Corps of Signals.

The other convoy which had joined us at Freetown included some really famous giant liners, the largest being the *Île de France*. Our commodore ship was the classy-looking *Andes*. During Christmas lunch (which, apart from the pud, was anything but traditional) both convoys got underway, the next port of call for ours, Cape Town; Durban for the other convoy. We also held an impromptu Christmas show in which I was glad to participate.

By day, there was the fascination of watching hordes of flying fish around the bows. At night, with black velvet skies seeming so close, one felt it almost possible to pluck at the myriad of glittering stars and could be lulled into an almost hypnotic state, staring for long periods at the phosphorous which permanently encircled the ship. Soon after leaving Freetown, the formidable battle cruiser *Ramilles* joined us – slap bang in the middle of the convoy. We felt a mighty lot happier and safer, I can tell you. Quite the reverse a few days later…

The *Orestes* had been dogged by repeated engine troubles, despite valiant work by RAF fitters and mechanics, so it was hardly surprising to awake to a dawn of incongruous silence. *Both* engines had packed in, the convoy was nowhere to be seen: the *Orestes* now a sitting duck – fair game for Jerry's Dakar-based Focke-Woolf bombers. Help! Except for the temporary return of a corvette, which exchanged many signals, we were alone for a full twenty-four hours before the engines coughed and spluttered into life.

Several days later, the lame duck rejoined her fitter companions, limping into Cape Town early in the new year. The essential spares and repairs needed afforded us some extra shore leave – six days, in fact – the highlight being a trip to the top of Table Mountain.

Between the Cape and Aden, the fire which broke out in the hold was fortunately brought under control, after giving off huge clouds of thick, choking smoke and fumes. Fortunately, indeed! The cargo down there consisted principally of tons and tons of ammunition. And now when I think about it, and how we joked – references to 'Steamboat Bill' and, 'I bet another dollar I go higher than you!' I know that such a situation today would have scared me stiff!

In rich contrast, a tropical rainstorm of vicious intensity in the Indian Ocean lashed us for about an hour, heaps of broken crockery being the only casualties.

Much off-duty time had been pleasantly spent by the majority of us taking part in sporting events of every kind. The RAF versus a combination of crew and army types. Included were some diminutive Chinese from the galley. What they lacked in stature they made up for in sheer cunning. I was in a tug o' war team that darn nigh pulled its guts out, until somebody discovered that the Chinese end of the rope had been securely fastened to a bollard! They were a good-humoured bunch, as I had discovered when chatting over piping-hot mugs of sweet cocoa which they served during the long, freezing spells of gun-pit duty. Cocoa never tasted so good!

Returning to the sporting events... The finals coincided with the Crossing the Line ceremony. A gigantic canvas bathing tub was erected for'ard and seawater pumped in for the dual purpose of the ceremony and the water sports, such as the greasy pole competition. There came an unexpected climax. More and more bodies plunged in, until the unsuspectedly rotten canvas was unable to sustain any more pressure. The panel facing the stern of the *Orestes* split wide open from top to bottom. Seated amidships, on upturned buckets, were members of a fatigue party, peeling spuds. A minor tidal wave swept down the deck, engulfing bodies, buckets and spuds while at the bottom of the tub, suddenly bereft of water, lay a heap of sprawling bodies! At both ends of the ship, it was a complete and utter shambles! Truly, a side-splitting and hilarious finale!

We sweltered in Aden for four days, going ashore in the evenings, the convoy having shrunk in numbers due to the departure of many vessels, more often than not bound for the Far East. Our nine week voyage ended with disembarkation on February 3rd, 1942, at Port

Tewfik in Egypt. We learned that the brave old *Orestes* was scheduled to go on to New Zealand, to be fitted out with cold storage facilities, and brave the now Japanese-occupied seas to transport a cargo of meat back to Blighty in June. I have often wondered whether she ever made it.

All in all, it had been a memorable voyage, in spite of the cramped and often near-primitive conditions. I had acquired a magnificent tan and felt as fit as a fiddle. In the years following, I travelled by ship, hovercraft and air without any adverse effects. But my fortunate capacity for being a good traveller does not blind me to the existence of those not so fortunate, for whom travel is totally denied or the pleasures of seeing faraway places blighted by the misery of air or seasickness.

CHAPTER THIRTEEN

SAND IN MY SHOES

Tewfik-Cairo-Alexandria – that was the route we took, a bunch of us eventually spilling out of a truck at Burg-el-Arab, about thirty-five miles south west of Alexandria,(known to all service bods as 'Alex'). We joined 203 Squadron, engaged on naval co-op reconnaissance duties, reflected in the squadron insignia of a seahorse, which was known by the veterans as 'Pregnant Percy', and the motto *Occidens-Oriensque*.

The squadron boasted many time-expired (overdue for return to the UK) regulars. I became increasingly convinced they were straight out of Noel Coward's 'Mad Dogs and Englishmen'. The war had brought about an extension of the tour of duty, from the peacetime two and three years for single men and married men respectively, to three and four years. Having served in much hotter climes than that of Egypt – Basra, Aden, Bahrain and the Sudan, for instance – long exposure to the sun had left its mark, summed up by one of the earliest Arabic words we learned, 'machnoon'. Whilst the spelling is probably wrong, in plain English this meant 'mad' – right round the bend!

I feel sure that there was a large element of sadistic glee expressed in the taunts of "Come over! Get some in! Get your knees brown!" The latter referred to the give-away of ghastly long shorts worn by new arrivals (quickly shortened by the local Arab tailor, bringing us in line with the desert veterans.) And the revelation, nay, almost certain prospect of a four-year stint in the Western Desert made one's heart sink to an all-time low. Within a few days I was in a group flown in a 'Wimpy' Wellington to the squadron's forward detachment way up the line at Sidi Barrani. But before that move we experienced sandstorm baptism. It raged for nearly twenty-four hours, with the density of a London peasouper fog obliterating everything. It cheered us no end when told, "That's nothing – it often blows non-stop for two or three days. Second only in intensity to sandstorms in Tobruk." Thank you!

As if that wasn't enough, more discomfort manifested itself in the form of fleas. Millions of 'em. No tent, blanket or article of clothing was ever entirely free of sand or fleas. The latter, however, were easily outnumbered by disease-carrying flies. Ugh! The detachment was short-lived. In March, I was back again at Burg-el-Arab and a day-pass to Alex opened my eyes to the darker side of the time-expired regulars, many of them pretty rough diamonds. They displayed all the arrogance of the 'send a gunboat up the river' and, 'one Englishman can lick a dozen wogs with one arm tied behind his back' mentality.

While certainly not condoning the bloodshed, violence and exploitation associated with the building of the British Empire, I must admit to a sneaking admiration for the worldwide legacy of the English language, the civil service and democratic system and British culture inherited by the outposts of the Empire, perhaps best summed up in the cynical expression I recall reading, yonks ago: 'When the missionaries went to darkest Africa to teach Christianity to the natives, the British navy followed close behind to make sure they understood it.'

I had sent several cryptic cables when joining 203 to tell of my safe arrival. Consequently, my return to base was more than welcome for, having been incommunicado for over three months, there was a small bundle of mail for me. Included were two rolls of sheet music. Unrolling them and taking in the titles, I exclaimed to my tent-mates, with amusement, "Hey! Take a shufti at these! 'Sand In My Shoes' and 'Oasis'."

Permanent buildings, erected by local labour, comprised only the officers' mess, the armoury, and the cookhouse, electricity being provided by mobile generators. The ORs' canteen was a mass (mess?) of large tents, known as EPI tents overlapped to create a large area, the ridges and joins heavy with wind-blown sand, revealed by the sagging bulges inside from which, without warning, sand would sometimes descend. The results were disastrous if your food or drink happened to be underneath the downpour!

There was home-made music emanating from that hotch-potch of canvas one evening. I wandered in, bought a beer and made my way to the raised platform where a five-piece outfit was playing. At the first opportunity I spoke to the pianist, mainly to ask if I could use the piano when off duty.

"Aye, lad," came the broad Yorkshire reply "but what about having a bash now?"

I said I didn't want to muscle in on the act, but then came the pleasing suggestion, "Let's do us duets, then. Do you know 'Tiger Rag'?"

"Sure."

"Right, lad. Thee tak top end," he invited.

I pulled up an empty drum, there was a simple four bar vamp in the bass register, and we were away. The lads stamped, clapped and shouted their approval, and so encouraged, we continued with our new-born four-hands-at-the-piano act until lights out. The Australian and Canadian beer, compared to Blighty's wartime watered-down brew, was pretty potent stuff – good 'singing' beer, so there were interludes in which some strange new songs and ditties reached my ears; mostly home-grown products, inspired by the wanderings of regular servicemen abroad.

The 'Wild Colonial Boy', the amazing feats of 'My Brother, Sylvest', and, as the titles suggest, 'The Harlot of Jerusalem', 'The Good Ship Venus' and 'O'Reilly's Daughter' are typically bawdy, obscene service songs. There was an amusing version of 'A Little Bit Of Heaven' reflecting, with more than a germ of truth, the genius of the Air Ministry's higher echelons for selecting the diabolically, bare, outlandish and uncomfortable regions of the world for RAF bases. 'Shaibah Blues' gave vent to frustration and homesickness in very forcible terms, and even in these anything-goes, much enlightened days, the lyrical content remains unprintable!

Between numbers, introductions were made, snippets of information as to who-came-from-where, civvy street occupations and gig venues, snapshots of girlfriends and wives exchanged. Jack White was the pianist's name, an inveterate pipe smoker, aged thirty-three. His home town was Morley, Leeds, where prior to RAF service, he had held a most unusual job promoting sales of sheet music by playing piano in the huge department store, Lewis's. Evenings and weekends, he gigged around with local bands, and in earlier days had done some seasonal work in the Isle of Man.

Fleas didn't bother me that night. Tired, but contented, having indulged in several bottles of the strong Aussie brew, I slept like a log. Beer, and a skin becoming ever-tougher in the sun, was an ideal, effective combination in combating nocturnal insect activity; one soon developed total immunity.

My thoughts centred on the immediate musical affinity – as if we had been playing duets for years, at that evening's impromptu performance. The next day, over tiffin, Jack told me that a concert party, to be known as The Lineshooters, was to be formed. I was invited to join the band, playing, as he put it, at 'top-end' and we would have our own solo spot in the show.

"Let's go over to my tent," I suggested. "I've got a whole load of dots I brought out with me, and I've since got some latest tunes from home."

We thumbed through the music. Jack was delighted when I, handed him the copy of 'Oasis' saying, "How about this? Just the job for a signature tune," giving his approval: "Reight gradely."

And so it was. Regretfully, I do not have the copy of 'Oasis' as it got lost with some other sheet music during the evacuation of Burg-el-Arab. Just a memory as a souvenir of a musical friendship and understanding which endured until postings in different directions parted us some eighteen months later. We graduated quickly from our arrangements of popular and standard music to the classics; the 'Sleeping Beauty Waltz' and 'Valse des Fleurs' ballet music by Delibes and many others.

Far from being the end of musical involvement, the posting abroad was another new beginning. How wrong can one be?

CHAPTER FOURTEEN

THE LINESHOOTERS

It was my first but by no means my last experience of desert concert party work, and I wouldn't have missed it for all the gold of ancient Egypt. Often funnier than the rehearsed show itself were the numerous times when something went wrong. The ad libs, the off-stage burlesques. We had topical scripts and ideas and parodied songs; for example, the George Formby 'My Little Stick Of Blackpool Rock' became a stick of 'Burg-el-Arab Rock'. Two glamorous bints (girls, to you) were played by Phil and Charlie, the latter a corporal of Maltese descent, who was absolutely dedicated and fastidious in each and every presentation. His send-up of Carmen Miranda was the high spot of the show.

Charlie's linguistic ability in English, French, Italian and Arabic was a boon. No one in his right mind ever paid the initial asking price for anything in Egypt: haggling over the price was a national and natural pastime. His command of Arabic, spiced with humour, was appreciated by bazaar traders in Alex, and, later, Benghazi. It was an entertainment in itself. After much gesticulation and a long harangue, he would obtain materials needed for props, costumes, and dresses at rock-bottom prices. For an agreed sum, the Egyptian tailor-cum-dhobie-wallah could be cajoled into making up the garments. Many items – backdrops, curtains, coloured lighting – although improvised, appeared as if by magic, with no questions asked, not even by the CO, re the source of supply.

The very nature of the squadron's role kept it based a long way behind the front line (then at Tobruk) and it had to be near the Mediterranean coast, so we were fortunate to have off-duty bathing parties, transported by a three-ton gharry. (Anything on four wheels was known as a gharry, although the word strictly refers to horse-drawn vehicles.) The Lineshooters having played at a variety of camps, army and navy included, were given permission by the CO to take the production on tour, taking in as many units as possible all the way up the 'blue' (an Aussie term for the desert) to Tobruk.

Two three-ton gharries, one open, one covered, constituted our home for the next few weeks. Audiences ranged from a few dozen to several hundreds, just as the facilities and situations were of two extremes, calling for some improvisations and adaptations of the show and its scenery. Everywhere, willing hands assisted the off-loading of old bomb boxes which served to carry all the gear, heaviest of all, of course, the piano. Even generator failures at Daba and Fuka didn't stop the show. Both times it continued with the aid of oil pressure lamps.

Southerly winds blowing directly from the heart of the Sahara Desert, known locally as the Kham-Sin, made it distinctly uncomfortable for travelling. It can be likened to the waves of heat unleashed when opening a hot oven or furnace door, but on a gigantic scale, and it created very humid conditions. We would arrive at each venue a tired, dusty and sweaty bunch of erks, yet remarkably we would "pick ourselves up, dust ourselves off, and start all over again," as per the song's very good advice. Enthusiasm never waned, the show keeping its verve and pace throughout. The piano, shrouded in protective canvas, travelled up front, behind the driver's cab, secured by ropes and supported on old rubber tyres. It was kept in tune by means of a tuning spanner, fashioned for us in the fitters' work tents.

We didn't make Tobruk, because the tour was aborted at Sollum where a signal had been received ordering our immediate return to base due to the all-out attack by Rommel. We stocked up with provisions and water and did an about-turn, getting back to base late the next day. Again, the conspiracy of time and events made the date unforgettable – it was June 15th, 1942 – my twenty-first birthday. All leave had been cancelled so there was no slap-up meal and cold beer in my favourite Alex restaurant, The Long Bar. It was tinned grub and warm beer consumed in the back of the gharry. Hardly a gastronomic delight!

A heap of mail and music awaited me, including a parcel containing a large tin, inside which was an equally large home-made fruit cake. Good old mum! I felt choked, knowing that probably several weeks' rations of dried fruit had been sacrificed on my behalf. But also in the tin were some tablets of soap. The scent from them had been absorbed by the cake! Nevertheless, my tent-mates and I made short work of demolishing it, washed down with the evening brew-up, on the primus stove, of chai (tea).

A letter from Frank told me that he was at RAF Shaibah. He had joined the camp dance band known as The Commanders. It was good to be in touch again.

In the two weeks of intense activity which followed, music took a back seat. All unessential kit and personal items were collected and transported in spare kitbags to Aboukir, in preparation for evacuation. There were some items I was loath to part with, but if I were to hang on to the bulk of my music, then there was no alternative: they had to go. With many fighter plane bases in enemy hands and our own base becoming ever-closer to the front line, it became cluttered with planes from other squadrons which had moved back. I was back again behind twin machine guns, mounted in a sandbagged gun-pit. Considering the conglomeration of poorly dispersed kites, casualties from strafing were miraculously few. Especially on the final night when the flare-path was lit for a supposedly friendly incoming kite. But a hail of machine gun fire soon disproved the classic wartime expression 'It's all right, it's one of ours.'

A convoy of vehicles pulled out on July 1st, mingling with thousands of others heading east on a strip of melting, hot tarmac, jokingly called a road, which crumbled everywhere under a weight and volume of traffic it had never been intended to bear. We should have been blasted into eternity by the Luftwaffe but, as at Dunkirk, the bulk of the Allied forces lived to fight another day.

Organised chaos! Tents had hardly been erected and dug in when the order came to break camp. We moved on to another stretch of sand, still in the Canal Zone, but now at Abu Suweir, by the Sweetwater Canal. Whoever gave it that name must have had a mighty grim sense of humour. You should have seen the colour of the water! It contained all known germs that could kill you dead!

Amongst the non-priority items left behind was the piano and concert party prop boxes. A retrieval party returned to Burg-el-Arab, now occupied by other Allied retreating forces. A unit of Aussies looked upon their newly-acquired piano as the spoils of war. A heated argument developed, threatening a split in the Allied ranks! It was only the supreme authority of the officer in charge after a talk with the Aussies CO that secured its return without having to resort to forceful methods!

The squadron's antiquated kites – Blenheims and Ansons – were being replaced by a fast, slim, pencil-like aircraft from the USA called the Maryland. Some were destined never to go into action, disastrous conversion flights taking their toll of brand-new planes and human lives. And another group – half-a-dozen officers returning in a Dodge truck from a swim – who should have known better than to play around with unexploded devices, tossed one around playfully. Truck and bodies went sky high just as the truck reached the centre of camp. I was at the burial service and parade at dawn, rifle loaded with blanks. Six hessian shrouds, dark brown patches of blood attracting hordes of flies; six who died not from enemy direct fire, but from human error.

The Lineshooters picked up the threads of entertainment again; there were occasional day passes into Ishmailia, but yours truly was laid low by the first of three bouts of debilitating and energy-sapping malaria. In October, we joined the massive movement of men and machines westward. Throughout the night of October the 23rd, we could hear and feel the rumble of the El Alamein barrage even though we were some forty miles behind the front line, now based at El 'Amiriya.

Another incident entirely due to human error, but fortunately involving no fatal casualties, was the crash landing of an old Anson which was doing night-time 'circuits and bumps'. It narrowly missed our tents before ploughing into the sand. A group of us ran out to rescue the two man crew, one of whom was injured. As we beat a swift retreat, together with the medics who had now arrived on the scene, from the smoking kite, there was a burst of flame which rapidly spread to three brand-new Marylands which faced the tented area and, for what seemed to be like a lifetime, we could do no more than lie flat on the deck while thousands of bullets and a firework display of pyrotechnics (distress flares) sprayed over us. Friendly fire? You must be joking! Someone must have got a right rollicking the next day for not supervising proper dispersal. We also endured a sandstorm of record proportions – three days and nights, with our tent becoming airborne on the final night. I went into dock again, stricken with malaria, but returned in time to spend and enjoy my first Christmas in the desert with 203. And so to the new year, and goodbye El 'Amiriya.

Our fourteen day journey to Benghazi took in the escarpments, rising several hundreds of feet above sea level at Sollum and Derna. In many places, old petrol drums (filled with sand and stones and piled up in pyramid form like huge cotton reels) plugged and propped up the escarpment roads, filling the tremendous gaps made by both sides in the conflict when in retreat. The improvised foundations didn't exactly inspire a lot of confidence, Furthermore, our gharry, driven by Jack (who, incidentally, was an armourer) had so much play in the steering that it just wasn't true! Each hairpin bend was, indeed, a hair-raising experience.

The squadron settled at Berka, one of three principal air bases in the area – certainly more pleasant than any others we had known. It was slightly more fertile due to its proximity to the sea and the amount of rain which fell in the so-called winter months. Except for some brief excursions to Tripoli, where it was heartening to note that the army had got its priorities right in trying to restore production at the local brewery, I was destined to move around in the next two years, yet to be confined to the Benghazi locale.

Jack often enthused about our act.

"When this lot's over, kid," he would say, "'appen we could get together in Leeds. We could 'ave two pianos – baby grands – in t'store at Lewis's."

The idea appealed to me, although I knew that I still had a lot more to learn.

For good measure, he would throw in other incentives, adding, "We could do us duets at Sunday concerts like, and wi' tons o' gigs in t'north, tha'll never want for work."

Such dreams were the first line of defence, I suppose, in periods of despair that required a lot of effort to shake off. A form of escapism, a stimulus and incentive to make the best of things today; tomorrow, we would make them come true. But tomorrow was a long, long time coming...

Recurring malaria put me in dock for the third time. My kay-dee shirt and shorts, fresh on that morning, were now a mass of dark brown patches: saturated. My body was on fire yet I shivered in the hot sun, teeth chattering. I managed to summon the energy to shower at the hospital, then collapsed into bed. When I came to, more than twenty-four hours of my life had passed me by, completely unaccounted for. It had been the worst attack yet. I was given fourteen days' sick leave. Jack, being due for leave, was able to come too.

Late next day, we got our first glimpse of Apollonia from the back of the gharry. The name had been given to the spot by the Italians. In a sheltered bay at the foot of a winding escarpment lay a small group of buildings, once used by them as a military hospital. On the way down and indeed on the beach too there were centuries-old ruins, many tall pillars and columns still upright. I was, and still am, ignorant as to their origin. Certainly all the evidence of roads, dwellings and baths was of a very early civilisation: Greek, Roman, or perhaps both, but certainly interesting. As was the high, natural rock formation known as Cleopatra's Pool, into which the Mediterranean ebbed and flowed.

Fourteen idyllic days. No parades; no bull; no uniform. Time-drifting days spent lazing in the water and sun. Sometimes a friendly game of football or cricket in the cool of evening and, for the first time in months, cold refreshing beer, albeit rationed. According to my dictionary, Apollo was not only a Greek god, but also, in later times, a Roman god of 'sunlight, music, poetry and prophecy'. Some snapshots I sent home caused my folks to comment on my malaria-inflicted loss of weight. Stupid! I should have realised that a drop from a well-built 160 pounds to about 140 in less than a year would be painfully obvious to them.

Again, a batch of mail and music upon my return from leave. News of cousin Millie's first happy event – a boy; brother Albert was in the RAC (Royal Armoured Corps) training at Catterick camp; and, surprise, surprise, Frank was expecting to soon move into the Middle East command.

CHAPTER FIFTEEN

RUMOUR, REGIMENTATION AND REUNION

The next six months were miserable ones. Overnight, I was drafted with all other ground gunners into a new squadron of the RAF Regiment, encamped about a mile or so from 203. When off duty, I would walk or thumb a lift from a passing Jeep back to my old squadron, just to be among old friends and to spend a while at the piano. Usually, I got a lift, for it seemed that every man-jack in the US forces had his own personal Jeep! 203 was now equipped with long-range kites – Boston Baltimores – and there were rumours galore about an imminent move to Italy. The underbelly paunch of the Baltimores caused them to be dubbed, most appropriately, 'pregnant Marylands'.

But in fact 203 went to India. Although I had set my heart on getting to Italy, I would have gladly settled for India – anything to free me from my new but wholly depressing and alien environment. Even the billets into which we moved were alive with bugs, and all attempts at disinfection were largely ineffective. Army NCOs were called in to drill and train us, but no one took kindly to starting all over again, being treated like a bunch of rookies, least of all yours truly. A process designed to turn us into a glorified army unit seemed doomed to failure in the face of us having become accustomed to other things, with anything up to four years of the RAF way of life. Hardly a week passed in which I did not submit an application for posting to Italy, or to remuster into another trade. Eventually, persistence paid off...

With two other erks also determined to improve their lot, I was given the chance to remuster, provided I could pass the written and oral trade test. We all succeeded, but shortly afterwards we became the butt of many derisory remarks, such as: "You bloody fools! You'll be left out here in this stinking dump. We're all going back to Blighty!"

They were right about going home; way out on the judgement of our independent action. I took up duties at nearby 247 Wing, in the operations room where, later, I received letters from the RAF Regiment bods in Blighty. They had been split up, right, left and centre, and new squadrons formed. Many weeks passed, but when the next letters arrived, they were not from Blighty. They came from Burma.

More important was the great news contained in a lengthy letter from Frank. It transpired that when he arrived in Cairo, he had discovered that there was a vacancy for second alto sax in the No.2 RAF ME Command Dance Band. Talk about being in the right place at the right time! Auditioned by the chief of RAF and Entertainment, Sqdn. Leader Hugo Rignold, and leader and first alto of the band, Ronnie Austin, he had just about scraped through. He was now in a probationary phase – sink or swim. The majority of musicians, being well-experienced, hard-bitten pros, were giving Frank a hard time, confirming what we had often heard – something akin to the acting profession (also overcrowded) sometimes being hostile to newcomers. Typical of disheartening remarks which Frank had to shrug off was 'Why don't you learn to play before joining the professionals?' One needed a pretty thick skin to survive.

'It would be great to see you. Can't you get some leave?' was Frank's plea.

It was about time I took some leave, anyway. Moral support was needed and although it would entail some five hundred miles of hot, dusty and uncomfortable travel each way, by road and rail, I was soon heading east, spending a few of the fourteen days, *en route*, in my favourite spot, Alexandria (but not to call in at Sister Street!). As any ex-ME serviceman will tell you, this was the officially recognised brothel under strict medical supervision, but, like so many blokes, still 'virgin soldiers' the very first sexual encounter being one which would be handed over on a plate didn't appeal. There would no doubt be opportunities of a more natural, genuine and satisfying, relationship with our own service girls at base camps. In fact, it was the married men who most frequently availed themselves of the services, just for quick self-gratification, crudely known as 'having a bang', or 'getting some dirty water off my chest.'

"I always keep my socks on," I recall one chap telling a group of us, much to our amusement, and curiosity. We naturally all wanted to know why.

"I put my wallet in one sock, my pay book in the other!"

It may shock some, this revelation of an official brothel, but, judged in light of what has since happened – the Pill, the promiscuity of the 'Swinging Sixties', the abandonment of the condom and the terrible spread of AIDS – one must admit that it was common-sense and responsible to provide such a facility. It was a necessary safeguard against servicemen tempted to frequent the many houses of ill-repute, naturally 'out of bounds' or, in Americanese, 'off limits' where they was almost certain to become infected with venereal disease. Referring to medals and decorations, there was the services' grim and humorous corruption of the Victoria Cross – 'VD and bar!'

Touts, pimps, beggars, peddlers and pickpockets abounded to lure and exploit the unwary, the unsuspecting. I recall this epitomized in a Tommy Trinder gag – a topical account of his arrival in the ME. Coming down the gangplank, he was accosted by a well-dressed Egyptian pimp who leered, "You want quiose[5] bint, effendi?"

"No, I want the harbourmaster," Tommy replied.

Still smiling, undeterred, and rubbing his hands together, the pimp said, "Ah, it will be difficult, effendi, but I will try."

Before we leave Alex, I must mention the forces' principal venue, The Fleet Club, with its vast beer garden, where equally vast sessions of tombola were played with not huge but certainly useful and handsome cash prizes for the lucky ones.

Some chaps would go on leave possessing no more than the cash for bed and breakfast in their pockets, plus some, to gamble on tombola or Housey-Housey, pooling their resources, hoping to pull off a big win to set them up and provide beer money for the leave. Some gamble! But I know that very often it worked. Curiously, it was many years after the war before tombola or Housey-Housey became a commercial, money-spinning craze under its new title Bingo.

Back to Frank and me. It was a memorable leave, mingling with the band at rehearsals and public performances. The band's speciality was the Glenn Miller sound, one of the programmes being recorded and broadcast by the BBC. A welcome change for me, and a morale booster for both of us, it was embodied in a souvenir snapshot of the reunion.

The ghastly six month era behind me, my aspirations for posting to Italy faded. I still hoped to get there, but it would have to happen of its own accord. At 247 Wing, we formed a concert party, the 'Guarcsia Gaieties', which took its name from a nearby local village. As many buildings were still intact, one of then was converted into a small, intimate theatre. Instead of travelling to other camps, it

---

[5] Nice girl

enabled the CO to invite personnel from them. We staged some remarkably good shows, the D-Day landings inspiring a revue optimistically entitled 'Happiness Ahead'. By far the most popular act was the duo, Bill Alban and Len Kenwood. By no means old, yet both as bald as badgers! They wrote reams of witty, topical monologues, delivering them much in the style of those two cads, Kenneth and George, the Western Brothers, against my light background of piano when required. They poked harmless yet often penetrating fun at everyone and everything, from the Air Ministry and the CO down to the humble erk and the base-wallahs in Cairo.

'Happiness Ahead' proved to be my last show with 247 Wing – and a very prophetic title in a personal sense. I have fond recollections of the finale. A Big Ben-dominated backdrop, the featured piano solo 'Midnight in Mayfair', followed by a drunken, dishevelled, happy figure in top hat, white tie and tails, singing what was surely the most original and happiest comedy song of the war, Hubert Gregg's 'I'm Gonna Get Lit Up When The Lights Go Up In London', the solo vocal and dance then being joined in with great gusto by the entire company. My incessant scribblings on to manuscripts often by the light of an oil lamp earned me the temporary nickname of 'Dots'.

It wasn't just music for the show however; I was preparing hopefully for better days, doing some revision from old textbooks on harmony, and from a copy of Lew Stone's *Harmony and Orchestration for the Modern Dance Band*, which I had received from home. It was probably the earliest sign of writer's itch which was to mature many years thence.

The war having moved far away from us, other welcome facilities became available, such as a mobile record library. A home-made radiogram was installed in a spare Nissen hut (which was like a furnace during the day, but a lot cooler at night) where I enjoyed immensely the peace and tranquillity provided by the weekly recitals of concertos, light music and symphonies.

One sphere of entertainment which did not improve was the occasional film shows. I am reminded of them when noticing Channel Four's black and white offerings such as *Kismet* and *Bitter Sweet* Someone by the name of Shafto (probably a Greek-Cypriot) had the forces contract, the instant dubbing in the vernacular was 'Shafto's Shoofties'! Such terrible films were enlivened only by the witticisms, a typical example being one in which a shapely, well-endowed star ripped off a strip of her well-filled blouse to dress the gunshot wound of the hero. Such generous exposure to sex-starved desert rats provoked a witty reaction from one wag, much to the delight of the audience. Addressing the film's 'baddie', he yelled, "Go on, shoot 'im in the other arm!"

CHAPTER SIXTEEN

AND THE BAND PLAYED ON

The aim of 212 Group at Benina Airfield was to form a dance band and a show by drawing on and combining the best talent from all the units within its control; so many strings were pulled, all in the cause of entertainment. My spell with 247 Wing concert party assured me of a place – a temporary detachment which turned out to be permanent. The company and conventional dance band contained several peacetime pro acts and musicians. Many of the shows were staged in a converted hangar, capable of seating an audience of several hundred. Hessian galore covered the metal walls and roof in a valiant, but not entirely successful bid to improve the awful acoustics. The biggest and brightest show and yet personnel postings to the UK, or to bases in Alex and Cairo, forced it to wind up in a matter of weeks.

But eight musicians remained – trumpet, four saxes, piano, drums and bass – adequate to undertake a tour, this time in the opposite direction to Tobruk, with Flying Officer Freddie Morton in charge. Another bod whose two years plus in Iraq had left him with more than a touch of the sun! On parade, it was 'Yes sir' or 'No sir' but off duty, he mucked in and became one of the lads, no standing on ceremony. The tour was only days old when postings to the UK cut us down to four. Fortunately, the one tenor sax left with us was George Forbes, a pro from Edinburgh and a very fine violinist to boot. Rudy Sage from Brightlingsea on drums, Ralph Hudson from Skipton on trumpet made up the quartet which continued with the tour.

Ralph's usual role was second or even third trumpet in a big band. Having to take the lead much of the time in a smaller outfit didn't come easy. So much so that at Apollonia, he mucked up the final brass passage of 'In The Mood' striving to hit the top C concert. We managed to cover it up by faking some comedy, but it was obvious that his lip on high notes was going fast. So we persuaded him to take up string bass. It was, in any case, more essential and suitable to our combination, and it didn't take him long to get the hang of it.

Our arrival at Tobruk was timely.

"We've got an extra night here, chaps," said Freddie. "The Officers' Club opens this evening with a slap-up dinner and dance. They would like us to go along."

The club had been installed in one of the few buildings declared safe. Following the background music for dinner, we had an excellent meal, then continued playing for dancing until about two in the morning. Female partners were there in great force (almost equalling the number of males), in the shape of nursing and NAAFI staff, and many of them, I might add, in *very* good shape! A marvellous evening ended when the booze ran out, and George was in his element as we played for the Eightsome Reel. But it *wasn't* the end...

As we packed instruments and prepared to get the mini-piano down two flights of stairs, music drifted up from the ground floor. There was a boisterous knees-up going on to the music of a five-piece Army ENSA band which had apparently arrived soon after us. We were invited to share what was left of the beer and, joining forces, played till gone four in the morning. Ralph was really and truly Brahms and Liszt! He was insistent about his ability to drive the three-ton gharry, but we bundled him into the back and Rudy took the wheel, Ralph mumbling and muttering, "Rudy won't let me drive. I'm all right, I'm not drunk."

Getting no sympathy, he became depressed about the Apollonia incident, bidding us, "Throw my bloody trumpet out of t'gharry; I'm no good, I can't play t'bloody thing!"

We recovered from our hangovers to do the show for two more nights, and so back to Benina.

Living month after month on so much dehydrated food (I can still see those dry, revolting, cardboard coloured strips supposed to be carrots), with a lack of fresh fruit and vegetables, plus eating local meat fit only for repairing boots, dozens of us went down with jaundice. Another spell in Benghazi Hospital, followed by one more idyllic sick leave at Apollonia. (Seems I can't get away from the place!) We hadn't lost our sense of humour though. It found its expression in a game of football. The teams? 'Yellow Peril' versus 'Dysentery'. We lost, five nil. Guess who played in goal?

Later in the year, we began playing for dinner and dancing at the Benghazi Officers' Club. We were paid for our services and got free meals and drinks into the bargain. (Good ere, innit?)

92

On Christmas Day, we organised our own party. Freddie joined us for a while, accompanied by his pet dog, a black, floppy spaniel, Sheila. There were evenings when she roamed into our tent, and we discovered how much she loved a platter of beer. We had plied her with the stuff on Christmas Eve so it was one more occasion when Freddie mildly, but good-humouredly rebuked us.

"You've been at it again you buggers!" he exclaimed. "She's had her head down all day long. Out to the world."

Earlier that day I had been back to the hospital again, but this was a much happier visit. There were three major wards and we spent about thirty minutes in each, entertaining, and playing request tunes for staff and patients.

At the Erks versus Officers & NCOs football match next morning, the going was soggy after heavy rain, the field dotted not just with puddles, but pretty large pools. The Erks were five up at half time, forcing the other team to resort to a second half of no holds barred. A gharry filled the goal mouth; several players mounted donkeys; and the game rapidly developed into a comic quasi-rugger affair. As the final whistle blew, twenty-two saturated, mud-splattered players made a bee-line for the referee – still virtually unblemished in white shirt and shorts. It doesn't require very much imagination to guess what happened to him!

At the camp concert on Boxing Day night, the Italian POWs[6] closed the first half with a presentation of a ballet scene from *William Tell*. They took their bow, and we all began to move off into the wings. In our wake, however, followed one of the group, unannounced, nervously clutching violin and bow. He began playing the opening slow movement of Monte's 'Czardas'. I knew it well. I crept quietly back to the piano and accompanied him to the end.

Through the medium of hand signs, a mixture of Italian and English, his professional status was confirmed. It transpired that George had been persuaded to lend him his fiddle, but the PoW had not played for the best part of two years. The tears ran down his cheeks as profusely as his thanks spilled out to George and me. Understanding his feelings in those supercharged emotional moments, I put myself in his place, and thought, 'What if I had been forced to

---

[6] Although Italy had, of course, surrendered in August 1943 there were still POWs awaiting repatriation.

endure three and a half years devoid of making music, even though it was but a humble offering?'

Christmas and the universal language of music had transcended all man-made barriers. The Italians are, of course, classed as being an emotional race – far more so than the phlegmatic, stiff-upper-lipped British. But the incident made nonsense of classifications. Whatever the race, there are those made of stone and those who are not. To hell with racial classification! Possibly because I was by far the youngest in the entire show, I was affected more than anyone else.

Moved to tears, I fled backstage to be alone with my thoughts for several minutes, filled with a curious mixture of emotions: happiness shared with another musician, regardless of creed or race, friend or enemy, awareness of why the world was at war, yet deep sadness, tinged with anger at the stupidity of it all. Thoughts that ran parallel to the First World War, recalling my father telling me how opposing forces would visit each other's trenches and dug-outs, sharing food, drinks and tobacco; swapping photographs and mementoes during the Christmas Day cease-fire, only to begin all the hellish slaughter and destruction again on the stroke of midnight.

The next evening, using the CO's shooting brake, we were off again to Benghazi Hospital, playing until the early hours, and we stayed overnight. Going down after breakfast the next morning, we found that some joker (or jokers) had deflated all four tyres! Consequently, it was well after ten that morning before we reached Benina, greeted by a fusillade of implicating jests from the lads, "Dirty lot of stop-outs!", "Some blokes get all the luck!", "Was the operation successful?" and, "Fancy having a nurse hold your hand and not even being ill!"

A superb Christmas was rounded off by our return to play for the New Year's Eve party and dance for hospital staff. Fantastic hospitality. Auld Lang Syne, not a few tears, and a toast to a speedy end to the war. And with war still raging in Europe and the Far East, one sometimes felt guilty about the good times. Still, I had tried to move on, but it wasn't to be. I was just one of hundreds of thousands who filled what was mostly a peacetime occupational role.

We would doubtless soon be moved on to the Far East. Would the war ever end?

CHAPTER SEVENTEEN

DESERTING THE DESERT

By March 1945 I had heard from Jack, now stationed in the UK, at Stansted. He offered to visit my folks, but, of course, I had to explain that they were still in North Wales. I also had a few lines from Les Brown who was now in the Scots Guards band, as a percussionist when on parades and marches.

At last, it was goodbye to the Western Desert. I spent a few weeks at a radar station near Alex known as 'Seagull' Camp, where music was in demand mostly for dancing, personnel consisting of roughly equal numbers of RAF and WAAF bods. After three and a half years of male-dominated communities it seemed a bit strange at first. But don't get me wrong – I wasn't complaining! There were gigs with a four-piece outfit – three of the musicians actually from an all-services big band – with which I eventually played for dances held at the Fleet Club. That was a welcome change too, becoming acquainted with all the latest orchestrations from Blighty, the big band numbers by Glenn Miller, Artie Shaw, Stan Kenton, Duke Ellington *et al*.

I had always preferred Alex to Cairo. Being on the coast, it was always noticeably cooler and fresher. (Except for the smell of the leather works which assailed one's nostrils when approaching from a westerly direction!) So the next posting to an MU at Trura Caves in the suburbs of the capital wasn't very pleasing. Inevitably, some trades were fast becoming redundant, and mine was no exception. I was engaged for a short while in a store-bashing capacity. Unexpectedly, there was a fortunate twist of fate.

I was hardly past the main gates when a gharry pulled up, the driver got out, removed his sun-glasses, and stared as if he couldn't believe his eyes! I stared too. It was George Forbes! The reunion was short-lived – four weeks, in fact, with musical activities limited to playing for kicks, except on Sunday mornings when a cellist joined us and we provided light music for a couple of hours in the pleasant lounge of the YMCA.

May 8th, 1945 was significant not only as VE Day to me, due once again to the collusion of time and events. It was a day when the oppressive Kham-Sin was blowing so forcefully that even the outskirts of Cairo had sand whirling around the streets. George and I sat in a bar after lunch, combating the stifling, sticky and energy-sapping atmosphere by downing cold beer. Back at Trura that evening, shortly after the VE Day celebrations, the most violent electrical storm the area had known for more than a century erupted. There was driving, torrential rain and the intensity and fury of the storm was spectacular and frightening. A complete section of the main road collapsed and even aircraft engines were carried hundreds of yards away. The timing of the phenomenon was positively uncanny.

Next stop – Heliopolis, 282 Wing of Transport Command from whence I made frequent excursions into Cairo to see Frank, and to meet his WAAF girlfriend Joan, a petite brunette from Taunton, Somerset. It was a whirlwind affair and, in next to no time, I found myself in the crowd of guests, mostly the band and ME Welfare Unit, at the wedding and the reception, at Claridges. Within a matter of weeks, the newly-weds were homeward bound, but I was unaware of their movements due to an unexpected move to Palestine.

I had become a footballing casualty. My right kneecap resembled an Egyptian melon. Failing to respond to treatment in sick bay, I was flown in a Dakota to Lydda Airport, thence to the RAF Orthopaedic hospital for a stay of several weeks. I hadn't flown since those happy days with 203 when scrounging a lift on training flights or to forward base in a 'Wimpy' Wellington. Perhaps that was why it seemed to be an extraordinary bumpy noisy flight. 'Every cloud has a silver lining' is the optimist's platitude. Mine became apparent when I was once again mobile and I went with a small party, led by the hospital padre and a local guide, to spend two highly interesting days in Jerusalem and Bethlehem. The tours were leisurely and unhurried, allowing ample time for me to make copious notes. The extension of these into a lengthy letter home was reproduced, much to my surprise and delight, in a local paper. The editor must have been hard up for copy that week!

Two or three weeks at a cliff-top rehabilitation centre, a stone's throw from Tel Aviv, helped to make some atonement for my dreadful weight loss in recent years. A now completely acclimatised body lazing in sun and water, day after day, resulted in a fantastic gain of eight pounds, aided, no doubt, by the availability, for the first time in years of two totally different beverages, Horlicks in the morning and

Guinness at night. (Sounds like a TV commercial, doesn't it?) The happy stay in Palestine was rounded off when I managed to get to a concert by the Palestine Orchestra before returning to Egypt.

Before I left Tel Aviv, the fateful atomic attacks on Japan had taken place. Unable to get back by air, I endured a laboriously slow return by road and rail. Arriving in the heat of the afternoon, I made for the Tedder Club, showered, mingled with the excited, seething masses in the capital, then made tracks for Heliopolis. Peace had arrived but, as we all know, not for long. Many other conflicts followed and as I write, ethnic cleansing blights the country we once knew as Yugoslavia; neo-Nazi racism raises its ugly head again in Europe. How can anyone who went through World War Two fail to be moved by the latest horrors to hit our TV screens? Similarly by clips of the Holocaust; the silent sentinels of human folly – seemingly endless rows of war graves; the misery of fleeing refugees; Burma rail-road atrocities; young fighter pilots 'scrambling' at a Battle of Britain airfield.

The fight for human rights, the freedom and dignity of the individual is endless. I recall another black and white clip – one from that full dress rehearsal for World War Two, the Spanish Civil War. A combatant wearing a headband, bandolier across his chest, rifle held defiantly aloft; the caption, 'It is better to die on your feet than live on your knees,' says it all.

CHAPTER EIGHTEEN

INTERMEZZO

Now back at 282 Wing, I started dating dark-haired, dreamy Michaela – a locally enlisted member of the WAAF, popularly known as 'Mickey'. She was Jewish, but had a cosmopolitan background. Her mother was German; her father, who was in the medical profession, was Russian. Add to the mixture, her birthday – March 17th, St Patrick's Day – and you'll see what I mean!

The Jewish race seem to have a distinct flair for foreign languages, born, I suppose, out of sheer necessity through centuries of persecution forever wandering the world seeking refuge in friendly countries. Michaela, a few years older than I, was no exception, being fluent in several tongues, well-travelled and a good conversationalist. (On holiday some thirty years later Olive and I, in a shopping arcade in Montreux, were fascinated by the linguistic ability of the Jewish proprietor of a general store. Perhaps limited to the demands of his business but, nevertheless, he switched effortlessly from English, French, German and Italian.)

Michaela was an enigmatic character who displayed contrasting moods of melancholy and flippancy. In keeping with such characteristics, I became accustomed to playing the role of second fiddle to an army officer, a tall, good-looking type aged, I guessed, about forty-plus. She enjoyed my company, as I did hers, but she had no compunction about breaking our date should the army type suddenly be off duty. I suppose I should have known better than to attempt to compete with the experience of an older (and married) man, whose rank and money outclassed anything material I could offer. The many better-class venues were strictly out of bounds – off limits to other ranks, even if some of them were quite capable of conducting themselves correctly and being appreciative of the better things in life.

In September, Michaela went home on leave, to Tel Aviv for the Jewish new year holiday. She lived with her parents hardly a stone's throw from the centre where I had been only a few weeks earlier! When speaking to her about the absence of a piano at the camp, she had remarked kindly, and, I believe, quite sincerely, "It's a pity you didn't know me then. You could have called any time and used our piano at home."

Yes; I often wondered later just how things might have turned out had we met prior to my Palestinian sojourn. Still fresh in the mind were the horrific pictures of the Holocaust, but our conversations seldom dwelt for long on such a distressing subject, so obvious was Michaela's sadness, mingled, I suspected, with relief that she and her family had escaped the vicious genocide.

One could hire practice rooms, equipped with a piano, in Cairo for a few akkers (piastres) per hour, courtesy RAF welfare. Needless to say, I made the most of this welcome facility, spending much time committing my first serious attempt at composition. In retrospect, it wasn't anything particularly brilliant, except perhaps that the piece, of about eight minutes' duration, accurately caught Michaela's enigmatic character in its twin contrasting themes, the slow sad one in a minor key having a distinctly Jewish flavour. I've since added a short ballet movement, and another featuring typical balalaika music, three movements comprising 'Intermezzo 45'.

Hearing it for the first time in the practice rooms, Michaela commented on the sad influence, but added an encouraging, "You must go on writing, don't ever give up. Maybe we'll meet again when you are on tour."

Mere pipe dreams, I thought. We made our way downstairs, the snogging (horrible word) session over, had coffee at a nearby cafe then, hand in hand, made our way back to Heliopolis, singing excerpts from 'At The Balalaika', 'Play Gypsy' and the exciting 'Czardas' from 'Maritza' and Michaela's favourite of the day, 'Besame Mucho', all in between mouthfuls of roasted corn on the cob.

Incredible! Yet another conspiracy of time and events. This one coincided with my mother's birthday, November 12th. There it was, in black and white on the repatriation list – my name. That was it – the last letter home to the family, now back in the Happy Hacienda except brother Albert, still in Europe. The old homestead had taken a few hard knocks but, mercifully, was a survivor in that war-torn district of London.

Strange, but until only a few years ago I had a constantly recurring dream – that of being totally alone on the shore, waiting for the ship to arrive and take me home. Everyone else had gone. Something planted in the deep subconscious, I suppose. After all, the boat home was never far from anyone's mind, as was the possibility that one might *never* return. Final goodbyes were made on the 18th November, 1945. I boarded the 25,000 ton Polish liner, the *Batory*. What a contrast between the outgoing and return voyages! Four berth cabins with H&C instead of hammocks, hung so close to each other that they produced a togetherness rivalled only by sardines! One kitbag and a case in place of the vast amount of gear we took out with us; an acute shortage of duty-free tobacco, whereas it had been plentiful when outward-bound. Suntanned not pale faces reflecting happy thoughts of the prospect of Christmas at home, as opposed to the 'I-wonder-what-will-happen-to-us' expression.

Regular serving airmen had told us of the time-honoured custom whereby topees were flung unceremoniously from the stern when a troopship left foreign ports, 'bound for old Blighty's shores' as in the song 'Bless 'Em All'. Topees had been left behind, however, and if there had been any I doubt whether the ritual would have been performed.

As we drew slowly away from Port Said, momentarily a heavy, ponderous silence, entirely out of proportion to the hundreds lining the decks, seemed to smother and engulf the liner. Then suddenly, it was broken by movement and voices, just as if we had simultaneously pinched ourselves out of a dream into stark reality. Yes, we really were on the way home! It was an unexpectedly swift route. A short call at Malta, gleaming, shimmering, pristine whiteness under a clear blue sky. Thence to Toulon, thirty-six hours by rail to Dieppe and the following morning, on the tide, all aboard the *Isle of Thanet Belle*, probably one of the armada of little ships which had survived Dunkirk.

We crowded on deck, wearing our Mae Wests, instructed to watch out for loose mines. But as dawn broke on that clear, frosty morning, all eyes were concentrated expectantly in one direction and one direction only – awaiting the magical moment when we would catch our first glimpse of the English coastline. At Newhaven, the customs officers were pretty lenient, letting dozens go by, stopping only one airman immediately in front of me to ask about the Continental-type accordion he had with him. I don't doubt that it was bartered for cigarettes, chocolate or bully beef. Insisting that he had taken it out with him from Blighty, he was given the benefit of the doubt. The incident was a painful reminder of my unfulfilled desire to see Italy, even at that late stage.

After Newhaven, Hornchurch, and by 30th November, home again, where my brother Albert was also on leave from Belgium. A mere eighteen days compared to the nine weeks on the eventful run to the ME four years ago. Four years? Was it really that long? Curiously, the time gap seemed to shrink, to become more and more compressed, as I made my way around, seeing friends and relatives. I journeyed to Morley at Jack White's invitation. He and his wife, Clarissa, lived in a typical Northern terraced house. As I entered the living room, the first object to catch my eye was a pewter tankard, suitably engraved – a souvenir from 203 Squadron Officers' Mess – on the high, old-fashioned mantelshelf, some pipe cleaners protruding from the top!

"You're lucky, Jack," I commented.

"What do you mean?" he asked.

"I packed my tankard with other souvenirs which went to Aboukir back in 42," I explained. "It was a daft thing to do. The kit bag was pinched by Gyppo clefty-wallahs when they broke into the store."

I continued, "Included was the sheet music of 'Oasis'. No use talking about it now – they've all gone for ever," I reflected, somewhat sadly.

Jack's wife had somehow formed the impression that I lived in far superior surroundings, a high-class neighbourhood of London's suburbia. She was distinctly uneasy at first, being openly over-apologetic about the outside loo in the back yard. I had always tried to get along with everyone, rubbing shoulders with people from all walks of life, regardless of status, colour or creed, in the past five years. I did my best to dispel Clarissa's erroneous notions.

Back in his civvies and back to work for Jack, so I had breakfast late next morning, after he had left. Surprisingly, Clarissa was most talkative; I seemed to have broken the ice. She made no bones about the fact that Jack had gone into a regular day job because, as she put it, most succinctly, "We'll not get wed unless thee get a regular job wi' regular brass." Security was obviously uppermost in her mind. Jack had compromised with the Lewis's music department by day, playing gigs in spare time.

I didn't know it at the time, but that word 'compromise' was to play a big part in my life very soon. Christmas was only a few days off, so I returned to London after a short stay, during which time I did the rounds of Leeds with Jack, and we talked about our proposed joint venture without any firm commitment, deciding to keep in touch pending news as to my eventual demob date.

During my final few weeks at Heliopolis, Michaela had faithfully kept every date. I might have guessed that there was a good reason behind the sudden, but pleasant change. When told of my imminent departure for Blighty, she admitted that her number one escort was already heading in the same direction. The night before I left, she handed me a thick, tightly-packed envelope, and separately, for obvious reasons, a business address at which I would be able to contact her 'Dream Lover' – my term for him, but an appropriate one, for without a shadow of a doubt she was absolutely convinced that, regardless of his family and domestic responsibilities, he would be back – permanently.

'What a line he must have shot' was my unspoken opinion. I journeyed south one afternoon, early in the new year, the letter being handed over in the seclusion of the upstairs cafe of the Odeon Cinema, Ashford, in Kent. (Had you told me that I would be treading the same ground a few years later when it was used for dinner dances and I would be playing there, I wouldn't have believed you. But that's what did happen!)

A cup of tea, a friendly chat, brief, yet spanning past, present and future, then I made tracks for home, leaving the recipient, now back at his office in a local estate agents, to read what was most certainly a sentimental romantic and yearning epistle. "When you've read it, I would make sure it is destroyed," was my well-meant advice, acknowledged by only a smile – a response which meant neither yes nor no. Even a kindly way of saying, 'Mind your own business!' Anyway, contrary to my fears, the meeting had not been an embarrassing one, even though Michaela had, of course, taken a terrible risk. Or did her obsession blind her to the wide-open possibility that her letter, in the wrong hands, invited blackmail? An ugly, but realistic thought. It was emotional dynamite, capable of destroying a whole family. I felt flattered by her placing so much trust in me. We exchanged a couple of letters – the finale, early in 1946 to a three-part intermezzo in which I had played second fiddle. But there are times when one has to if harmony is to be created.

So ended a mildly romantic encounter, one of many which befell erks, brown types and jolly jack tars alike during the war years. Simply someone of the opposite sex with whom to share conversation, laughter, memories, walks and social occasions, after having been denied female company for several years. As Rodgers and Hammerstein observed most accurately, in just one line, 'There is nothing like a dame.'

Some years later, I penned a simple little theme – 'A Minor Affair' – for no other reason than that it was in the sad-sounding key of A minor. And that title most aptly summed up the pleasant, memorable, but brief relationship with the dreamy, dark-haired Michaela.

We leave Heliopolis with a remarkable if not unique story related to me by tent-mate, Archie, a Geordie corporal in the medical bay. He was assigned to RAF air/sea rescue launches, which were pretty nippy craft (as I discovered when taking a trip in one off Derna). Archie's launch picked up a crew from an inflatable dinghy in the North Sea and he noticed the long stare and puzzled face of one of the crew who eventually said, "Say, haven't I seen you somewhere before? Wasn't it in Canada?"

Indeed, it turned out that he had, and it was in fact in Canada! Archie had rescued the self-same Canadian airman when stationed in Canada on rescue launches in the earlier part of the war. As they say in show biz, 'Follow that!'

CHAPTER NINETEEN

FROM MINOR TO MAJOR

It was a bitterly cold, cloudy day when I strolled through Central Park *en route* for Frank's place, which was situated off the other side of the High Street. It was good to be home, but already I was hating the climate, sorely missing the eternal eastern sunshine although I was glad to be rid of hordes of disease-carrying flies and mosquitoes, to be able to sleep without the intrusion of fleas, bugs, scorpions and, at one time I recalled, as my memory jumped around, even locusts. I had to admit to myself that during the last few months abroad, given essential facilities of a shower whenever one pleased, a decent bed, proper sanitation, refrigeration and a wider variety of food, life had been quite bearable, even pleasant. Thinking back to the sun again, I touched on the fact that for almost four years there had been no wondering, 'Shall I need a brolly? A swathing of greatcoat, scarf and gloves?' Oh, the wonderful bodily freedom of just shirt, shorts, and desert boots, month in, month out! I had been spoiled for ever!

Thoughts swiftly changed again, jerked back to the present as I gazed at the ploughed-up playing fields where I had so often engaged in sporting activities with schoolmates, still filled with the fruits – or rather more accurately, the vegetables – of the 'Dig for Victory' campaign. Still very much in evidence too were the now desolate, abandoned sites which had housed ack-ack gun emplacements, searchlights and barrage balloons. I hurried on out of the park gates and into the main thoroughfare, observing the ugly, yawning gaps where once had stood houses, shops, a club, a church. Dominating all was a derelict sprawl, the site of a vanished landmark, The White Horse public house, where the number 15 bus route from town terminated.

At Frank's place, his father, a carpenter and cabinet maker, was pottering between garden shed and side door when I arrived. Happy pre-war memories were revived when I commented on the old Morris in the side-way, in mothballs, so to speak, jacked up off the ground to protect the tyres. We hadn't been chatting very long before Frank's mother, his wife Joan and his sister Olive joined us, and on went the kettle for a cuppa. They had returned from a visit to Frank at RAF Halton.

Both girls were still in the WAAF awaiting demob, the latter a teleprinter operator and looking far more attractive in civilian garb was petite blonde Olive, whom I last remembered when in the somewhat thin, gawky and giggly not-long-out-of-school stage of life. What a transformation! 'I don't know what I saw in you,' is the well-worn jest between married couples, and reference to it is pertinent here when it comes to dancing – something at which Olive was, and still is, very good. It was ages later before I got around to serious attempts to improve, so that I could trip the light fantastic with more style. Up till then, I guess that I had merely tripped! But it's a well-known fact that being on the outside looking in – in other words, years of *playing* for dancing – tends to produce a breed of musicians who, regardless of their excellent sense of rhythm and timing, paradoxically, are the world's worst hoofers.

The period between January and May was made enjoyable by the variety of activities and the change of scene. I had very limited duties to perform where I was now stationed – the former Battle of Britain HQ at Bentley Priory, Stanmore, and being billeted at RAF Uxbridge was another stroke of good fortune. It was, and still is, of course, the home of the RAF Central Band. Befriended by a drummer – a diminutive Jewish chap named Lew – when trying my skill at a two-manual organ one evening, I was soon in on the dance band scene. I gigged around the Middlesex locale on private engagements with him, mostly with four or five-piece outfits. I endeavoured, not very successfully, to improve my dancing at local hops, doubtless leaving many a WAAF partner hoping that I *didn't* come here often!

I was ideally situated. Home in just over an hour at weekends, or for heading north to Luton or Bedford to meet Olive whose camp was at Chicksands Priory. (Yes, we were right ones for priories!) I recall getting my head down for a few hours in the guard room there after the fateful 'D' watch Saint Valentine's Day dance, boarding the first bus in the morning and arriving at Stanmore bleary-eyed and unshaven. But parades and inspections were now virtually non-existent, such was the demob-happy atmosphere. Naturally, the last waltz had to be the oldie 'I'll Be Your Sweetheart', which poses the question 'If you will be mine' and the declaration 'All my life, I'll be your Valentine'. 'Bluebells I'll gather, take them and be true'...

Bluebells? You must be joking! At two in the morning in the middle
of cold, damp February? Not at Chicksands Priory! And why waste
time gathering bluebells? Joking apart, the time, the place, the means
of expression, bluebells or no bluebells, what do they matter? Love
was the perennial flower in bloom and, to quote Tennyson, 'In the
spring a young man's fancy turns to thoughts of love.' Well, perhaps
springtime is more conducive to love-making but ours had all begun in
December, so it happens anywhere, any time. 'Any time's kissing
time' to quote the ballad from 'Chu Chin Chow'.

Measured by today's standards, when anything which hasn't been
pressed into a recent single hit song must be old hat, 'I'll Be Your
Sweetheart' would be dismissed as sentimental slop. Yet I fully
expect that modern equivalents 'I Want To Be Your Teddy Bear' and
'I Wanna Hold Your Hand' will be similarly relegated. Song-writers
have been, and still are, coming up with new ways of saying 'I love
you'. Although moon and June are now very much out of fashion,
love is still, world-wide, the most popular theme.

In Victorian days, a young maiden was invited, in genteel tones, to
'Come into the Garden, Maud'. Compare the song with the
humorous, but blatant abrasive persuasion of the pop song, 'Come
Outside'. Whether you class the songs in the category of love or lust,
the fact remains that they are synonymous – only time separates them.
Ending on a more cultured note, I can do no better than to quote the
immortal bard: 'All the world loves a lover.' He knew what he was
talking about. St Valentine rules, OK! Or does he? Nothing, it
seems, is sacred. Are natural and spontaneous romantic encounters of
the human kind now threatened by man's introduction of electronic
monsters, 'chips' with everything, widely advertised as the ideal
media for finding a life-partner?

FINDAMATE

Verse 1:   Would you like to join our list of suitors?
FINDAMATE's the leading agency,
We mix you with the chicks on our computers,
Compatibility we guarantee.
That's the kind of ad I find amusing.
Just for kicks, I put it to the test,
But stupid are computers playing Cupid,

Can't wait to get the story off my chest.

Chorus 1:   I made a date with FINDAMATE,
For FINDAMATE to find
The kindamate that FINDAMATE
Designed with me in mind.
But ev'ry date was oh, so desperate,
My mate to be, my destiny,
I guess I'll wait till fate creates one just for me –
Naturally.

Verse 2:   Looking for true love and true romances?
Lonely people throw away despair,
We make the technological advances –
The modern answer to a maiden's prayer.
But just how many misses become missus
Just because statistics make the date? And just how
many guys get tasty dishes
When love is handed to them on a tape?

Repeat Chorus 1

Verse 3:   Now that ad is even more amusing.
In the end it happened naturally.
It was fate that did the pick 'n' choosing,
What a joke it all turned out to be!

Chorus 3:   I made a date with FINDAMATE,
The principal to see.
And the one who founded FINDAMATE,
She foundamate – in me.
It's so ironical, it's comical!
Now I make the dates for desperates,
To findamate for them that FINDAMATE
Couldn't find for me!

Repeat, fading... I made a date with FINDAMATE, I made a date
etc., etc.

CHAPTER TWENTY

DECISO

Time had passed quickly. Demob day for me – May 6th 1946 –
was just around the corner, yet my mind constantly wrestled with the
glut of opportunities, bouncing around like ping-pong balls inside my
head, not to be stilled until I made a firm decision. I had spent a
weekend in Taunton, where Frank and Joan, now back in civilian life,
were expecting their first-born in July. The prime purpose was to
discuss the formation of a dance band under Frank's direction – an
exciting venture, but so was that which Jack had offered – and, to
complicate matters further, Lew the drummer also approached me.

"You're in the same Demob Group – No. 33 – as me, aren't you?
How about joining me in Yarmouth, end of May? I've got a sixteen
week season there."

I thanked him for the offer, promising to make up my mind in
good time. It was nice to be wanted, but I had to keep options open.
The RAF also came up with an attractive three year term of service,
war years included for pension purposes. The carrot, dangling
tantalisingly, was the chance to remuster into other trades. A vocation
with the Central Band could be a rewarding one, although I'd
probably have to learn to play another instrument, and after three
years I could quit or go on for the jackpot.

But the poor rate of pay was most off-putting. I wonder how
many others considered then dismissed the idea, little dreaming of the
vastly improved status that would be attained by the services in a
matter of just a few years. But I had had enough of uniformity and
conformity so I threw out the idea. One ping-pong ball less bouncing
around in my mind. Frank's offer (and, I suppose, a 'keep it in the
family' influence) finally won the day.

Immaculate was truly the word to describe the band's appearance
and performance. The black and white façade of substantial, wide
music desks was echoed by black dress trousers, topped with
specially-made double-breasted, single button style white jackets, with
sweeping wide lapels. The final touch of elegance – buttonholes of
red carnations. A far cry from the scruffiness which was to assail the
public eye in the rock and roll and pop era. Not that one plays any

better smartly dressed, but appearance and presentation are all essential in showbiz. Sometimes the band was augmented to fulfil important dates such as The Winter Gardens, Weston-super-Mare, but generally gigs were at smaller and less imposing venues.

It soon became clear that it would be ages before the government derequisitioned and restored the many larger halls and premises, those which accommodated local functions, hunt balls etc., so in a matter of a few weeks the band folded. I was on fully-paid demob leave until mid-August; just as well, for my gratuity and other cash benefits which initially had seemed generous didn't go far. The cost of a new, decent civilian wardrobe, due to inflation, was now between four or five times the pre-war cost. The horrible demob suit I gave to Arthur, my youngest brother, for two reasons. Firstly because of a lack of clothing coupons and secondly because he would soon be off on his national service stint.

Back to London, where I did the rounds of Charing Cross Road, and that dingy little turning, Denmark Street, known as Tin Pan Alley. I didn't strike oil until late afternoon when I called at Francis, Day and Hunter. No vacancies, but Johnny Franz (then accompanist to singer Ann Shelton) directed me to a newly-formed music publisher in Greek Street – the Strauss-Miller Company. It was based at number eight. Formerly a restaurant, the premises hardly ranked as prestigious, but, with properties in short supply, I suppose it was very much Hobson's choice. I landed the job as a copyist and pianist, making it clear that I wanted to move on to the more interesting and lucrative field of orchestration. Since it was only a few months old, if the company prospered I would prosper too. I was in on the ground floor.

"What a fantastic break!" exclaimed Frank and Joan when I returned to Taunton that Saturday to do my final gig with the ill-fated band. Yes, it was a fantastic break, but also the first of life's many compromises, and a happy one.

I was soon at home in the friendly, happy atmosphere of the first floor office. It could be divided at will by the ceiling-to-floor length red and gold curtains, the front area being occupied by songwriter and arranger, Art Strauss, Sonny Miller, who did the lyrics, and pint-sized Hilda Ell, known by everyone in the business as 'Ellie'. Her main role was secretarial, but she also did some plugging and artistes' contact by phone. There was a lovely boudoir grand piano in one corner whilst at the rear of the office sat professional manager Tommy Hudson, arranger and songwriter Bob Dale and yours truly. They were all much older than I and seasoned hands in the music biz.

As usual, special orchestrations were always wanted by yesterday; there were contrasting hectic and slack periods, but everyone mucked in – never a dull moment. The starting time of ten each morning and no Saturdays suited me fine, particularly in the new year when my activities as a freelance pianist really took off, due to the many new contacts I'd made. It was sometimes necessary to take home a score and take off the parts (for which I was paid overtime) in readiness for rehearsal the next morning. It was an enjoyable perk, taking the parts along to a theatre in the Moss Empire chain, or to one of the BBC studios – mostly the Paris in Regent Street – and being present at rehearsal by the artiste or artistes concerned.

The scene was made more colourful by the perpetual comings and goings of show-biz personalities. Sometimes it was a purely social call and a chat over a cuppa – other times it was acts looking for new material or a speciality number. Vocalists with a big band or in a radio show came in to fix a suitable key for one of our songs, in preparation for a forthcoming broadcast. It all happened there, from the big-timers to the tatty music hall acts. Prominent among vocalists were Dorothy Squires, Ann Shelton, Donald Peers and Vera Lynn. (Thirty years later Dame Vera's presence brought back echoes of publishing days. She and her party were staying at the Castle Keep Hotel, Kingsgate, prior to doing a Sunday concert at Margate's Winter Gardens. As resident band we played through dinner, after which there was a brief conversation, a 'thank you for the music', with her husband and ex-Ambrose sax player Harry Lewis expressing the hope, in the words of the Musicians' Union slogan, that we would continue to 'Keep Music Live'.)

A layman entering the office in the midst of a hectic, busy spell could be forgiven for thinking, 'This is a nut house!' The switchboard buzzing, piano being played, a background of non-stop conversation and laughter, punctuated by Art's animated vocal grunts, noises like a steam engine, impersonations of instruments, all designed to convey to Bob at the piano how the next four or eight bar phrase of the orchestration would shape; where accents would fall; brass, strings, woodwind or percussion, or perhaps the reed section, and so on. To Bob and me it all meant something, but to the non-musical onlooker..!

One more page of the score completed, I would then write the individual parts, transposing where necessary. Veteran songwriters Leo Towers and Don Pelosi were frequent visitors, who, I recall, always expressed fascination at the speed of transfer of music to paper, asking, "How on earth do you work so fast – and accurately with all this racket going on?" I suppose one could describe it as being mildly schizophrenic – a knack of concentrating on dot scribbling, yet being aware of what was going on in the other side of the room.

Payment of 'plug' money to bandleaders and artists continued after the war, top spot then being the radio programme *Music Hall* which, to the best of my recollection, went on air at eight o'clock on Saturday evenings. The artist doing our current song would receive (you'll note I say 'receive', not 'earn') anything between fifty and one hundred pounds in hard cash as plug money. Chickenfeed now, I know, but an awful lot of money in 1946/7. Payment of such monies had always been frowned on by Auntie BBC, so the instigation of an agreement with the Music Publishers' Association the following year to outlaw all forms of incentive and inducement came as no great surprise. Now in a music world far removed from that of more than forty years ago, it is of course, the DJs who have the power to make or break a song. Whether the agreement still exists, in perhaps an updated form, I don't know. What I do know, however, is that it would be naïve of me to believe that plugging is a thing of the past; it is the methods which have probably changed.

Back in the seventies, when discussing the chances of getting one of my works into a popular radio programme, the professional manager of a name publishing house told me, "A couple of crates of Scotch for so-and-so [the producer] would do the trick, but we don't do business that way. Merit should be the overriding factor." If only it were so!

Probably best-known to my generation are Toronto-born Art Strauss's two hit songs 'They Can't Black-out The Moon' and 'Cinderella Sweetheart'. But during the war years a great deal of his time and energy had been devoted to doing arrangements for the big bands of the day, led by Stanley Black, Billy Cotton and, in particular, Bert Ambrose. His favourite hobby horse was the indispensable role of the arranger. One doesn't have to be well-versed in music to realise that a simple melody or a work of a more serious and enduring

"Sprogs", Blackpool, 1940 (top)

Invalid's Walk, Llandudno, 1940 (bottom)

Just two of many RAF shows.
Cardiff 1940 (top), Benghazi, 1943 (bottom)

203 Squadron Band, Burg-El-Arab Western Desert, April, 1942
(Jack White, centre) (top)

Christmas Menu, 1942 (bottom)

Reunion, Cairo, October, 1943 (top)

August, 1945 (bottom)

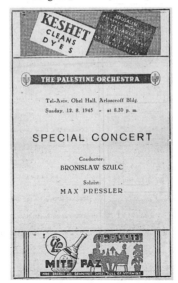

RAF 212 Group Band (top)

Guarscia gaieties, RAF Benghazi (bottom)

THE ORCHESTRA OF THE ROYAL MARINES SCHOOL OF MUSIC
Leader: Band Colour Sergeant J O'Neill

under the direction of

Lieutenant Colonel G A C HOSKINS OBE MVO ARAM RM
Principal Director of Music Royal Marines

NATIONAL ANTHEM

March from	THINGS TO COME	Bliss	Overture	OBERON		Weber
Suite	BALLET EGYPTIEN	Luigini	Fantasia	GREENSLEEVES	Vaughan Williams	
(i) Allegro Non Troppo (ii) Allegretto				Conductor:		
(iii) Andante Sostenuto (iv) Andante Espressivo:				Band Corporal B G STARR		
		Allegro Non Troppo				
	Conductor:		Tone Poem	FINLANDIA		Sibelius
	Sergeant N S AL-HADIDI					
	Oman Royal Guard					
Solo	TRUMPET TUNE AND AIR	Purcell	Film Theme	ARTHUR'S THEME		Bacharach arr Davis
	Soloist:			Conductor:		
	BCSgt J YATES ARCM			Band Corporal C J DAVIS		
Symphony	No 35 in D Major KV 385	Mozart	Selection	SOUTH PACIFIC		Rodgers
	"HAFFNER"			Conductor:		
	(i) Allegro Con Spirito			Sergeant A M AL-SABA		
	(ii) Andante			Bahrain Police		
	(iii) Minuetto					
	(iv) Finale		Two Portraits	RHAPSODIE TRISTESSE		Worland
	Conductor:			IN THE SHADOW OF VESUVIUS		Worland
	Band Sergeant C S Sproston			A LIFE ON THE OCEAN WAVE		Russell
	INTERVAL			Conductor:		
	(Coffee available at the rear of the Church)			Lieutenant Colonel G A C HOSKINS OBE MVO ARAM RM		
				Principal Director of Music Royal Marines		

Excerpts from Thursday concert programmes,
Royal Marines School of Music, Deal (top)

East Kent Light Orchestra

"Note Mozart Calendar"

On a gig – Winter Gardens, Margate (top)

Olive having a swinging time in Montreux (bottom)

The "Loose Ends" and "Cameos" (top)

Bolivian buskers, Bad Ischll, Austria (bottom)

nature, without the skill of an arranger, a score for the conductor and parts for each instrument or voice, bands, orchestras, choirs and backing groups, irrespective of size, would not be able to breathe life into the work – a blending of tone, colour, light and shade, and expression into a coherent and acceptable sound. The importance of the arranger will be seen to emerge more and more in the chapters ahead.

For his part, Sonny Miller's lyrics contributed to such hits as 'So Deep Is The Night', 'Russian Rose' and 'When The Gang Meet Again'. He was also responsible for the lyrics in the musical *Wedding In Paris*. Sonny was as Scouse as they come, especially within the office precincts, but in the business his obsession with all things American, included his car – a huge Oldsmobile saloon – and a phoney Yankee drawl! Bob Dale, who joined the company soon after demob from the RAF, had been part of a threesome for some years, later turning out a hit 'On the Five Forty-Five' under the pen name Mark Warren in 1948. Here was a streak of coincidence – Bob had been stationed at a balloon site in East Ham! By no means had I been a lone piano-plonker in RAF days. Bob mentioned gigs he had done in the East London locale, especially at Herbert's School of Dancing, which I knew well, adding the jest, "I got my 'props'[7] playing there!"

Which prompts me to add that in the post-war years, when the inevitable and commonplace question was put to me, "What did you do in the war, Daddy?" I quite truthfully and unashamedly answered, "I played piano most of the time," because, although ever mindful of those who hadn't been so fortunate, I was aware and appreciative that, in many ways, music being the mother of resourcefulness had helped me to survive the rough-and-ready experiences.

---

[7] Promotion to Leading Aircraftman — a propeller worn on each arm.

CHAPTER TWENTY-ONE

CHANGING FORTUNES

Shortly before Christmas, Olive and I were married, spending the honeymoon at Ventnor, Isle of Wight. White it was too – with snow. It was a freezing day, with light falls of snow, as we gathered at the Norman church of St Mary's in East Ham. It was the prelude to one of the coldest, longest, snowbound winters on record, the discomforts heightened by fuel shortages and widespread power cut-outs well into March 1947. But if winter was unforgettable, so was the summer which followed. Nature redressed the balance swiftly with a long-lingering glorious display of warmth, light and colour so sorely needed in drab and uneasy post-war Britain.

The other celebration was sparked off when a corny waltz, 'Sweetheart, We'll Never Grow Old', which Strauss-Miller were currently promoting, hit the number one spot in the pop music charts – and I do mean *music*, based on the sales of sheet music, not records. It was no mean achievement for a firm just one year old. It set the bubbly corks a-popping, as countless show biz people dropped in to offer congratulations. Whereas I was now in a fortunate phase in the see-saw of life, a very unsettled Frank, with his family, came back to town and began picking up a few gigs. We were sometimes joined by Freddy Hooper, an excellent string bass player who lived next door.

Every gig one undertakes is not necessarily all honey, pleasurable and straightforward. And in those early days of building up connections, hardly a week passed without encountering new faces, new places. A classic example, bang in the middle of the great freeze-up, was a gig at Epping Town Hall. That same evening Frank and Freddy had one at a venue somewhere out in the sticks of Hertfordshire, so we all journeyed in Fred's jalopy and it was arranged that they would pick me up at Epping after midnight on their return journey.

I was already miserably cold when the gig finished. The heating had been woefully inadequate. Outside, it was snowing hard and the minutes ticked by to half an hour; then a whole hour had passed. Had they forgotten? Had I missed them? Or had they broken down before reaching Epping town? I gave up pondering what had gone wrong and trudged along to the local cop shop, where I explained my dilemma.

The sergeant on duty was sympathetic and offered practical advice.

"Have a doze here until the milk lorry comes through – usually between five and five-thirty in the morning."

Grateful for the mugs of hot steaming tea provided. I stayed awake by engaging in conversation on a range of topics, mostly everyday mundane items, but it was a time-killing aid.

"I'm not supposed to give any lifts," grunted the lorry driver when I waved him to stop, "but in weather like this... well, hop in, mate."

So, coming home with the milk that Sunday morning, I reflected that the only small redeeming feature of the gig had been the surprise at meeting a sax and clarinet player, a lot older than I, who knew Bob Dale very well – a jazz enthusiast. I had learned an 'oldie' to add to my repertoire, 'Someday Sweetheart', the tune still buzzing around inside my head. One seldom went out on a gig without learning something. It happened all the time; no one could claim to know it all.

Frank and Freddy had not arrived home until three in the morning, delayed by engine trouble and a flat tyre, so all three of us had experienced one of those gigs best forgotten. Until now, that is, when one can look back and laugh at it all, thinking, 'Why did we do it? We must have been mad!'

Weather conditions apart, one rarely got through any year without being the victim of last-minute cancellation or double bookings, involving one individually or a whole band. Usually, it is poor lines of communication – Jack, on the committee, who thought Joe was booking the band or making a cancellation or vice versa. Result: a glorious cock-up. Not forgetting the 'characters', the less dependable type of musician who lets you down at the last minute or turns up late or not at all! And those who take a booking, then put in a deputy so useless that the band is better off without him!

Comics of the day flitted in and out of S-M den. Charlie Chester (hawking songs), Harry Lester, Izzy Bonn, Harold Berens. The latter, I recall, had us in stitches with humorous reminiscences. There came a fitting finale as he related an incident "on the boards... and just as the act was getting interesting, a stagehand threw the switch – in the wrong place! Complete blackout!" And obligingly, bang on cue, someone at the power station did just that! The office was plunged into darkness and, when we had all recovered from fits of laughter and candles were lit, all one could utter was the age-old showbiz challenge, "Follow that!"

Yes, even in that long icy spell there were lighter moments. Other financial benefits manifested themselves, such as private copying which Art put my way. This was very well-paid work which I did at home, mainly from scores for recording sessions by the big bands, attempting to survive in a much changed society, with a lot more changes in the musical climate too just around the corner. Even for superb bands like the Ted Heath outfit. How we enjoyed the Sunday concerts at the London Palladium in those immediate post-war years!

Bob, no longer interested in gigging, passed on a date nearer my home than his - at Ilford, where I met one of his wartime musician pals. It turned out to be a fortuitous date. I was invited to put in my own four-piece band on a regular basis. One night a week snowballed quickly with the addition of many other club functions, plus backing cabaret acts. The initial contract was for three months, but it was in fact eighteen before we parted company, but amicably, and of my own volition. It was time for change, to seek fresh fields and broaden experience.

Another opportunity presented itself when I received a letter and contract from Joe Crossland, the saxophonist who had been with the Group big band in the ME. He offered a six month run at an entertainment complex on the east coast of Scotland, with the option of a further six months. Accommodation was available, a four-berth caravan. Olive and I discussed the offer very briefly. We were expecting our first baby and the venture was out of the question, so I had to write accordingly to Joe. I was flattered by the offer. It was nice to know that I had been remembered by a seasoned pro, obviously impressed with my playing in those bygone days.

Coming out of the Ilford club proved to be good timing. One of the new contacts made was to endure for nearly thirteen years, terminating only because of my move out of London. Drummer Vic Hewitt, an ex-naval type, who lived opposite Barking Park, ran the big band, but at weekends there were always two, three or even more engagements to cover with smaller groups. Hence the location and type of function varied a great deal. Prominent were the full band gigs, taking in virtually every West End hotel of note, from the Savoy downwards. (The Hilton was then but a blueprint.) There were usually three of us beginning as early as 6.30p.m. for the reception and then playing for dinner. After a break for our own meal, the rest of the outfit would join us, playing for dancing and backing cabaret until midnight or later. My ability to sight-read well, to busk and to switch with ease from light music to that for dancing paid off handsomely. The variety and quality made every gig a pleasure, time simply speeding by, as it always does on enjoyable occasions. It was a band – a happy one, with, as the fully justified blurb read, 'East London's Brightest Band'.

Over the years, there were some resident jobs, such as the Saturday dancing club at the Doctor Johnson, Barkingside. Earlier, it was the Robin Hood Tavern, where I thoroughly enjoyed the mini Palm Court type of programme we played each Sunday, for two hours at lunchtime, using a seven-piece outfit with strings... memories of an early shot at orchestration of the then popular 'Too Young' in a contrasting rubato, beguine fashion, drawing the compliment, "It's very full; sounds very Fred Hartleyish," from the lads. Memorable too was the occasion when a member of the audience came armed with what surely must have been one of the first of post-war tape recorders. A huge bulky and heavy contraption, something of a novelty then, but with the undreamed of advances since made, all records and recording is now taken for granted, and sadly, in unthinking and unscrupulous hands, subjected to misuse, abuse and musical piracy.

I was soon doing more than half of my freelance work with Vic's band, a fine rapport having been established at the outset, especially with lead alto and clarinet, Les Logan. It compelled me to ask Les on the very first gig, "You played some other instrument before taking up sax, didn't you? Perhaps piano, or guitar?"

"That's right, Spanish guitar originally. Sax and clarry later, during the war," he replied.

My guess had been prompted by his evident knowledge of harmony and chord structure. The bulk of instrumentalists merely learn to read music and play, but were sadly lacking when it came to harmony and chord sequences. The years Les had spent on guitar, where such knowledge is a must, were reflected in his immaculate musicianship.

Some of our frequently visited venues included the historic King's Head at Chigwell, the American base at Wetherfield, Garon's

Restaurant, Southend, and the Athenaeum (previously a cinema) at Muswell Hill.

Reverting to the West End, there was an instance when we had to travel by Underground for an engagement (at Frascati's, I believe it was) because our petrol ration coupons had run out – testimony to the amount of work we were doing.

A good time was had by all. So much so that on the return journey Les and two others became entangled with instruments soon after setting foot on the main escalator at Tottenham Court Road. All three, followed by cases and big bass drum, effected an undignified descent, landing in a heap at the bottom! The incident had a shaky but sobering effect on them; with the discovery that, miraculously, no one was hurt, concern was relieved by a laughter which was fed by many other apt and humorous comments on the way home.

It was customary, indeed an unwritten law, to provide a meal for those musicians who had played for reception and through dinner. But there were wide variations in both food and service. At St Ermyns, for example, we were treated well. We could order a drink and choose from the extensive and attractive menu in the main restaurant. At the other end of the scale, at the Connaught Rooms, it was a traipse down a rear staircase, to be seated with waiters and other kitchen staff in a noisy, hot atmosphere, and to be grateful for what we were about to receive – often the leftovers.

Having left the scene more than thirty years ago, it may well have since changed for the better, I don't know. But the two examples, expressed in musical terms, certainly smack of 'Poet and Peasant' treatment.

Frank did a spell at the Mecca Ballroom, Southend and shortly afterwards his marriage foundered, Joan and baby returning to Somerset. A life fraught with the uncertainties of finance, accommodation and frequent upheaval was not for her. You win some, you lose some. Changes came thick and fast. Frank switched from alto to tenor sax, eventually taking a summer season at Sherry's, Brighton, and settled in Hove, running a guest house (having found a new partner in Irish-born Margaret) mostly for showbiz people. He spent several years with the Syd Dean Band at the Regent Ballroom, during which time he was joined by Freddy Hooper on bass.

In the late summer of '48 Olive and I, plus baby daughter Rita, moved into the ground floor flat we had bought. During our stay, the family circle was shocked by the death of cousin Millie from typhoid. I was saddened, because she was, in my eyes, very much a young person.

The S-M publishing venture folded, but my association with it had lasted for several years, during which time I had gained a great deal of invaluable experience and know-how. Its demise was mainly due to the inability to build a 'standard' catalogue – tunes which establish themselves, and continue to sell and earn royalties, to keep the firm ticking over in lean times when it didn't have a hit number in the charts. Art and his family made for the USA; Sonny freelanced around, as did Bob, with whom I kept in touch, meeting again in 1956 when visiting the ITV studios where he had obtained the post of music librarian. The sad, downhill trend gave rise one morning to Sonny's quip, "Oy vey! There's no business like no business!"

Another reason was the lack of interest displayed in the USA in material which Art took over trying to get name band recordings. An expensive sea trip (including family) which yielded naught. Too early, of course, for there was to be no reversal of American domination of the popular music market until the sixties, when Lennon and McCartney were destined to dramatically change not only the status quo but pop music itself. Only Lennon and McCartney? Sure, there were four Beatles who produced the famous Merseyside sound, but, without the conceived originality and genius of the two principal songsmiths, The Beatles may well have been just another group, not forgetting, of course, the large part played by George Martin. Once again, we are back to the arrangers.

Fitting at this juncture are the lyrics of a song written in the late fifties for a competition with Soho as the subject. Once more, a sixty-four bar theme of the kind associated with Cole Porter's style and a beguine rhythm (since replaced by the bossa nova). On a personal note, I would add that, of those few writers who wrote both words and music single-handed for shows, Mr Porter has my vote, especially where witty lyrics are concerned.

118

THIS IS SOHO

It's a hive, look alive, the moment you arrive – this is
                                    Soho.
Have a treat, happy feet, and promenade each street, this
                                    is Soho.
There's a metropolitan, cosmopolitan, zing-a-ling
                                    everywhere,
And that old mysterious, sweet, delirious touch of spring
                                    in the air.
All that's best, east and west, the customs and the rest,
This is Soho, this is Soho.
From the start, ev'ry heart, they all become a part
                                    of this Soho.
                                        (Of this Soho.)
The maze of light, the dazzle and the glow,
The days and nights of never-ending show.
At first, a day, and then you find you're here to stay,
                                    and say
This is Soho.

CHAPTER TWENTY-TWO

CON AMORE

From notoriously seedy Soho to the suburban respectability of Gidea Park, Essex, where we were to live for the next five years in a little thirties-built semi. And with the arrival of son Brian on Christmas Eve 1952, we noted the family foursome which represented the four seasons, birthdays falling in April, June, September and December.

Added now to existing connections of Vic Hewitt and the gig agencies of Stan Bloomfield and Howard Baker was that of Ted Bent, trumpet player (and womanising vocalist!) in the new locale. He used Harry James's 'Carnival' as his signature tune, but there the similarity ended! We had a first-class drummer in Len Parrish. As with Les Logan, he and I were soon on the same wavelength. His drumming, never excessively heavy, was rock-steady. He had an intelligent anticipation of accents, crescendo and diminuendo, never drowning a soloist with a series of over-busy breaks and noises, which contribute nothing, but which is so commonplace in much of today's percussion world, irritating, obliterating words or melody, or both. And his Latin American rhythms were second to none.

I wasted no time in introducing Len to the Vic Hewitt scene and whenever possible, on the double dates, requiring only a small band, the rapport which flowed between Les, Len and me produced a much appreciated, delightful sound for dancers. And we all derived a great measure of satisfaction from creating it. If four were required, the addition of fine string bass player, George Trilbey, reinforced and enhanced the rhythmic quality. We had our fair share of playing for Sunday dance clubs, which were becoming increasingly popular. At one of these, at the promoter's request, I got together a Victor Sylvester type outfit, which featured Louis Becker, who previously had been with me at weekends, playing music from the shows and a wide variety of light music. A first-class violinist, as one would expect of a Welsh Guards bandsman, who played clarinet when in the military band, and on the march. To the extremes of the East and West End venues were added those nearer home – Upminster, Hornchurch, Brentwood and Chelmsford.

The most vivid memory of the era, however, was being stranded in the evil, great smog which smothered London in the early fifties. We endeavoured to get back into Essex, having played that night at Toynbee Hall, Aldgate. At The Cauliflower pub, Chadwell Heath, we gave up, pulling on to the forecourt and dozing until about six in the morning, when the smog thinned a little, and we pressed on, cold, tired, and hungry. Although Don Solomons, Ted's alto sax and clarinet player, enjoyed his liquid lubrication as much as he enjoyed playing – sometimes a bit too much – he fortunately didn't have to drive home.

At the Great Eastern Hotel one evening when Don, as usual, had reached a point of blissful obliviousness of everyone and everything around him, he reeled off a succession of hot choruses of his favourite, 'How High The Moon'. It wasn't only the moon that was high! The 'Mexican Hat Dance', popular then, was in full swing when Don left the stage and joined the antics of the dancers. On stage, the rest of us shuddered, closed our eyes and uttered a silent prayer as Don's sax flew off its sling and hit the deck with an ominous thud. As if that were not enough, he side-footed it with the aplomb of a centre forward. It slid across the dance floor, ending its journey with another thump against the front of the stage, to be retrieved by Ted.

As one man, we thought, 'Disaster!'

Don, with a sickly grin on his face, rejoined us, Ted ticking him off no end. Don didn't turn a hair. (He couldn't, now I come to think of it, anyway, being more than a little thin on top!) Picking up his sax, he surveyed it with bleary eyes (something after the fashion of that sax-playing character in *The Muppet Show*) and blew. Luckily, the mechanism had survived OK.

We all like to enjoy our gigs, our music, a convivial jar or two, and some comical touches can be an asset. Like one night at the Castle Keep Hotel when a diner asked, "Can you play 'In The Old-Fashioned Way'?" It evoked the swift witticism from Ron, our bassist, "At my age, that's the *only* way I can play!" which was appreciated all round. Harmless fun compared to Don's behaviour back in the fifties which was totally irresponsible, though it seemed great fun at the time.

Although a high standard of musical performance was obviously the prime requirement, in those days band leaders and agencies took into account a gigster's appearance, dress, general behaviour and the ability to get on well musically and otherwise in the outfit. Turning up late on a gig, playing lots of wrong notes, bad reading due to too much drink, unreliability, scruffiness was just not tolerated. There was an ever-increasing demand for my services and, setting aside the financial rewards, I was deriving great creative and aesthetic pleasure from my music-making. Even so, an asset can become a liability at times. Times when there is conflict with the family and domestic environment. Times when, with the best will in the world, it is difficult to strike an agreeable, workable balance; a mutually acceptable compromise. One cannot be entirely insensitive to such situations. Earlier I wrote about someone having to play second fiddle in order to create harmony. Not an easy role for one's better half and not surprising, therefore, that Olive so often found it difficult to live with, not always sharing the leader's sense of commitment and dedication. The duet very often turned into a duel! In music, as in life, alternating passages of *calmato* and *agitato*, *giocoso* and *dolorous*, *legato* and *staccato*, consonance and dissonance.

I guess we're all conversant with books, songs, plays and history referring to the eternal triangle. The woman in love with two men; the man in love with two women. Olive had often said, sometimes teasingly, sometimes not, "You love your music more than you love me." (Sounds like that old St Bruno TV commercial, doesn't it?) Bruno.

"Not so," would be the quick denial. "I guess I love both."

The truth of the denial is supported by the evidence of enduring partnership and prompts me to ask, "Which one would you opt for, ladies? Sharing your man with another woman? Or sharing a man and his music? The one always searching for 'talent' or the one born with talent?"

A tribute in song ends this chapter. A boy/girl duo originally written for a song festival and since used in some local shows, using an expression which was fashionable in the seventies.

TOGETHERNESS

Chorus: Togetherness, as close as two can be.
Togetherness, no third party, we agree.
No mystery about this happy combination,
For the key is simply perfect harmony.

Togetherness, to each other we belong,
Just one woman, one man and love's sweet song.
We won't tangle with the eternal triangle –
We are blessed with togetherness.

Verse: A pair of love birds upon the wing.
They have no love words, but how they sing.
But we have words as well as music to express
The way we feel about togetherness.

Repeat Chorus: Togetherness etc., etc.

CHAPTER TWENTY-THREE

MAESTOSO

All gigsters have their favourite venues. I'm no exception for I firmly believe that it is not only environment that matters but, more importantly, atmosphere. I hold the opinion that inanimate objects, just like living things, receive and transmit vibes, absorb and radiate atmosphere, friendly or hostile. To feel at ease, at one with the venue and the audience produces a sensitivity which, in turn, finds expression in one's musical outpourings. You may be inclined to laugh, sneer or exclaim outright, "Rubbish!" But who can deny having sometimes felt entirely out of place in certain company, or in surroundings which evoke the commonplace protest, 'This place gives me the creeps'?

The two long-lived resident engagements related in subsequent chapters will give credibility to my beliefs.

In this context, first and still foremost comes the Seven Kings Hotel. It was in the mid-fifties, several weeks prior to moving back to East Ham, when I undertook some odd Saturday dates at the hotel. The quartet was led by fiddle player, Charles Phillips. His father had been a musical director for a very long time, mostly in pit orchestras and particularly in and around Cardiff. It was a foretaste of things to come – great things, and, above all, an opportunity *at last* to play *my* kind of music and to awaken the dormant writer's itch.

George Trilbey, whom I mentioned earlier, played bass and his powerful baritone voice, eminently suited for the hit ballad numbers in show music selections, made him an obvious choice for inclusion. On alto and clarinet was Jimmy Phelan, who travelled all the way from Clapham on Saturdays, his mode of transport being a commodious old ex-taxi cab which he had christened 'Henry'. Sunday evenings were covered by Les Logan on reeds. With that added incentive, when asked if interested in doing all the work there, all the time, I grasped the invitation firmly in both hands. Not that it was going to be easy to begin with. Although the tone Charles produced was sometimes lacking in warmth and finesse, he was a first-rate musician. Somewhat temperamental and easily agitated, mostly due to the constant coming and going of freelance pianists who, in truth, were competent only in dance-band work full stop, and thus far removed from Charles's demanding professional standards. This much I learned from Les when he first approached me: "We've had pianists galore, none of them any good, but Charles was impressed with the odd Saturdays you did recently."

Impressed? If he was, he hadn't shown it, but I was flattered just the same. I knew that I hadn't made any major blunders, but there had been times when I was most certainly 'feeling my way', relying on my sight reading to get me through. The majority of commercial orchestrations place great reliance on the pianist filling in all the cued-in passages of other instruments not present in smaller combinations. The part was not generally defined as 'piano conductor' for nothing. Through the few dates I had done, I was conscious of the potential of the mini-orchestra (for want of a better expression) and the conviction that light music was my forte, and always would be, was proven by three and a half happy years of making beautiful music. For me, the pinnacle of solid achievement, a superior era not since matched, nor ever likely to be in the unbalanced musical climate which has since taken over everywhere.

My very first visit to Charles's home in Romford was a mind-boggling experience. The front room was a miniature music library. Shelves and racks on three walls were stacked high with orchestral scores and parts of every kind, ranging from works by the classical giants and light music of the past fifty years to a multitude of show and film selections, spanning a period from Gilbert and Sullivan to the then current *Annie, Get Your Gun* and *Oklahoma!* Much of it had been inherited, of course, from his father and what Charles didn't have in the library wasn't worth having. Thus we were able to present an entirely different programme each weekend, save the repeat of a few personal favourites or request items. It was impossible for us, or the listeners, to ever be bored with such a wide variety, a veritable musical kaleidoscope. This was proved so many times in the complimentary remarks overheard during the interval, or in the drifts of conversation which reached our ears while on stage, the emphasis always being on our versatility.

Far more subtle than vocal appreciation and applause was the heightened perception. One developed an expertise for selecting the real music lovers, divining their thoughts and gasps of "I don't believe it!" Perhaps a sharp intake of breath, absolute astonishment, as we switched from say, 'Ebb Tide' to Charles's brilliance in 'Gypsy Fiddler' or 'Diona' then into something by Novello, Coates, Léhar, Farnon, or operatic and ballet gems, George bringing the house down with a spirited 'Granada'. A mixture such as 'The Dream of Olwen', 'La Boutique Fantastique', 'Moonlight on the Alster', 'Claire de Lune', 'Guys and Dolls,' Leroy Anderson's 'Belle of the Ball' to name but a few. Music of the gods!

The childhood involvement with the classics and light music, sustained by Daisy's insistence that I never let go, was bringing its rewards in every way. It had been of paramount importance in my proving equal to the irresistible challenge posed by being thrown in at the deep end with three older, very experienced musicians. I treated it as a heaven-sent opportunity, wonderful good fortune, and soon came to realise that, given a goal, a target, albeit self-imposed, nothing is impossible, adopting the approach, epitomized in the song title, 'Anything You Can Do, I Can Do Better'.

But my realisation had come too late. There were echoes of RAF days when Les mentioned a friend of his who had stayed on and gone into the Central Band immediately after the war. Now a sergeant, with married quarters at Uxbridge for only twenty-five bob per week and an excellent rate of pay, plus lucrative engagements, official and otherwise. He had just signed on for the final term. C'est la vie! I was happy and contented with the niche I had found. There was still a long way to go. Forward, not backward, thinking about what might have been.

The enormous lounge of the Seven Kings Hotel, with its high decorative ceiling from which were suspended glittering chandeliers, was a fit and proper setting for my kind of music or, more accurately now, *our* kind of music. We would chat during the short interval to some of the regulars, discovering that some had travelled a fair distance for the musical treat, as far away as Woodford, Romford, Brentwood and Chingford.

'There isn't another place for miles around where you can sit in pleasant surroundings, have a drink, a conversation without shouting above the so-called music. It's well worth the journey,' was the general consensus. Yes, it was unique.

With the tall casement doors near the stage open in spring and summer, it was even more pleasant. No matter what the season, the main tables were graced with flower arrangements – *real* flowers, none of yer plastic daffs! Waiters in black and white attire hovered and pirouetted skilfully and efficiently 'twixt bar and tables on the thickly carpeted floor. There was always a buzz of conversation, but I cannot recall it ever reaching proportions which seriously interfered with the music reaching the ears of those seated in the main part of the lounge nearest the stage.

Charles kept the library up to date. Included in the new music was a selection from the fabulous *My Fair Lady*, months before it opened at Drury Lane, Charles's brother in the USA having sent it over. You may recall that Chappells, the publishers, had imposed a ban on all performances, recording and music released in the UK pending the opening night. Concluding the first half of the programme with the selection one evening, we were making our way down for a beer when a middle-aged chap invited us to join him. We took up his kind offer, the conversation opening with an appreciation of the music, then completely out of the blue, he asked, "How long have you been playing music from *My Fair Lady*?"

We exchanged uneasy glances, all thinking the same thing – "We're going to be clobbered, he's a rep from Chappells. How else could he know the songs?"

Charles answered smugly, even cheekily, "Oh, several months now," and went on to explain how he had come by the music.

Then, to our relief, the stranger spilt the beans. "I'm on leave from the boats. I've seen the show three times. Marvellous stuff! I didn't expect to hear the music tonight, as I thought that performance in this country was prohibited at present. Nice surprise, fellers. Have another drink," he concluded generously.

Phew! We returned onstage, chuckling over the most unusual incident. Needless to say, *My Fair Lady* reigned supreme just as long as we did at the Seven Kings Hotel, once the memorable tunes became universally known, George's vocal conclusion of 'On The Street Where You Live' never failing to please.

The residency had now become a refuge, a haven of resistance from a new dimension which was to grow to deformed and overrated proportions, courtesy of Mr Bill Haley. It was during that era when a small, scruffy group of rockers mingled with the regulars early one Saturday evening, looking decidedly out of place. We ignored the trouble-provoking shout of "What abaht some rock?" initially, but, when it went up a second time, accompanied by foul-mouthed derisory remarks which were having an unnerving effect on some of the older patrons, it got the response it deserved.

I went down to their table and advised the mickey-taking gang that, analogous to the drunk on the familiar record of 'Cigarees and Whiskey', who wanted to hear 'Temptation', we didn't play that kind of music here. There were so many places where people listened with their feet, had their eardrums split by excessive volume and garbled words.

"They call it 'going for a quiet drink' I believe," was my sarcastic remark. "I suggest you go join them and enjoy yourselves – that's more your scene – and stop spoiling other folks' enjoyment."

Two burly waiters were more emphatic. "Drink up, and get out," they ordered.

The group retreated, muttering, in disorder from the lounge, *molto presto*!

With the proliferation of rock, skiffle (and piffle), the Seven Kings venue became even more unique while the three chord trick, record-aping merchants went on rocking and rolling, many of them thankfully drowned in a sea of oblivion. R&R may be enjoyable to dancers, but it is far from musical and I find that, after playing a couple of numbers, the sheer monotony is unbearable. The fast-changing music scene was perhaps put into a nutshell during the interval by a group at a nearby table to us, whose conversation we couldn't help overhearing.

"It's a shame," said one. "They've got more music and talent in their little fingers than all the pop groups rolled into one."

Another added, "Yes, but just because they're not young, noisy and bashing drums and guitars, they get a fraction of the money that overpaid pop stars get."

That's right, we didn't earn a fortune. Nor did we have the gear, the hair or the amplification. More than a decade later, when multi-track guitarist, Wout Steenhuis, who lived nearby, put me in touch with a prominent music publisher whom I visited, things hadn't changed. In fact, they had gone steadily downhill. He put it much more succinctly, saying, "It's the age of mediocrity, Bill."

Another sign of the times was the vast number of homes disposing of their front parlour pianos, instruments which had taken pride of place in home entertainment and social gatherings of all kinds. One retail chain of stores, I recall, took old pianos in part-exchange for TV sets! Most of them went to the scrap heap. Some in better condition had exteriors updated and interiors reconditioned. One well-known local branch of piano makers took up the TV challenge by holding a 'Piano Week' exhibition in Ilford. That was a unique engagement for me. I drifted around playing selected pianos during peak times and, once I'd drawn an audience around me, the salesmen moved in and I moved on to the next piano.

I was there at the opening when popular fun-man, Sid James opened the exhibition. Soon after, he stood with the manager, gin and tonic in hand, as I played the best piano there – a concert grand. Commenting on its tone, Sid asked the manager the price. When he got the reply, he pointed at me, and with a grin said, "Does that include him?"

"No way, Sidney!"

The kind of solo playing I enjoyed was the two hour spot at the Seven Kings Hotel on Thursday evenings – presenting a wide variety of music strictly for listening. Today it's known as The Piano Bar. It was round about this time when, quite by accident, an amazing coincidence came to light, linking past and present. A friend of mine had asked me to provide a small band to play for his daughter's wedding reception, taking place on a Saturday afternoon. I suggested to Jimmy that he could come over from Clapham earlier than usual, play for the wedding, have a meal at my place then on to Seven Kings in the evening. Somehow, there was an oblique reference to the Middle East during tea-time talk, which naturally swung around to Olive's brother, Frank, and his RAF days at Shaibah.

"Not Frank *Ireland*?" questioned Jimmy, eyebrows raised in surprise.

"Yes," I answered, "but how come you know the surname?"

"Gosh, I ought to, I was with Frank in the Commanders Dance Band at Shaibah!"

And observing Olive's fair features, he remarked, "Of course! I can see the likeness now. Another blondie, like Frank."

There was an inevitable round of exclamations, laughter and platitudes about the world being a small place, and I rummaged in a drawer and produced a bundle of photographs. Triumphantly, I handed one to Jimmy.

"There you are! Takes you back a bit, doesn't it?"

Nearly fifteen years in fact. The odds against such an encounter must have been enormous. Jogging along in 'Henry', it continued to be the main topic of conversation, Charles and George being equally amazed and amused when told of the incident.

The reader might also be amazed on another count. Two musicians in the same outfit for best part of two years without the link being discovered? Easily explained: chit-chat was limited to the few minutes before setting up and tuning-up; the interval was limited to ten minutes, and at the end, we were often waylaid by enthusiasts to talk music and perhaps make a request for the next night or next weekend. It took a social occasion to bring the connection to light.

Charles had a passion for heavy, high-powered motorbikes. His idea of bliss was to scorch mile after monotonous mile (sorry, kilometre) along Europe's autobahns. At my place one afternoon to try over some new music, we had tea, then proceeded to the hotel, yours truly perched most uncomfortably on the pillion of a huge, snorting mechanical monster. Charles's fast, aggressive driving had me wondering if the journey would be made even shorter – the final one into eternity!

The gig boys had long since given up trying to get me back into the old circle! "No use ringing Bill Worland – he's got the job where he can play what he likes most, the way he likes it," was their apt conclusion.

A majestic three and a half years had elapsed when, for the last time, we bowed out with the familiar signature tune, 'Rendezvous'. To Charles, Les, George and Jimmy – for having made such a cherished memory possible – my eternal thanks.

CHAPTER TWENTY-FOUR

DOLOROSO

Soon after our return to East Ham, we holidayed in the Brighton area, staying at Frank and Margaret's place in Hove. The long stay afforded a chance to stroll around that wonderful and bizarre Eastern importation, the luxurious indulgence of Regency days, the Royal Pavilion, one rainy morning. Although visited several times since, its architecture and fabulous contents are still a source of fascination. The very first time, I thought, 'What a great musical it would make.' A real life story of the Prince Regent and his contemporaries, with a Pavilion setting and the obvious title *Prinny* – but no one seems to have considered its potential from a musical standpoint.

A couple of years later the changing face of pop music had put an end to Syd Dean's mammoth run at the Regent Ballroom. As Frank said, "Syd's still playing all the old 'Lallys' and all we get is a handful of dancers on the floor, but as soon as the pop group come on, it's packed with youngsters."

He stayed with the band which, from time to time, had to play at other ballrooms in the circuit, one of them in Leeds. I had lost touch completely with Jack White, so asked Frank to look him up in Morley or at the Lewis's store. He became the bearer of sad news when returning and calling on us. Jack, he was told, had died several years previously in a car crash when coming home late one night from a gig. With sales of records fast outstripping that of sheet music, and the subsequent installation of listening booths, the job at the store had died too. The ravages of time left me sadly mulling over how I might have fared had I gone north, back in 1946: 'Que Sera Sera'...

I was out of touch too with Daisy, because of the preoccupied years at Gidea Park, which I determined to atone for by an immediate visit. But she was preoccupied too – with an elderly gent, whose name I cannot even recall, more dominant in my memory being the very first introduction, arousing some suspicious, even hostile feelings within me. I felt outraged when I observed the horrible, dark-patterned cheap wallpaper which had replaced the serenity of pale blue distemper in the sunny front room. Told that it was the work of the stranger on the scene, it was difficult to stifle derogatory remarks.

Conversation about music was limited, but I did manage to draw some response from Daisy about one Len Colvin, in Johannesburg. Len had been a pupil and a dance band pianist some years before me. He suffered dreadfully from rheumatic fever, but his acceptance of a musical job in South Africa had brought success and also considerable improvement in health in the kinder climate of that continent. He was undoubtedly the apple of Daisy's eye and I flattered myself that I was a close runner-up. A clip from a recent *Melody Maker* which I showed Daisy prompted her to hand me the latest letter she had received for me to read.

I continued to pop in whenever visiting my parents, but the 'man-about-the-house' was forever around, always, it seemed, doing his best to speed my departure. I noticed too, on a subsequent visit, that he now possessed a large and fairly new car... Daisy did, however, make me a present of some albums of music, much of which, even to this day, I simply have not had time to study and learn to play to a satisfactory standard. Music from student days as evidenced by dates stretching back to the early twentieth century. She continued to ply me with other books and albums on other visits. On one hand, I felt that there was something wrong; on the other – what business was it of mine?

Out of touch again, due to the off-putting attitude of you-know-who, whose resentment, it was plain, grew with each and every visit I made. Therefore it was in roundabout fashion that I heard Daisy was dying of cancer. I telephoned the hospital. Too late. She had gone. A chat with a friendly, helpful ward sister revealed to me Daisy's most uttered concern during her merciful short stay: "I must take care of my hands, I must take care of my hands." A poignant reminder of the times she had told me to take care of mine.

I met the only surviving relatives – her niece and her husband, when they arrived from Belfast. They disclosed in great anguish how several thousands of pounds in cash, bonds and other securities had been withdrawn in a remarkably short period of time, the bank manager seemingly powerless in his efforts to advise, to change the reckless course of someone who appeared to be determined to have a final fling, behaviour completely out of character. Other valuables were also missing, including a coveted war medal, a DSO, or something akin to such an award. Legally, there was nothing they could do. Had Daisy been conned out of a small fortune, or had she given it willingly? Obsession, or affection, so late in life for a stranger who had effected such drastic changes?

We never knew, and I don't suppose anyone will ever know. I took a small memento – a black and white perpetual calendar, a souvenir of bygone days from the Salzburg Music Festival, which had the figure of Mozart at the keyboard and a few bars of music as its motif. Fashioned in Bakelite, not plastic, it had been given to her by a former pupil and had always stood on top of the piano together with other bric-a-brac. Abruptly, *fine* had been written to another two chapters of my life. I paid my last respects, joining the small group of mourners at the City of London Cemetery in May.

My intuition had proved to be entirely correct in one sense. Yet I had failed to divine the motive, the awful finality of the various gifts of music. But not completely... The news of Daisy's passing had triggered an immediate flashback in my mind to an uncanny experience a couple of weeks earlier. It was the year 1957 and, having turned to writing light orchestral music, there had been two closely related times when ideas poured so effortlessly from my fingers to the keyboard that it seemed unbelievable. I was hard put to match the creative flow with my manuscript scribblings. There was an overpowering impression that I was not alone; hands not under my own control were being guided by an unknown and unseen presence. Any hark-back to the incidents, even as I write, still sets off a shivery physical reaction.

I had told no one, attempting, in my ignorance, to dismiss the first as pure fantasy, imagination. A repetition so shortly afterwards convinced me, left me in no doubt whatsoever that they were clearly psychic experiences, supernatural links.

Sceptics are entitled to their viewpoint, so often formed by total ignorance and not having been exposed to occult or similar phenomena. Subjected personally to such experiences, they would soon have a change of mind, becoming acutely aware of the cosmic and ethereal forces, so often beyond human ken. It would be easy to get carried away on so fascinating a subject, but here I will content myself by simply agreeing with the theory that modern civilisation, with its materialistic base, has considerably diminished the qualities of the sixth sense (the third eye), divination, intuition, telepathy and all related subjects, inherent in hunter and hunted, in primitive man. The facility to 'tune in' is a faculty possessed by all, but in the vast majority is a wasted, unused and untapped source of power and energy.

I also have an unshakeable belief in continuity – the natural order of things, the seasons, cycles, birth and rebirth as nature intended ever since the Creation. The current up-surge of interest in the art of relaxation, yoga, meditation and natural health foods, centuries-old teachings of the ancients, is significant as people seek to combat the ill effects of food for the body, rather than food for spiritual thought in a mad, mad, mad world. That there is another better one ahead (though not necessarily all milk and honey) I have no doubt; just one more stage in the refinement of the human soul. As the song has it, 'Got A Lot Of Living To Do'. To experience is to live.

Returning from my digression into the unknown... Everything changes, of course. There were many times visiting the 'Happy Hacienda' in East Ham after we had moved to the coast when I would stroll up the road just to cast my eyes again on the place where so much time had been usefully spent avidly absorbing every morsel of musical knowledge. Learning then, still learning today.

Daisy's house had been converted into two flats, the exterior now in different colours, but to me it was still in green and cream; still a brass plate on the wall; a sunblind over the front door. I had only to close my eyes to reproduce the image, as clear as any colour photograph. The same goes for that sunny front parlour with its pale blue walls, always seeming to simply ooze a calm, cool and relaxed air into the room.

Outside, no longer the quiet of the thirties. A busy area, even buses belching their diesel-fed way along the adjoining thoroughfare, and, in common with so many towns with old terrace houses which lack garages, the roads littered with parked cars. Despite all the changes, I guess that I'll always see the picture mirrored in my mind's eye. Sentimental fool that I am, I can draw an analogy with the feelings of the Jerome Kern/Oscar Hammerstein song 'The Last Time I Saw Paris', specifically the last line of the song: 'No matter how they change her, I'll remember her that way.'

Upon reflection, choosing late '55 in which to dabble in song writing was a daft decision. New fashions were being rapidly established, becoming the yardstick by which everything was measured. Even seasoned professional writers who could not or would not change were finding the going tough, so what chance had a

raw recruit, offering run-of-the-mill songs? Fortunately, insight from
the Strauss-Miller days prevented me from falling into the trap which
repeatedly ensnares so many new beginners who simply dash off one
song after another without stopping to think, 'Is it worthwhile doing?
Has the idea already been done? If so, can I do it from a more
original angle? Is it commercial and, above all, is it in keeping with
current trends?'

So my output in two years ran to a mere dozen tunes, some of
which I destroyed in disgust; furthermore, due to the lack of a first-
class collaborator on lyrics, I gave up, turning my attention to
instrumental compositions of a melodic nature. Much harder work,
but it did not deter me. Trying to write songs was partly influenced
by an organisation known as the 'Eddie Payne Close Harmony
Songwriters' Club'. As the somewhat long-winded title suggests, the
principal function was to bring together composers and lyricists. For
a modest fee, one could got an assessment of one's latest 'it-must-
surely-sell-a-million' creation!

Eddie, mainly a freelance MD and songwriter whom I had briefly
met when he was peddling songs around the Alley, Strauss-Miller
included, now resided in Ramsgate, writing, producing and conducting
summer shows. In reality, a continuation of something he had done in
far more austere conditions during a long stint in a German PoW
camp. Little did I dream that many links would shortly be restored in
that south-east corner. One of them was with Eddie who staunchly
declared himself a 'fugitive from the three-chord-trick merchants' and
the unadulterated rubbish being churned out in the name of music. I
could understand his feelings. But I did have certain reservations; he
had none.

For several weeks I was inundated with shoals of lyrics, which in
cold stark figures presented a ratio of ninety-five per cent chaff, five
per cent wheat. Essential knowledge of rhythm, metrical form, binary
or ternary form, stresses, accents, beats to the bar was appallingly
non-existent. So I knew that, if and when I tried song writing again,
I'd have to do my own words. George, Len and I cut a demo disc of
a song in 1956. Such records were then the exception rather than the
rule, so we had certainly moved with the times. Before the Seven
Kings residency ended, some of my early light music was performed
at the hotel, and in 1958 we did an LP record, along with other items,
one being George's vocal of 'Granada'. It's now a nostalgic museum

piece compared to my latest digital tapes. Bob Dale, now librarian at London-based TV studios, listened to my pieces, his suggestions for improvement helpful and encouraging. I saw him again in the sixties, for the last time. He died shortly afterwards.

Summer of '59 was permanently overcast by the knowledge that my father's life was ebbing away. After a long illness, we said our farewells on October the 1st, a day which produced the kind of weather befitting his generally cheerful disposition, sunny and warm. Not a cloud in the sky. And brighter times were ahead too. Our house went on the market early in the new year, and we prepared to move to the south-east coast, to live by the sea – to leave behind the rush-and-tear of London and its hordes of ant-like commuters. A London town which, even for one spawned in the heart of its cockney land, had rapidly lost its appeal as a place in which to work and to live. Ring out the old – ring in the new!

CHAPTER TWENTY-FIVE

NEW PLACES, BUT OLD FACES

A new decade had dawned. A dot on the map, shown as Broadstairs (population 21,000) was our objective, having taken a liking to the town when on holiday. Since house-hunting had met with no success by the time our London abode had to be vacated, Olive and the children joined me in early March. Pro tem, we took a short lease on a small house until July, when we moved into a lovely old four-bedroomed residence, built in Edwardian days, enviably situated within minutes of the charming, picturesque seafront. Tiny, but still the envy of the Ramsgate and Margate resorts. But now even Broadstairs reflects the outright encouragement of supermarkets and hypermarkets, the high street having several empty shops and a surfeit of estate agents and building society offices. And it has all happened in an alarmingly short space of time.

Our offer, substantially below market price, for the Edwardian house was accepted, the bargain further enhanced when discovering that the property had been the show house way back in 1910. At number eight, a little further up, near the top of King Edward Avenue in a house known as Helmdon, resided Ted Heath's parents. No, not the band leader, but the ex-prime minister. When Mr Heath became PM and leader of the Tories, they moved on to a larger and more expensive place, more in keeping with his newly-won status. The move produced some corny humour in the gig circle. Quips such as "I see Ted Heath's moved out – there wasn't room for two pianists in the same road."

In the years of consolidation, composition had to be thrust into the background. Olive's folks enjoyed long summer holidays with us, her father, as ever, pottering happily around, his life-long skills as a 'chippy' contributing many additions and improvements. By 1963, the lure of the seaside town became stronger than ever. They pulled up London roots and took a nearby flat. Our extra bedroom proved to be a blessing. People we hadn't seen or heard of for yonks turned up in force once they knew that we were by the sea. Another 'Happy Hacienda' but complete with occasional unexplained happenings, and a friendly ghost, which both Rita and Olive encountered!

"It's not like London, you know," secretary Billy Bell told me when I got around to transferring to the Thanet Branch of the Musicians' Union. "A lot of work in the summer season, but a lot less out of season."

He was an articulate Geordie and ex-trumpet player of the old school and vigorously pro-Union – a prominent trait I had observed so many times before in his generation of pros, fostered, no doubt, by the poor conditions of employment and pay which had relegated professional musicians to near-peasant status, their unhappy lot between the wars. As I well know, a typical instance was the employment on cruise ships, when many had to undertake onerous duties far removed from music-making. The MU was fast becoming a recognised and responsible body to which we could turn for help and advice, to get free legal representation when necessary, which is more often than you may imagine. There are crafty and unscrupulous employers, just as there are employees. Without the MU we might still be treated like minstrels playing for our supper.

I auditioned successfully for a fifteen week season with jovial portly drummer-entertainer, Al Collins, in Margate. Al's capacity for ale was largely responsible for his rotund frame, which gave rise to the dubbing, 'Al-Cohollins!' A joke which Al related had even funnier echoes on the opening night.

A group of rough and tough sailors went ashore at Shanghai. They were greeted by one helluva racket of exploding fireworks and crackers.

"What the hell's going on?" they asked one of the natives.

"Chinese New Year," he explained proudly. "Ellybody happy."

"Aw, fuck your Chinese New Year," grunted one sailor.

"And fluck your Melly Clistmas too!"

It was time for Al, assisted by sax and clarinettist, Harry Segal, to do the then popular Michael Miles 'Mustn't Say Yes, Mustn't Say No' quiz. Harry went backstage to fetch the large Chinese gong used in the quiz. There was a loud b-o-i-n-g and a crash. Harry emerged, having picked himself up, gong in hand and choking with laughter, and said to Al, "Fluck your Chinese gong!"

The winter months, mostly on a freelance basis, were spent usefully, getting to know other musicians, later forging alliances which would spell musical enjoyment, and the assessment of various venues, their atmosphere and the quality or otherwise of their pianos.

'A Concert by the 5th Battalion Buffs TA Band' the posters announced. In small print below: 'Conducted by Bandmaster Louis Becker.'

"It must be somebody with a similar name," I explained to Olive. "It can't be Lou from the Welsh Guards."

It was most intriguing. Curiosity had to be satisfied, so we all made for the Broadstairs bandstand the following Sunday. Every seat was soon filled that fine September afternoon. A scene reminiscent of childhood holidays and the bandstand in Central Park, East Ham and with so many of the tunes associated with youthful days shown in the programme – tunes which I lovingly classed as 'deck chairs and ice cream' music!

The ritual of tuning-up gave way to applause as the bandmaster made for the rostrum. It *was* Lou! Resplendent in dark blue, red-trimmed uniform, which, buttoned up to the neck was a veritable sweat-box on such a hot day. The applause was acknowledged with a brisk salute of a white-gloved hand and the concert got underway. We mingled with the bandsmen during the interval. Woodwind and brass-blowing musicians were now consuming thirst-quenching tea and soft drinks.

Lou was taking a breather, removing headgear and unfastening top buttons when I approached him with a loud, "Hello, Lou! What are you doing in this neck of the woods – and conducting a Terriers' Band at that?"

He countered with a grin, "What are *you* doing here – on holiday?"

I explained we were living not a stone's throw away from the bandstand, and learned that Lou had moved to Ramsgate after successfully gaining an appointment as Professor of Music some years previously and was now teaching at the Royal Marines School of Music in Deal.

Still puzzled, I returned to the second part of my question, "How come you're conducting a TA band?"

"Oh, I'm not the regular conductor," Lou explained, "just depping for Bob Driscoll. He can't make it today."

Bob, I later learned, was the military band expert in the Thanet locale. It had been an entirely unexpected and pleasant encounter. Early in the new year came another, bridging an even wider gap in time.

Resident at St George's, in the Butlins group of hotels, was Bert Hayes, also involved in BBC productions *Crackerjack* and *The Basil Brush Show*. Over the years, when BBC rehearsal and recording commitments clashed with the hotel residency dates, I deputised for Bert. On the very first occasion, I arrived early in order to case the joint, as it was new to me, then I waited in the bandroom for the others to arrive. Who should turn up but violinist and tenor sax player Charlie Palmer, who had been in the RAF ME No. 2 Band with Frank! The expressions of mutual surprise were followed by a continuous swapping of news items, a fifteen year span remarkably compacted in the space of a few hours.

Finally, a trio of remarkable reunions was completed in 1964 at The Pavilion, Broadstairs. In defiance of modern trends, the resort still employed a light orchestra. Its size and the number of performances gradually dwindled over the next twenty-odd years, however. I had gone along just before the start of another long summer season by Cecil Barker's Orchestra. (On the way down, I recall the house in York Street, obviously plagued with Dickens buffs in the past, which bore a plaque reading 'Charles Dickens did not live here!') Cecil's orchestra reigned supreme, enjoyed by residents and holiday makers alike for more than a score of years until his untimely death in the seventies. Simply as a biographical note, Leslie Wheeler, violinist and MD from Margate, took over and, after his death, was succeeded by Johnny Trefny for a brief while. Bert Waller took over what was left of the outfit, on Sundays only, until its demise in 1988.

Having written to Cecil during the winter, he had kindly agreed to try out several of my compositions which I had specially orchestrated for his nine-piece outfit. He played them during the season, and they were also used by the trio which did a short programme each morning while holiday makers sipped soft drinks and coffee on the delightful adjoining Garden on the Sands. I was pleased with the outcome, for the arrangements had been done as a try-out, a prelude and preparation for scoring the pieces for much larger BBC house orchestras later. Rehearsals were underway when I arrived with my manuscripts.

Lo and behold! There was George Forbes, on second fiddle and tenor sax, as large as life – and a bit larger in stature too and, nineteen years on, not much of his carroty-coloured thatch left, either!

The orchestra finished the piece it was playing and, in my excitement, I'm afraid that I leapt on to the stage to greet George, ignoring Cecil for the moment. I turned to apologise and say hello. He was good-natured however.

He grinned widely, enquiring, "Where did you two meet before?"

"Benghazi," came the dual response.

"Benghazi?" echoed Cecil. "That's amazing. The odds against you meeting again after so many years must be tremendous."

Most Sunday lunch times that season George and I had plenty to talk about – mostly music – but slipping back, George said, "This is certainly a much better place in which to meet," sipping his drink and sinking back into the luxury of a deep armchair.

George loved comfortable, congenial surroundings. He had been hard put to adapt to desert life. "A terrible existence!" was his expression for it. He added, "Those years, those places. I'm sure it was all a horrible dream."

Recalling my very first effort at writing in 1945, he wished me luck for the future. I was touched by his sincere appraisal: "If the pieces you did for us are anything to go by, your writer's itch should soon pay off."

Compliments, compliments. A lot were to come my way in the next few years, but the itch, in terms of material success, eventually did pay off. One has to have a lot of patience and confidence. And, most of all, the stamina to stay the course.

CHAPTER TWENTY-SIX

THE OLD ORDER CHANGETH

In spite of Billy Bell's statement, I was never short of work. A tremendously busy and varied decade of freelancing, spells of running my own band and residencies followed, the pace and volume gathering when, with the entry mid-way into the sphere of composition, something had to give. I jettisoned the summer work during 1967 in order to concentrate on writing. The most notable residency, mostly 'out of season', was that at the San Clu Hotel, my host being Ex-Battle of Britain flyer, John Robson. The lounge and foyer abounded with aerial photographs of many kites, chiefly fighters, immortalised by the Second World War. The hotel catered for many important and lively dinner-dance functions, annual highlights being the International Rotary, Royal Temple Yacht Club, Licensed Victuallers and the Dramatic Society, the latter sometimes graced by Jack Warner (who lived at Kingsgate), enlivened by his after-dinner wit.

Generally, we were a trio – piano, drums (George) and on bass Reg – but for bigger functions we added tenor sax. The San Clu's stationery bears the heading which will appeal to ex-RAF types – 'Cluless, Ramsgate'. Anything but clueless! There was a cosy, intimate, happy atmosphere; the two grand pianos were always in tune, and one's efforts to entertain never went unappreciated. Many delightful, memorable years, second only to the Seven Kings era.

Another very capable and versatile pianist was Alex Inman who, until the late sixties, played during summer with the old time and modern sequence band at Butlins. The switch-over provided me with several seasons of enjoyable work, depping for Alex at his winter venue, the classy Chez Laurie roadhouse on the Thanet Way, regrettably long since gone. There were still a few opportunities for playing light music, one of them being at Slatter's Hotel in Canterbury, in 1966, memorable for the many parties of American tourists on a 'See Europe in ten days' tour (or something equally ridiculous, time-wise). I got requests like 'Play me sump'n from *Oklahoma!*", the inducement being the tip of an old-fashioned dollar – two half-crowns placed on the side of the piano.

Speaking of our American cousins, the USAAF was preparing to pull out of its Manston base as we moved to Thanet. There were mixed feelings among the locals, but, generally, people were sorry to see them go, especially those in business and musical circles, very much aware of the increased trade and employment their presence had generated. I quote, "They livened-up this more dead-than-alive hole," the ayes easily outnumbering those of the "Lock up your daughters" and "Yanks, go home" brigades, particularly the girls, who had never been at a loss for dancing partners at the Dreamland, Coronation and Grand Ballrooms. They've all disappeared into history, the Grand at Broadstairs being the last to close, grimly hanging on until March 1984. I was with the band which played the very last Saturday night shindig.[8] The proposed demolition and redevelopment has not yet happened. It's still a silent, boarded-up, mouldering monument to the halcyon days of dancing, as is the souvenir – a poster from the early fifties – dancing, *six nights a week!*

Dover, Folkestone (the Leas Hall), the Coniston at Sittingbourne, the Star, Maidstone – all became familiar haunts outside the Thanet area, not forgetting the Imperial, Hythe, which, in my eyes, still retained an air of comfort and relaxation, clinging to the grace and grandeur of a bygone age, fast slipping away everywhere else. Sid Craven, another saxophonist-cum-fiddle player with a wealth of recording and broadcasting experience, was invaluable on so many of my gigs and, along with his friend Alex Inman, is sorely missed, both having departed this life far too early. One likes to think they are still making music somewhere in the Grand Beyond, wherever that may be.

At The Winter Gardens, the orchestra for nearly fourteen years under the baton of Cardiff-born, Ivor Novello devotee, Leslie Wheeler, had its role on a permanent basis terminated in the early sixties. True, local lads were later used for concerts and pit orchestra work, but the size of the orchestra and number of engagements rapidly dwindled. It was the thin end of the wedge. The package show was beginning to make its impact. I was lucky enough to have my fair share of such interesting work before it all passed into history. The next blow, not entirely unexpected, was the death of the East Kent Light Orchestra.

---

[8] Update: now blocks of luxury flats

Heavily subsidised by the MU it gave a number of Sunday concerts per year, during the period October-March. That restriction was the prime reason behind its failure to attract audiences large enough to make it viable; stuck with winter dates only, Billy Bell was never successful in his dogged efforts to convince local authorities that it would be far more lucrative if they were able to rehearse more, invest in an up-dated repertoire; and that it would benefit all if concerts were given when the weather was kinder and the Thanet towns packed with holiday makers,

MU involvement was just one of hundreds aimed at maintaining acceptable levels of employment in a profession where an ever-expanding technology of electronics, automation and recording techniques was taking a dreadful toll. Another facet of its 'Keep Music Live' campaign was to encourage the younger generation of musicians, by the creation of chances to gain experience, to learn their craft through the finest medium – the LIVE performance. The EKLO was the very epitome of a worthwhile cause. Amongst the pros, ex-pros, semi-pros, teachers and Royal Marine and TA bandsmen was a generous sprinkling of young students. Remembering with gratitude all I had learned from the old 'uns in the game, the MU's efforts deserve much praise. Not ignorant of the havoc which technology has created, and continues to create in other directions, it must be admitted that we live in an age where music is taken for granted. Push a button, flick a switch...

Just as Les Wheeler lorded over orchestral and local operatic society activities (signature tune naturally being Novello's 'Love Is My Reason'), so Bob Driscoll was the brass and woodwind supremo. Undaunted by the dissolving of the TA band, he gathered together the remnants and enthusiasts of all ages and formed his own outfit, mixing established and new material for concerts for many years. We are back, once more, to the arrangers...

"Take your partners for the 'Geriatric Gavotte' followed by the 'Rumba Rheumatica'." Yes, it's fashionable in avant-garde circles to make fun of the old time and modern sequence scene, and I must admit that I still find it amusing, even ludicrous, the number of 'new' dances that seem to be born virtually every few weeks. Old time is now a dead duck, save for a few established favourites, the Lancers, quadrilles, etc., consigned to the archives way back. But modern sequence thrives, mostly for those of my generation, and there are some dances where good standard tunes can be used. Tangos, rhumbas, cha-chas and other novelties bring a welcome variation entirely divorced from the modern ballroom scene. But today, that's all covered by records too. On a personal note, seeing the menfolk outnumbered on numerous occasions by the ladies, mostly widows, who dance together, I was reminded of Joyce Grenfell's witty observation of dancing bust to bust in her song 'Old Time Dancing'.

Returning to pop music: record-aping groups mushroomed overnight. Contrary to fears that conventional bands would suffer loss of dates, their initial impact was not sustained, many of them breaking up before they had paid for expensive equipment bought on the never-never. At The Winter Gardens, it became the custom to book both a group and a dance band, the latter taking refuge when the group went on, as a protection against having eardrums split. Usually, in the bar, as far away as possible – across the road in The Rose in June. Ironically, as the seventies marched on, we *all* lost out, especially the groups, to discomania. It was a comfort, however, during the good years at the San Clu and other venues to have a couple of drummers who had moved with the times, making it possible to select beat numbers which could be presented reasonably without sounding corny or dated and without the risk of inviting rejection or mickey-taking by the younger set.

With so much emphasis on drum and bass guitar, any attempt to play such stuff with a rhythm section devoid of any feel for the new idiom, stuck with, say, an old-fashioned off-beat, was courting disaster and would be downright embarrassing. The number of younger people attending functions was bound to grow, as it did, and they had to be catered for. Like age, the approach to music is a quality of mind. Those unable or unwilling to present a 'right-across-the-board' programme (back again to compromise!) faded from the scene, made redundant by bands who could. Like ours, their versatility stemmed from a strange mixture; the experience and young-at-heart approach of the old blending effectively with the young, full of modern know-how, but keen to play the music of bygone days as well. One still having something to learn from the other, personal prejudices dissolved in combined efforts to play and present the best of both worlds.

Into the local MU branch came the hordes of youngsters, membership soon being curtailed for many. I recall most vividly the statements made in fun, and in anger, all critical, of the mediocre sixties by showbiz personalities who had come up the hard way. A classic example: 'In my day, we began at the bottom and worked hard for years to get to the London Palladium. Now, without a ha'porth of talent, they *start* at the Palladium!'

In line with that remark, I relate an amusing episode culled from the memory of a Sunday morning general meeting of the branch. It revolved around a question of manning levels, previously agreed with owners and management of the principal entertainment venues. The minimum for Dreamland was, at that time, I believe, five musicians.

The leader of a new beat group numbering only three had been given some gigs at the ballroom. So the group was invited to the meeting to discuss and hopefully solve the problem. All suggestions and efforts to enlist the group and to augment it became bogged down – one hour of fruitless discussion, A protest by the leader that additional instrumentation would kill its 'individual' sound revealed, after some searching questions, that there was nothing original about it anyway. The repertoire was in fact limited to a handful of tunes aped from hit records!

"But we're goingter learn ter read music later on," the group's leader added casually. Howls of laughter, mingled with a hubbub of indignation, derision, sarcasm and a host of uncomplimentary rejoinders were flung from every quarter,

Veteran committee member and chairman, Eric Bing, struggling to restore order, suggested that with the emphasis on beat music, what about the addition of a string bass. This too met with resistance, in the expression, "No, it ain't the same."

"What do you mean, it's not the same?" asked Eric.

The leader, looking decidedly uncomfortable, shuffled to his feet, then somewhat hesitantly replied, "Well... it ain't got frets, 'as it?"

More uproar, with members literally rolling about with laughter! The meeting had also touched on the illegal mingling on engagements of members of the MU and non-members, producing the maxim, 'Make sure the musician is a member.' One can strive only so far to be tolerant, sometimes to a point where tolerance becomes a vice, not a virtue. The sheer nerve, the bumptiousness of a group intending to undertake gigs which, with its self-confessed pitiful limitations it was totally unqualified to accept or fulfil, made me see red. Musicians engaged by major ballrooms when I was a teenager were competent,

and had the ability to play best part of four hours nightly without
repetition of tunes.

When all the rhubarb subsided, I rose from my chair and addressed
the chairman, saying, "I regret to say that if this morning's
proceedings hint at the kind of intake we are likely to get in the future,
why bother whether the musician is a member? Would it not be far
more important to ensure that the member is a musician?"

Amid further uproar, I took my exit home to a Sunday lunch
spoiling in the oven. This amusing extract from 'Letters to the
Editor', *Melody Maker* (1938) clearly demonstrates that there were
'cowboys' around even then!

> I recently played at a gig, and after the job, the
> leader paid me five shillings and threepence, I
> protested to him. He said that five shillings and
> threepence was pro-rata[9] pro rate, because I was
> only a *demi*-semi-pro!

Manning agreements, in truth, were a restrictive practice which
soon became an anachronism of course, unworkable when groups and
bands, far more professional, with distinctive sounds and styles
appeared.

Nevertheless, I still come away from the few local shows I've seen
with an empty feeling where the musical accompaniment is concerned.
At best, it's usually piano, electronic keyboard, bass guitar and drums
(which, nine times out of ten, threaten to split one's eardrums) and
pre-recorded and synthesised backing tapes.

Many gifted musicians were unable to accept or cope with the
rough justice being handed out by the kind of changes dealt with in
this chapter. One of them was Jimmy Stein, a mild-mannered,
bespectacled chap who later sold up and emigrated Down Under. Not
only did he play all the reeds from clarinet and soprano sax right down
to baritone, he was also a competent percussionist; not just a
drummer, but tympani, glockenspiels, xylophone, tubular bells – you
name it, Jimmy played it. The changes had brought about a condition
which had him constantly looking over one shoulder at the past and
carrying an enormous chip on the other.

---

[9] Ten shillings and sixpence or half a guinea.

This amusing but perfectly true happening illustrates his staunch professionalism. He was with me when we played for the opening night at a swish new restaurant. During the evening, the head waiter hovered near the band, trying to be matey in between numbers. Come the Latin American session, he grabbed the maracas and began shaking then violently – out of tempo, of course. We stopped playing and Jimmy, eyes glinting furioso behind rimless specs, demanded, "What do you think you're doing?"

"Oh, I always play maracas in the LA numbers," he asserted airily.

"Not with my instruments, you don't!" countered an irate Jimmy. "You put then down," he ordered fiercely.

We fell about with helpless laughter as he hurled the final insult after the retreating waiter, "I don't come into your kitchen and play with your bloody knives and forks, do I?"

Another noteworthy incident, but of quite a different nature, was the belated discovery that one of the characters on the run after the Great Train Robbery with the fugitive, Ronald Biggs, in the early sixties, had been staying at the Endcliffe Hotel, Cliftonville, where I was doing the summer season. The hotel fairly swarmed with photographers and reporters, gaining a lot of free publicity on a national scale. I undertook the long Christmas booking as management had agreed to provide full board and accommodation, gratis, for the band's families. So we enjoyed an exceptionally good holiday. The fancy dress competition on Boxing Day night threw up some interesting and clever entries, but of course, it had to be the family occupying the room previously used by the notorious character who made the most of it! But they were beaten into second place by a suitable group of adults and children, attired in the magnificent pomp and splendour of the royal family, linking the birth, that year, of Prince Edward with the then topical slogan the banner proclaimed, 'National Productivity Year'!

148

CHAPTER TWENTY-SEVEN

DIVISI

'TOO LITTLE LIGHT MUSIC BROADCAST' – so ran the heading of an article in *The Daily Telegraph*, 6th August, 1965, dealing with the BBC's overemphasis on music already popular, and the overwhelming preponderance of pop programmes, giving no opportunity for new music. But, you may well ask, 'What is light music?'

I will try to answer the question honestly, balancing the limitations of the layman with those who have some musical background, but by no means wishing to create the impression that I am a know-all on the subject, as this is just an effort to expand, in terms of titles. With such a broad spectrum, one could easily fill a giant catalogue, but a short selection spanning several decades may be helpful.

Mozart's 'Eine Kleine Nachtmusik', waltzes by Léhar – 'Gold and Silver' and 'Wild Roses', The 'Knightsbridge March' and indeed most of Eric Coate's works. Dances from 'Merrie England' by Edward German, and, 'Montmartre' from the Paris suite by Haydn Wood. Incidental music from 'The Merchant of Venice'. Suites such as 'Robin Hood' and 'In Malaga' by Frederic Curzon. The works of Gilbert and Sullivan, and a wealth of numbers from shows and films old and new. Also qualifying: Richard Rodger's 'Slaughter on 10th Avenue' and, more recently (the items tending to become shorter in duration mainly due to radio and recording requirements), Ronnie Binge's 'Elizabethan Serenade' and 'Holiday for Strings' by David Rose. Leroy Anderson's 'Belle of the Ball'. Still with the contemporaries – 'The Dream of Olwen', 'Ebb Tide', 'Sleepy Shore' and 'La Mer'. 'Portrait Of A Flirt' by Bob Farnon and a couple of personal favourites, the theme from the 'Pink Panther' by Henry Mancini and Ron Goodwin's '633 Squadron'.

The next hurdle to overcome is the plea, 'But I don't know half of them.' By title alone, no. But were I to play the first few bars of any one tune, I warrant the reaction would be, 'Oh, yes! I know that one! So *that's* what it's called!'

Generally speaking, those with a true and realistic conception of what comprises light music are mostly to be found in the older generation which remembers the days of musical equality. On a descending scale the younger the person the greater the likelihood that he or she will have soaked up totally erroneous and misleading definitions, the majority of them fed on a diet of pop and rock for which BBC channelisation must shoulder much of the blame.

Those falling in the latter category need not feel insulted, inferior, outraged or ashamed. This woeful state of affairs is the logical end-product of more than three decades of brainwashing on a massive scale and, since 1970, channelisation. But youngsters *do* get older and, in not a few, taste sharpens and broadens, even change completely, as I have observed in my own offspring. Brian plays piano, but favours the pre-war 'standards' and now selectively listens to a lot of Radio 3 programmes. Rita, who used to play in a folk group (keyboards and other instruments), sings great choral works like 'The Messiah' and 'The Creation' in the Thanet Festival Choir. So the denial of the existence of a large audience for light music, old and new, is nothing but a travesty of the truth. It follows that there will *always* be one, as is the case for jazz, the big band sound, country and western etc.

Quoted here, *verbatim*, is a statement on light music by the then Master of the Queen's Music, and President of the Light Music Society, founded in 1957, Sir Arthur Bliss.

PRESIDENT'S INTRODUCTION

The world of light music is a wonderfully varied one. It embraces the music that Haydn and Mozart so often wrote for their patrons' entertainment, and it equally welcomes a song by Gershwin and a march by Sousa. Light music wins its audience by a melodic beauty, a rhythmic vitality, a freshness and sparkle of orchestration, weaving its spell by sheer charm. It can be music which has been loved and enjoyed for many generations or music written today with the same conscious aim to please and entertain not only once, but continuously.

It is evident that good light music can give all of us immediate enjoyment. Yet it is all too easy for us to take this pleasure for granted. In doing so, we run the risk of allowing music of certain periods or styles to slip into neglect, or to allow standards of taste and presentation to fall. In contemporary music, it must not be forgotten that the living composer of light music needs just as much active support as his colleagues in other branches of music.

The Light Music Society brings together all those who have the interests of light music at heart. Its aim is simple: to ensure by every means it can that light music, in all its forms, makes the fullest and most worthwhile contribution to the happiness of the community.

But the living composer of light music received scant support from the BBC. 1973 sounded the death knell of the Society.

In late 1965, discussions between representatives of the Composers' Guild, the Light Music Society, the Songwriters' Guild of Great Britain (now known as BASCA – British Academy of Songwriters, Composers and Authors) and the BBC resulted in an agreement whereby new light music would be considered for inclusion in what were to be known as 'Repertoire Rehearsals' by the BBC Concert Orchestra. Composer Ernest Tomlinson and live wire secretary of the Songwriters' Guild Victor Knight played prominent parts in the talks. My contribution began early in 1966. Generally, individual items were limited to between three and three and a half minutes' duration with suites of up to fifteen minutes. Where possible, items accepted for promotion would receive five broadcasts within the month. But there was no payment for the arrangements or parts – not even a hire fee. So the BBC acquired a substantial repertoire, all for free!

The ACCS (Arrangers, Composers and Copyists Section) of the Musicians' Union quite rightly frowned upon the agreements. On the other hand, it displayed little understanding of the composers' dilemma. Like a salesman promoting a new product, one had to submit samples. A mundane comparison, I admit, but it serves to illustrate my point. As one can imagine, it was no joke scoring and writing parts for thirty-five or fifty-five strong orchestras, then, after rehearsal and playback of the recording, the composition being given the 'thumbs down'. The scheme soon ran into trouble. My first acceptance was in May 1966. The first broadcast? APRIL 1967! After many phone and postal reminders. It became acutely obvious that accepted items would not receive the minimum quota of airings originally planned or promised, thus the royalties would in no way be commensurate with the composer's time and creative effort.

Compare all this with the creation of a potential money-spinning pop song, at the most thirty-two bars of a single line melody with words, a repetitive 'hook' line, chord symbols, plus a demo featuring perhaps only a vocalist and a small backing group. However, BBC Radio being the largest and the only shop window in which to display musical wares, composers were truly faced with a Hobson's choice situation. Despite many obstacles combining to hinder progress, dogged persistence brought about acceptance and transmissions of four pieces. 'Shopping Spree' – favourable comment likened it to the Bob Farnon style; two bossa novas, 'Pepita' and 'Happy Hacienda'; and 'Brighton Belle' – descriptive of the locomotive adored and used by many showbiz people, who were soon to lament the end of that gracious lady's reign. Also a suite of nine minutes' duration, 'Tres Señoritas'. Its three movements, 'Miguela', 'Carlotta' and 'Conchita', were inspired by a painting entitled *Spanish Ladies*.

Five other pieces were declared 'unsuitable' so rejection and acceptances just about struck a fifty-fifty balance. Other more ambitious items were never sent. It was too late. The scheme was unjustly thrown out when Auntie Beeb (as she was now known) discarded her twin-sets and skirts for mini-skirts and hot pants. However, mine was a fair achievement, I suppose, for an unknown in the highly professional and competitive field of composition and orchestration.

Dodging back to May 25th, 1966, my visit to BBC's Yalding House address revealed that my very first submission, 'Shopping Spree', had been accepted, its title making it an obvious choice for the 'Breakfast Special' programmes.

In contrast to that heart-warming news, the appointment I had with a leading publisher led to a revelation of quite a different kind. It was a director of the company to whom I handed several scores. He pored over them for a moment and I guessed what was coming as he looked up, squirming with ill-concealed embarrassment in his plush, upholstered chair, asking, "Haven't you got any tapes?"

He then admitted he couldn't read a note of music!

I was quick to point out the impracticalities. Being orchestral music requiring so many players, it would cost a small fortune just to record two or three items. Demos of pop songs – yes, they were a feasible and viable proposition, but my kind of pieces – they were the publisher's responsibility, part of the promotional process once taking the copyright, not mine. I also pointed out that only when a piece had been broadcast, might one get hold of a recording, but this was most difficult in view of the BBC/MU agreement on tapes made by House Orchestras. On the other hand, it was up to publishers to show some interest in the Repertoire Rehearsals, to push items in the mutual advantage to themselves and composers.

With great difficulty, I restricted myself to maintaining a polite conversation, picked up my scores and departed with a final expression of strong disapproval of the time-wasting, catch-22 situation. Olive was with me and, once outside, gave vent to her feelings, comparing the limitations and incompetence of people in high positions which they were unqualified to hold with my own abilities. To me it was just the first incident of its kind. There would no doubt be many more nerve-jangling 'beat-your-head-against-a-brick-wall' experiences to follow. We jostled our way through crowded Oxford Street to look around 'Coats and 'ats' store. (To the uneducated, C&A!) Then back to the Dominion Theatre to see the film of the Rodgers and Hammerstein hit show, *The Sound of Music*. As the opening music swelled gloriously, the colours were as mixed as my emotions as I sat there misty-eyed reflecting on the frustration of the publishing office encounter and also the joy that *my* first sound of music had got off to a good start.

Emotions of a very different kind spilled over during the next decade. But family concerns and griefs are intensely private and personal. Without any intention of making light of the problem-laden years which followed, suffice it to say that no useful purpose can be served by dwelling in detail on family and domestic problems and crises which all too easily become highly-charged emotive dramas, with long drawn-out illnesses and departures in the circle. An excruciating stop-start period of far more 'downs' than 'ups', hardly conducive to a creative effort. Reality and sympathy had to be evenly balanced. Stretched as tight as the emotional tightrope I walked, I was far more fortunate than some. And, somehow, I kept my balance, my equilibrium protected by an umbrella of hard work and creativity.

The last impression I wish to create is one of self-satisfaction or smugness. I was perhaps fortunate in having the ability to pour emotion into something tangible, to get it all out of my system. Nor would I wish to seem pompous. But, without realising it at the time, all the agony and ecstasy of nearly ten years was summed up in a two and a half minute entry in the year 1975 in the final of the last of a long series of Southern Television competitions for songs, carols and hymns on given themes. Subjects in which I had had a fair measure of success. The fruits of adversity, I suppose one could call it.

THE AGONY, THE ECSTASY

1. The agony, the ecstasy of love,
    The joy, the tears, demanding years of love.
    His was no passing passion – that seems to be the fashion –
    But a grand design for all mankind to follow, for all time.
    Love is the wine of life – too good to waste.
    Divine – yet sometimes bitter-sweet the taste.
    But earth would be a poorer place if we could never face
    The agony, the ecstasy of love.

2. The agony, the ecstasy of love.
    The joy, the tears, demanding years of love.
    His was no passing passion – that seems to be the fashion –
    But a grand design for all mankind to follow for all time.
    Two thousand years ago the seed was sown.
    And ev'ry finest hour that man has known
    Springs from the seed, the flower,
    The unseen pow'r from heav'n above:
    The agony, the ecstasy of love.

CHAPTER TWENTY-EIGHT

SOLO

It was a hard and lonely road that I travelled during the next ten years despite the new faces and places, the new contacts made and the occasional gregarious gathering. Writing music was a piece of cake compared to the frustrations encountered when trying to promote it single-handed. The many battles were all part of a valuable learning experience, from which I believe I emerged much the wiser and stronger.

The BBC kindly invited composers and publishers to the Repertoire Rehearsals, usually held at the Camden studios in north London. I went along many times when my pieces were being rehearsed and recorded by the Concert Orchestra. It gave me the opportunity to hear, and to be self-critical. To be really hard on oneself, not to mention the chance to listen and learn from the efforts of other hopefuls. At this point my personal hopes were centred on a suite about Broadstairs entitled 'Seven Bays'. An extract from a letter from Leslie Osborne of KPM Music gives a dual confirmation of the appeal of my work and of the restrictive policies which put the new light music scheme in a straitjacket. Dated 19th July, 1967, it began:

> I have been carefully through the manuscripts which you sent me of the 'Seven Bays' suite and the other items. I think some of them are most attractive but I am not so sure that it would be all that easy to secure performances of works of this nature in view of the present content of BBC programmes.
>
> At the same time, as they do have considerable merit, and I always endeavour to do what I possibly can to help a composer (particularly if he is British), I am wondering if you would allow me to photograph the scores and send them to BBC producers and musical directors for them to review with a view to giving them a performance.

The 'Seven Bays' music embraced the strong Dickensian connections with the town of Broadstairs – the annual festival, and the residence of the famous literary figure at Bleak House. The BBC did not, however, share Leslie's opinion or his enthusiasm. Or, if they did, then one can only assume that the suite became a victim of circumstance – turned down so as not to add to the most embarrassing backlog of items thus inviting further criticism of its failure to meet the original aim of the scheme.

As another prominent publisher put it, "The BBC is making suitable noises, and, under pressure, appearing to do something about new light music, but it won't last long. The BBC doesn't like criticism, or being told what to do. I've been in the business long enough to know the score."

(Leslie Osborne, although long retired from publishing, died recently, and proved that age is no barrier, having co-written with Simon May the title music for *Howard's Way* and *Eastenders*.)

Clearly, there was no point in seeking publication, thus parting with half of my broadcasting royalties. I had now accumulated many useful contacts; I would make my own concentrated and aggressive promotional ploys, as opposed to none at all or half-hearted ones by publishers. The one exception would be KPM where I valued the experience and sincerity displayed by Leslie, even though he doubted that my 'Tres Señoritas' suite would ever get on the air. He happened to hear the first broadcast in 1969, characteristically phoning me to offer his congratulations. Other transmissions followed, and the very popular first movement, 'Miguela', had some separate plays, yet still not in keeping with the minimum promised. Leslie's reply to a query about guest conductors, December 1968, revealed another barrier: "...until a permanent conductor is fixed, they are having guest conductors and it is almost impossible to find out who they are until they are named in *The Radio Times*. As programmes are recorded several weeks in advance, such information is useless. Things are not getting any easier!"

Around that time I recall a broadcast by Leslie recounting a lifetime in music publishing, in the series, *Life is Nothing Without Music*. Reference to Ray Noble, also working in publishing then as a staff arranger, underlined my previous assertions about the indispensable men who 'put it all together' in orchestral form. Also the influence of the classical masters. Leslie related how he and Ray would go to a concert at the Albert Hall, the latter armed with miniature scores, which he would follow, carefully marking certain phrases which were of particular interest. No intention to pinch a melody, simply a studious and intelligent method of applying some aspects – perhaps voicings, tone colours, rhythmic patterns – in future arrangements, all in the cause of the betterment of popular music. The criteria for membership of the Performing Rights Society was proof of sustained involvement in composition and, more importantly, sufficient works broadcast, televised and/or published to warrant the Society collecting and distributing royalties on one's behalf. In March 1968, I was elected as a Provisional Associate member, which, in turn, gave me full membership of the Songwriters' Guild. Number one objective had been realised – much more quickly than I had anticipated.

I regularly attended PRS meetings and luncheons, and that which took place in July, 1970 at the London Hilton is particularly memorable, being graced by guest HRH The Prince of Wales, and presided over by Sir Arthur Bliss, our president, and Master of the Queen's Music. It was a huge, glittering gathering attended by not only everyone who was anyone, but also quite a few nonentities like me. I found myself allotted to the enjoyable company of Tony Roberts, son of songwriter the late Paddy Roberts, and the bubbly *Carry On* star Barbara Windsor.

The prince, in his reply to Sir Arthur's welcoming speech and the presentation of a handsome, red and gold bound volume, *Music for a Prince*, was in good form. He made witty reference to the musical aspirations of his royal forebears: "I understand that Henry VIII dabbled at composing music," adding slyly, "when he wasn't otherwise occupied!"

In May 1969, Kenneth Adam, former Director of Television, headed a lengthy article 'The BBC is Drowning in a Sea of Pop'. It was highly critical about the proposed set-up. The future of the orchestras and the coming of local radio stations was covered in another article by Brian Dean, in *The Daily Mail*, 2nd June. There was no shortage of letters of condemnation from the public, including my own contribution, published three days later as the 'Letter of the Day'. The sheer volume of July press clips, unanimous in their criticism, precludes complete reproduction. The song had ended, but the melody (or should it be 'malady'?) lingered on when in December,

1969, the leader in *The Daily Telegraph* called on the BBC to 'raise public taste and increase public knowledge by programmes of unchangeable quality... All the piffle and trash it can leave to be put out by others, or not at all.'

My letter to the Director-General of the BBC, Charles Curran, was passed 'down the line' to his subordinates, at that time Kenneth Baynes and Douglas Muggeridge. The latter wrote:

> ...You raise a number of extremely interesting points and I feel it would be best if we could have a chat about them. Perhaps you would be kind enough to ring my office in the next few days to arrange a time to come and have a talk with me.

The meeting took place on Friday 10th July. It would be tiresome to set out in full my report of the meeting. One big grouse was about the removal of approved new Repertoire Rehearsals items from programmes by producers on the grounds that they were not well known or popular. It was hypocritical to invite new items if they were to be thrown out at the whim of producers stuck with the policy of 'play something familiar'.

"Listeners tend to lose interest and switch off or over to another station as soon as something they don't know comes on the air," I was told. I just could not believe my ears! What an indictment! Were all those recent expressions of protest in the Press sent in by unthinking, unintelligent, ignorant morons?

A copy of my letter, followed by a copy report of the meeting, sent to the Songwriters' Guild were well received. The letter was described by Secretary, Victor Knight, as "excellent". The report drew the adjective "masterly", and I was congratulated heartily by the Council, to whom the report was read. Additionally, the Guild sent a copy to the Light Music Society. True, I was not, at that time, a member of that Society, yet no acknowledgement was ever received, nor any invitation extended to enlist the nonentity who had apparently, dared to steal its thunder: going to the top nearly three years in advance of its own belated efforts to stop the rot!

CHAPTER TWENTY-NINE

AUNTIE KNOWS BEST

In the May, 1970 *Journal of Performing Rights*, Stanley Black's article, 'A Plea for Sanity', drew attention to the dangerous gap – that between pop and nostalgia – which continues to widen. Opinions which were parallel to mine should strike a sympathetic chord in the minds of all those who would like the musical scales (pun not intended!) to become more evenly balanced. It began:

> I am often asked (by people who should know better) whether my attitude towards 'light' or 'popular' music differs from my attitude towards 'serious' music. This question is one which I find both amusing and irritating. Amusing, because there is the implication that one whose professional work embraces both ends of the musical spectrum must be some sort of schizophrenic freak; irritating, because one senses the condescending sneer that anyone who can be involved in both jazz *and* Messiaen must of necessity be a 'dabbler' in both.

Like Stanley Black, I share schizophrenic dabbling with an ever-increasing number of musicians and writers, far superior to me. (Just two names that spring to mind – Previn and Bernstein, for example.) In a biography I read recently there was a passage relevant to our present subject: 'George Gershwin had one foot in Tin Pan Alley, the other in Carnegie Hall.'

And this 'dabbler' has one foot in Tin Pan Alley, the other in Grand Hotel! Personally, I have yet to hear of an orchestral musician who has one instrument for Bob Farnon or Eric Coates and another for Beethoven or Debussy. Stanley Black's final paragraph emphasises the gap – that which should have been filled with light music –

> "How tragic it would be if, instead of gradually enlarging our musical public by carefully weaning, we

either drove those millions even further into their world of pop-groups and *Bless This House* or – as seems very likely at this point in time – antagonised them completely and irrevocably.

The abolition in 1971 of a license fee for home and car radio, replaced by an increased combined license, was a sensible decision in relation to the prohibitive cost of collection, simultaneously providing the BBC with a very convenient escape route from previously-levelled criticism re its preoccupation with pop for the mostly non-contributing section of the community.

And it wasn't only the press. I recall Max Bygraves wisecracking in a TV show, "Have you listened to BBC radio programmes lately? Anyone would think there was nobody over the age of sixteen listening in."

Today, the gap is even wider. Music for eggheads and pinheads. Or to use a description which all ex-service personnel will remember, "Like a NAAFI sandwich – one on top, one on the bottom and sweet FA in the middle!"

And the wisdom of the license decision was cancelled out, to use a much employed phrase of the era, 'at a stroke', a madcap mandate allowing Auntie to misappropriate the extra revenue, more than five million pounds on the furtherance of local radio. I don't think that we need both BBC and commercial stations. Having both, we were told, would help to raise and maintain a high standard. Rubbish! They all purvey the same musical fare.

In the autumn of 1970, I began a three year phase during which (save for the times when I joined the Pavilion Orchestra, to feature some of my works, and depping for Bert Hayes during the season) I cut out all other engagements deciding to concentrate on writing. Time was short and, at the end of my three year stint, Auntie was still ringing the changes – fast! All to the detriment of new light music writers. First, the instrumentation of the Scottish Light Orchestra, then the Midland, was drastically changed. The effect was twofold. All new writers' special orchestrations became redundant, and the new set-ups were entirely unsuitable for the performance of light music.

It was during one of my visits in Cairo in 1945 that I was introduced to RAF ME musician, arranger and composer of the No.1 Band, Frank Cordell who, following his return to the UK, became successful through the creation of jingles, film scores and backing arrangements for many recording stars. He was absolutely scathing about the BBC's strangulation of outlets for more adventurous MOR or light music compositions. In an article entitled 'Frank Talk' (1972) he wrote:

> The BBC's London-based Radio Orchestra has been wading through lowest-common-denominator musical mud for so long that one has come to accept their output as the well-meant but fairly appalling musical norm.
>
> The change of policy is an execrable move... more so because Norrie Paramor (who is a likeable chap), also happens to be a council member of the Light Music Society, and, by accepting (inaugurating?) the change within the orchestra and thus placing the performance of new light music orchestral works outside its capabilities, he is literally cutting the throats of the composers who are writing new works for possible performance, some of whom are members of the body on whose council he sits.
>
> It is a similar set-up with the Scottish Variety Orchestra. Their new conductor, Brian Fahey, is also a highly likeable chap – and a skilled arranger – but he is completely representative of the school of well-drilled purveyors of en masse pop arrangements.
>
> Unless someone, somewhere, sees the light, the outlets for composers of light orchestral music will quickly vanish. My terminology, i.e. 'light music' does not necessarily confine itself to the well-worn areas of Eric Coates, Gilbert and Sullivan etc., but includes, in fact, anything which may be termed adult music for enjoyment.

Producers of programmes like *Friday Night In Music Night*, *Grand Hotel* and *Sweet and Swing* were all tarred with the same brush, all playing down Memory Lane. When the regional orchestras became redundant, I added extra parts to my arrangements to meet the requirements of the surviving Concert Orchestra where, due to constant change of producers of *Melodies for You* my persistence paid off, getting pieces included in this popular Sunday spot. The breakthrough was perhaps helped by the fact that, by then, two of them had been used in British films.

I wrote to Albert Semprini asking him to spare me a few minutes of his time when appearing in a Sunday concert at Margate Winter Gardens. No reply, but I went along just the same, as it happened that I was booked to play in the pit orchestra that night. Leslie Wheeler was helpful in introducing me. I sent polite reminders re two BBC-approved scores which Semprini had taken with him, but they were ignored. Nine months later, without a word of apology, I got them back. It was due entirely to the fact that purely by chance and without request on my part, kindly Leslie Osborne, one of the few genuine, sympathetic souls I came across in the business, provided me with Semprini's private address.

Later another well-known MD and publisher took a fancy to a Latin-flavoured piece entitled 'Pepita'. But it was promises, promises all the way. I couldn't wait for ever. I did my own thing, getting several broadcasts while he was still thinking about it! Having literally sweated blood in securing the first airing of my Spanish suite, he displayed interest in that too, but the contract was dated so as to share royalties on the very first airing – and *I* had done all the spade work! That just wasn't on. I returned the contract, unsigned, stating my reasons. A pity it was the end of that association, but one has to learn, not remain the soft touch. I intended to press on regardless, not rewardless.

> I regret to say that I have very little opportunity these days to play new compositions or arrangements, the only ones being either my own or those requested by the gramophone company for specific reasons. Sorry I cannot help, but I wish you all the luck.

The above letter, a personal one from maestro Mantovani (then living in Dorset) was the response to mine drawing attention to BBC approval and broadcasts, offering scores and tapes of the compositions. My offer was not even taken up, the music dismissed without even a fair hearing. *The recording company pays the piper...* The maestro no doubt made a fortune from the worldwide sales of millions of records, but few are aware that the creator of the famous Mantovani sound was arranger and composer (of 'Elizabethan Serenade' fame) Ronnie Binge. Back to the arrangers again...

The next, from Malcolm Lockyer in July 1972, is one more glaring confirmation of BBC policy. (It was addressed to Norman Mead, Organiser of Orchestrations at Aeolian Hall, and forwarded to me.)

> Dear Norman,
>
> I have had a look at 'Happy Hacienda' and whilst I think it is a good composition, well scored in the light music idiom, I cannot see where you can place it in our next quarter's commitments. As you know, most producers are all in favour of scores from the top twenty or thirty for their programmes, i.e. Charlie Chester, 'Open House', Tony Brandon, etc. I can only suggest that Bill Worland makes direct contact with someone like Max Jaffa. We are all going through this frustrating spell so Bill is not alone!"

Suffice to say, I tried Max Jaffa. No dice. Same old reasons, *ad nauseum*!

In March 1973, I wrote to Norrie Paramor enclosing the same scores as above (which so far, had received all of two broadcasts!). I offered to supply an arrangement suitable for the instrumentation of the newly-created Midland Radio Orchestra. Two weeks later – Saturday, 7th April to be exact – Norris telephoned me. Yes, he liked the number and the arrangement, but... Here we go again, but with a variation on the well-worn theme. It transpired that, from the start, Auntie had decreed that the MRO's role would be confined to playing special arrangements of current hits, and those which had made their mark *only since the coming of Beatlemania in 1962. NOTHING ELSE!* This was resisted and a compromise was reached – the pre-1962 hits would also be included. Norrie was very pessimistic about the prospects of being able to use 'Happy Hacienda', despite it's having won his personal approval. As a gesture of goodwill (and consolation, I suppose), when I expressed my intense disappointment and vigorously denounced the policy as being no less than a restrictive practice, he asked me to do special arrangements of three 'standards' for the new library. It was appreciation and recognition of my arranging skills, but I also knew full well that it was an effort to get me off his back, to appease me.

This extract from one of Norrie's letters completes the picture. It is dated 29th October, 1974, in reply to a tape containing not only 'Pepita' but also several other items.

> ...I have now listened to all the items on the tape including your suggestion, 'Pepita'. Yes, the orchestra could play this well, but if I asked you for an orchestration it would be doubtful if it would ever see the light of day. The producers who select their own programmes have very strict requirements from which they will not deviate... I am sending your tape back which I, at any rate, enjoyed listening to.

Auntie pays the piper...

Mantovani, at that time, held a prominent position in the Songwriters' Guild, and Norrie Paramor a similar one on the Council of the Light Music Society – QUISLINGS!

I formed the impression from my contacts in succeeding years that, given a free hand, had the choice been left to musicians, the content of so many programmes would have been vastly different. Now, since it was an obviously hopeless task, I ceased all contact in 1976.

February 23rd 1973. A top-level meeting took place at Broadcasting House between BBC officials and representatives of the Composers' Guild, the Songwriters' Guild and the Light Music Society, the latter having three representatives, including Chairman Ernest Tomlinson. It is not a difficult task summarising the very lengthy report, as much of it went over ground covered by my strenuous solo effort nearly three years earlier, and the changes which I had believed to be imminent were now *fait accompli*. Radio 4 programmes *Morning Melody* and *Invitation to Music* were unjustifiably killed off, the Beeb refusing point-blank to consider their retention by transferring them to Radio 2. An extract from a bulletin of the Light Music Society, by Steve Race, February 1972:

...the other programme I enjoy tremendously is *Invitation to Music* where I simply take off my jacket, pour myself an after-lunch drink and say whatever comes into my head about the music being played. It's a direct communication between myself and the individual listener, and it's something only radio could do. I look forward to it tremendously.

Breakfast Special, Roundabout and similar broadly-based series also came in for the chop, as did the regional orchestras. The Societies and Guilds were rendered powerless. There were neither programmes nor orchestras remaining to play or promote the cause of light music, new or old. Exit musicians, bring on the DJs!

There had to be some modification of Lord Reith's concept and rigid attitudes, but things have gone too far. That section of the licence-paying public which has tastes other than pop and the extremes of Radio Three have little or no alternative. Stanley Black's article, referred to earlier, also had something to say about the many who couldn't care less about communicating.

In my opinion, it would be applicable to many non-musical personnel and non-musicians who play records hour after hour, probably paid far more handsomely, in fact, than many skilled writers and performers of music.

As I wrote earlier, I had no illusions of an overnight breakthrough, and I certainly never dreamed how deeply I would become involved in the battle for a fairer deal for new light music. A crusade which put me on a treadmill, a self-imposed, even masochistic, if you like, phase. I had my eyes wide open, but such involvement served only to open them even wider. On behalf of fellow composers of Repertoire Rehearsal days, with abortive scores, having given up creating works for a non-existent market, I offer lyrical and musical comment.

MELODIES OF MINE

Verse: I'm not in the same league as Beethoven, Bartók or Grieg.
I'm not highbrow, or lowbrow, but know how
To make melodies easy on the ear.
Tunes I've created, will anyone hear?
Tacet, they've waited, year after year.
No more tomorrows, make it today,
Before I am clay – orchestra play!

Chorus: Melodies of mine, born of heaven and of hell,
What a story you could tell, melodies of mine.
Gathering dust, and yellowing, each page,
Instead of mellowing with age.
What would I give, if you could live
Before I die!
Melodies of mine, when I'm gone, will someone find
All the treasures of my mind, for the pleasure of mankind?
Will you be encored?   Or will you still be ignored?
Melodies of mine, when I'm gone.

Bridge: Nostalgic slop and teenage pop for the old and teenage.
In despair, search the air, for something in-between-age.
Is Radio Three your cup of tea? Your Hundred Best
                        Tunes?
Melodies for you?
Nothing new – overplayed request tunes,
Long overdue to be laid-to-rest-tunes.

Repeat chorus: Melodies of mine etc...

In conclusion, a couple of bouquets – one to Alan Tongue, a helpful producer at Belfast, in the early days, and the other to Iain Sutherland, who was based at Glasgow. Replying to a critical letter in a Society bulletin, a colleague of mine, Ronnie Bridges, wrote:

> As a light music 'plugger' (amongst other occupations), I very such regret that Mr Reynolds [the critic concerned] has seemingly ignored the

166

magnificent work done by Iain Sutherland who conducted the orchestra from 1960 onwards. During his Glasgow sojourn, Iain proved a true devotee of Light Music and gave many delightful performances of new British works in this vein... this should at all times be remembered with gratitude.

I'll drink to that, Ronnie!

A quote from Iain's letter of March 1975, sent from his home in Harpenden after he had quit the BBC for a freelancing role, is a sad, but fitting finale.

> ...I'm afraid there is nothing I can do to help you 'fight the good fight' in the light music field these days – it is a disaster area... I wish you good luck in your quest.

* * * * *

"The public doesn't want new music: the main thing it demands of a composer is that he be dead."
ARTHUR HONEGGER (1892 – 1955)

CHAPTER THIRTY

THE QUEST GOES ON

Auntie Beeb having driven the final nail into the light music coffin, I took a stab at the recorded libraries of various publishing houses. For a while I had to be content with compliments, not cash. Some typical replies.

From Chandos Music Limited:

> I have listened to the tape and find it delightful music, well orchestrated, but, knowing the present situation at the BBC, it is rather hopeless trying to exploit it.

And from the Southern Library of Recorded Music Limited:

> I have now had an opportunity of listening to your tapes and looking at your scores, and, whilst I personally liked some of the numbers, I regretfully have to tell you that, due to BBC policy, with the accent on pop, they are not in the style that we get asked for these days.

I sent some songs, in manuscript form only, no demos, to Walter Ridley of EMI Records. His reply reads:

> I have played through all your material and must say that I think they are very well written songs, but regretfully, I am unable to consider them for any artists under my banner.

Samples of appreciation, not just a rejection slip, by musicians and staff arrangers of well-respected firms. Equally, an appreciation of the difficulties, lack of incentive or channels for effective promotion.

But once again, dogged persistence was rewarded when half a dozen of my pieces were accepted by Atmosphere Music Ltd, and it paid off handsomely: royalties still come in, even today, from this source, from tunes written thirty years ago!

There are, of course, some songs which appear to be 'tailor-made' for certain singers or groups. In the case of individual artists, one has to ascertain initially the record company with whom he or she is under contract. Also the A&R representative (the abbreviation for Artists and Repertoire) who has considerable influence – perhaps too much influence, one is sometimes tempted to believe – in the selection of material. So it follows that one's song can be rejected, as it often is, without even having been brought to the notice of the act or artist concerned. Pop groups, almost without exception, write their own doggerel. Alternatively, they have a close relationship with others who are equally expert at writing it for them, with emphasis on the group's sound and style. Also, there are the hordes of singer-songwriters. In fact, the trend is towards DIY recording. There are tracks, not just demos, oozing straight out of the independent, well-equipped studios and into initial airings on local radio stations.

I would not pretend to be able to write out-and-out pop, nor would I want to. One writes best that which one genuinely feels. Not just art for art's sake, nor for the lowest common denominator, but aiming for the true MOR market. A classical background can inhibit as well as inspire. The full orchestral and big band sounds are those which can turn me on; groups and gimmicky noises can't. It is an indisputable fact that there is a huge volume of music from the shows, the theatres and films which has endured and continues to endure without ever having found its way into the charts – the top twenty pops. Personally, I would rather be remembered by a handful of such tunes which, for want of a better expression, 'keep coming back like a song' than the five-minute wonder, destined to go the way of all flesh.

There is, of course, the far wider scope which situations in the book of a show create for writers of lively imagination and wit. I found it most interesting to read in Sammy Cahn's entertaining book, *I Should Care*, the method he and co-writer Jimmy Van Heusen employed when commissioned to do words and music for a show or film. They would each take a copy of the book, read slowly through it, marking pages which suggested a situation where a song could come in and, when finished, compare notes. So often, they coincided! There have been not a few occasions when my songs have drawn the comment (or criticism – please yourself!): 'It's not a commercial idea, but would make a great show number.'

My venture into the world of the musical play was short–lived, due mostly to the stubbornness of the 'other half'. A London journalist and writer, whom we will call 'Jack', advertised in *The Stage* – 'Book and lyrics ready. Composer wanted.' The setting was an eastern one, very well adapted from a well-known play. An excellent book, good dialogue etc., but the lyrics...! Even with the best will in the world, I found it impossible to work with them in the original form, which betrayed scant musical knowledge. Uppermost, I had in mind the successful songs from *Kismet* as the standard to work to, even though the melodies had been borrowed from *Borodin*. I created five of my own songs, two of them duets, in a short space of time, such was my enthusiasm. They still said what Jack had intended, but, without being trite or banal, were easily remembered and in keeping with the era and settings. Jack was adamant, however, that lyrics were his department. A couple of years later I spotted the ad again and rightly guessed that it was Jack. I made contact seeking a compromise, but it was no go. Pity. I'm sure it could have made the West End.

Written 'to order' in 1970 for a Blackpool song competition that never was (due to its sponsor pulling out), and a show number, if ever there was – 'The Golden Mile'.

You can imagine how memories of summer 1940 flooded back as I recalled the fantastic, unquenchable, happy-go-lucky atmosphere that prevailed during some of the darkest days of the war, the town heaving with humanity. Unashamedly razzmatazz, Blackpool, nevertheless, has been little affected by the popularity of holidays abroad, still unbeatable in terms of friendliness and sheer entertainment value.

THE GOLDEN MILE

There's a great big smile on the Golden Mile.
Fun begins right here, in top gear, ev'ry year.
It's a wide and wonderful playground,
A while-the-sun-shines-make-hay ground,
Such a happy-go-lucky, live-for-today sound.
So come spend a while on the Golden Mile.
We can make life swing, do our thing, a-ring-a-ding-ding,

In this something-for-all, we-don't-care town
Walk tall, have a ball, let our hair down –
We can do it in style on the Golden Mile.

My original lyric contained the line 'carefree and gay sound', since
changed for obvious reasons, although personally I find the current
colloquialism extremely distasteful. And two other lines ran 'All year
round our money we save up for this annual rave-up'. (Which is
exactly what the factory and mill workers *had* to do, way back to get a
holiday – the Good Old Days?)

There's a lot of fanciful, romantic nonsense said and written about
many great composers – analysis of the inspiration behind this or that
symphony or concerto. I'm sure that much of it never existed as far
as the composers were concerned. Were it possible for them to hear
such commentary, they would be doubled up with mirth. In common
with the isolated personal experiences in this book, inspired moments
are the exception rather than the rule. If every composer, famous or
otherwise, had sat around waiting for inspiration to strike, the world
would have been denied much beautiful music. Admittedly, the
masters had all the time in the world. Today, the ever-changing
trends and commercial pressures largely dictate that literary and
musical creation is just another job. One has to look, listen and
experiment, constantly putting on a thinking cap. Einstein, who put
the proportions behind genius as one per cent inspiration, ninety-nine
per cent perspiration, got it in one.

I have never had a bedside pad and pencil, although I will admit to
sometimes waking suddenly at some unearthly hour with the answer to
a problem which had evaded me all day long – such as a snatch of
melody, a lyrical line or two – simply because I had dozed off to sleep
with it still on my mind. Happily, I have the knack of storing the
answer, able to 'call it up' the next morning.

During those Western Desert years, reading material consisted
chiefly of out-dated magazines and books from home, such as *The
Reader's Digest* and *World Digest*. The pages were grubby and tatty –
well-thumbed evidence of their having been passed through countless
servicemen's hands. I adore genuine witty remarks, especially the
'off-the-cuff' ones. Not all funny, but sometimes penetrating, ironic,
sad, even profound, much of it today from radio shows, chat shows,
ad writers and cartoonists, and so often the phrase or turn of phrase is

unbelievably simple, forcing one to comment, 'Why didn't *I* think of that?'

The remark that stuck in my mind from 1943/44, is attributed to the sage of Oklahoma, Will Rogers, at a literary luncheon appeared among a welter of other stories, anecdotes, in a Digest magazine: "Kissin don't last – cookin' do," he observed. When country music made its first bow and became increasingly popular, I got around to turning the phrase into a full–blown number, in humorous vein. If you believe, ladies, that the way to a man's heart is through his stomach then this song is for you. Later, it was featured, along with the 'Golden Mile', in my BBC Radio Kent broadcasts.

KISSIN' DON'T LAST – COOKIN' DO   (boy/girl duet)

Verse 1: Boy: As I was readin' quotes an' anecdotes
By wise and witty guys,
Those tongue-in-cheek philosophers
Who cut us down to size,
I found Will Roger's recipe for matrimonial bliss,
Down-to-earth simplicity, what he said was this:

Chorus 1: Both: Kissin' don't last – cookin' do
Kissin' don't last – cookin' do
Boy: So keep your honey in the hive.
Keep him sunny, keep him live.
Both: Kissin' don't last – cookin' do.

Verse 2: Boy: The gals who wheel and deal the sex appeal –
That kind ain't hard to find.
But those who cook, the way they look,
They sure can blow my mind.
Girl: The meat is sweetest near the bone,
For starters, that's OK,
But man can't live by bed alone,
The same course night and day.

Chorus 2: Both: Kissin' don't last – cookin' do
Kissin' don't last – cookin' do.
Boy: Now time has flowed, it's ringin' true,

Ole Will, he knowed a thing or two,
Both: Kissin' don't last – cookin' do.

Verse 3: Boy: I guess that just like vittles that we eat,
The livin's à la carte.
The sweet an' sour, the bitter-sweet,
But you can win my heart.
Girl: Just make a wish for any dish
From cordon bleu to stew. [Pronounced 'stoo']
My expertise, which aims to please,
Is saying 'I love you'.

Chorus: Both: Kissin' don't last – cookin' do
Kissin' don't last – cookin' do.
Boy: Before you dream of shoes an' rice,
Think twice – remember Will's advice,
Both: Kissin' don't last – cookin' do.

Verse 4: Boy: Say, you're the kinda gal I'm looking for,
An' I can hardly wait
To fix the venue, fix the date,
An' see what you've in store.
Girl: But if it's spice an' all things nice,
The after dinner sort,
Well, that ain't on the menu,
But there's always food for thought!

Chorus 4: Both: Kissin' don't last – cookin' do
Kissin' don't last – cookin' do
Boy: There goes the dinner gong, so long!
There ain't no mo' to this here song,
Both: Kissin' don't last, Kissin' don't last,
Kissin' don't last... cookin' do.

In 1971 the Performing Rights Society gained recognition for its services by winning the Queen's Award to Industry. If there had been an award *for* industry, my widespread activities and untiring efforts in the Seventies would have made me a winner hands down! Sandwiched between the works for the BBC and all the time-consuming promotion was participation in song festivals, the search for other sources of performance, a lengthy run in a TV series and some recordings for the then BBC Radio Medway. These, in turn, were transmitted by Radio Brighton and London. I notched up far more successes than failures in terms of performance. These, covered in a subsequent chapter, secured objective number two. In the five year period as a Provisional Associate member, I had accrued the requisite performances and royalties to move up to associate membership – confirmed by the PRS on 1st June, 1973. I have no doubt at all that, given a more favourable BBC climate, I would later have made full membership status,

Colonel Paul Neville, Principal Director of Music, Royal Marines, Deal, kindly included some of my works in weekly concerts. You will see from a couple of reproduced souvenir programmes how incongruous my name appears, sandwiched as it is between Tchaikovsky and Rodgers, Rossini and Bach. Humbling but happy experiences, being in such illustrious company. Paul, after retirement from the Marines, became Principal of Music at the Kings School, Canterbury, and, following retirement from that post, remains active, conducting the Kent Concert Orchestra and the St Cecilia Strings. In more recent years, his successor, Lt. Col. Graham Hoskins, was equally co-operative, even to the point of recording, at his own volition, some of my work during rehearsals. There might have been a lot more, had it not been for a combination of events. Graham retired in March 1989 and there was great uncertainty about the future of the Deal-based marines; the possibility was of a merger with RAF and Army bands and schools of music.[10] Finally, on September 22nd, 1989 came the murderous IRA bomb outrage. Currently, it is Col. John Ware who maintains the continuity in the Thursday concerts, now much reduced in number.

There were some more BBC Medway broadcasts; much burning of the midnight oil, doing special arrangements for a seven-piece outfit which included versatile musician Eric Greengrass on trombone and vibes. In contrast to the extremely difficult situation for new material on a national scale, there was no objection whatsoever to the use of original works on the local scene. For example, seven of ten pieces recorded in one instance were my own. It just didn't make sense! More performances came via the Brighton Pops Orchestra (a dance

[10] The Royal Marines School of Music is now based in Portsmouth.

band and strings combination) at the Dome, in 1973. Conducted by Don Pashley, it was an excellent orchestra, but it was one more courageous 'Keep Music Live' venture doomed to bite the dust at an early date.

And almost a year later, when both Olive and her mother were in hospital, the bitter-sweet taste of life played tug-of-war with my emotions as we recorded another Medway slot which included 'My Funny Valentine' and 'Here's That Rainy Day'. It was St Valentine's Day, and a year previously my mother had died after a long illness. So for me there was a double significance. Comments were passed about the 'sobbing' alto phrases, and the sad-sounding trombone solo in the latter song. Yes, it showed. But only I knew why.

It was around this time that I began using the pseudonym 'Ron Groves' in respect of songs. How did I choose the name? Well, I suppose nostalgia played a part; those 'Good Old Days' when I lived at number sixteen, Grosvenor Gardens, East Ham. A shuffle of the letters gave the anagram of Grosvenor. Change of name, change of luck it would seem, as will be seen in the following chapter.

CHAPTER THIRTY-ONE

FESTIVALS

This was an enjoyable period, since I was often called on to write 'to order'. Two instances: an entry for 'A Song for Scotland' drew praise from Leslie Osborne, but not from the adjudicating panel; then a novel competition – to create a signature tune for a Sydney commercial radio station. My entry had a strong razzmatazz beat and, out of several hundred entries from all over the world, it made the shortlist. A writer from the USA carried off first prize. That was a real challenge. The word 'Sydney' doesn't exactly inspire in the same way as, say, 'Chattanooga Choo Choo', 'By The Time I Get To Phoenix', 'San Francisco' or, indeed, the many American places with Spanish/Indian influenced names, so ideal for songwriters.

SCOTLAND!

Scotland! Where there's a smile that's cheery
To welcome you at ev'ry door.
Mountains that you can climb till you're weary,
Castles to explore.
Scotland! Where you can see salmon leaping,
The heather swaying in the breeze.
Scotland! Where Robbie Burns is sleeping,
And fishermen brave the angry seas.
A hundred islands scattered just like stepping stones, I've seen.
Loch Lomond and the Hebrides, Ben Nevis, Gretna Green.
The seagulls wheeling overhead in ev'ry fishing port,
And Loch Ness with a monster that's never yet been caught!
Scotland! You never fail to enchant me,
No matter where my footsteps tread.
Scotland: I pray the good Lord will grant me
In the years that lie ahead.
My life I'll be spending, until it's ending, in
Scotland! Scotland! Scotland, my island home.

And from the Highlands to Down Under:

SYDNEY, NEW SOUTH WALES

There are songs that they sing, of Paris in spring,
And New York and London – they've got ev'rything.
But wait till you see Sydney, New South Wales.
It's a wide-awake place that's setting the pace,
A hive that's alive, a cosmopolitan race,
So happy to be in Sydney, New South Wales.
If you're looking for a place in the sun
That's second to none – you're on the right track.
Other cities you'll see, but I guarantee,
Like an old boomerang, you'll always come back.
Where the bridge spans the sea, there always will be
A sheltering harbour, a city that's free,
In Sydney, Sydney, New South Wales.

Continuing our musical tour, on to Gibraltar from whence came
the cheering news that my song 'Suddenly' was one of ten selected for
the finals in December. Three years later, I made the final again.
This time with a strong ballad 'But That Was Yesterday'. Both songs
became 'starters' in a long line of near misses, and an ever-growing
collection of Certificates of Merit.

BUT THAT WAS YESTERDAY

Candlelight and wine in some romantic setting,
So nostalgic, just when I'm forgetting
All the things we vowed would last for ever,
But that was yesterday.
Lots of pebbles on the beach, so round and shiny;
Weekend cottage, by the sea, so tiny –
Happy moments that we spent together,
But that was yesterday,
But that was yesterday, but that was yesterday.
The flames of love that burn too fast
Can never last all life through.
But that was yesterday, but that was yesterday.
The lessons that we learn – too late –

Are in the past that we knew.
Someday I will find a love to last a lifetime,
And I'll tell myself, 'This is the last time,
Ev'ry other love was just a pastime, but that was yesterday,
But that was yesterday.'

In 1972, the odds against winning were dramatically shortened when two songs selected from more than 1200 entries found their way into the finals of the Castlebar International Song Festival – 'Fact or Fiction?' and 'Viva Roma'. Entrants had to supply their own vocalist and provide the score and parts for the backing orchestra at the festival. Through the good offices of the Songwriters' Guild, I engaged a singer, a native of Gibraltar, and I also booked the flight and accommodation for Olive and me and Frank and his wife, Margaret. Frank was now doing very little playing, having gone into antique and good class second-hand furniture business.

We were looking forward to spending a week on the north-west coast of Ireland in October. But, as so often happens in real life, the joy was short-lived... It seems that Murphy's Law prevailed. Mr Ten-per-cent, the singer's agent, having obtained engagements of a more lucrative nature, put paid to his participation in the festival. Meanwhile, both the ladies became ill, so the holiday was cancelled. At very short notice, I had to take pot-luck with two local singers of whom I knew nothing except for their vocal range. This meant last-minute scoring in different keys. I got the dots away in time wishing the singers the best of Irish as well as the best of British, but heavy-hearted, with an instinctive feeling that my chances of success had been drastically cut. They had! Hence two more Certificates of Merit. The lyrics to 'Fact or Fiction' appears in the more appropriate chapter 'Religioso'. 'Viva Roma' is set out below, together with the letter of praise received from the USA. Ted Danz, the Managing Director of the American Song Festival, wrote:

You might be interested to know that your lyric made it to the second level of judging. It has been read and evaluated by at least four of our judges. It certainly received recognition as being an excellent lyric, and as you know, the judges are real 'heavies' in the music business.

178

> This level of judging signifies that your lyric was among the top 7% of all the thousands received, and possibly just short of being one of this year's prize winners. To say the least, this in quite an accomplishment. Congratulations! We would therefore...

And so – one more certificate for the collection! Once again, so near, yet so far from the real thing. Encouraged by such praise from the experts, 'Viva Roma!' did the rounds of the publishing houses and record companies in the UK. No *dolce vita* for my song. Like the Christians of old in the arena, it had been thrown to the lions and given the thumbs down!

VIVA ROMA!

Round the world I've been and seen a hundred cities, maybe more.
But my travelling's done, there's only one
That I am heading for.
Life is living in the gay, eternal city I adore –
Viva Roma! Viva Roma!
Like a bella signorina, like a haunting melody,
She has lingered in my memory, but soon I'm going to be
In her warm embrace for ever – lucky, lucky, lucky me!
Viva Roma! Viva Roma!
This is a dream come true at last – no fairy story.
Filled with wonder, and I can tell.
My future I will find where past is present glory,
Always under her magic spell.
I will care for her and share with her
The sunshine and the wine,
Knowing when I'm gone that she'll go on
Until the end of time,
Capturing so many other hearts the way she captured mine.
Viva Roma! Viva Roma!

1976 – the year of the great drought. August and September – a super holiday in beautiful Switzerland, Montreux-based, with trips to Geneva, and a breathtaking climb of and descent from the ski resort,

Gstaad, returning home in time to take off again – a second chance in the annual Castlebar event.

I had visited Ireland a few years previously, just a short stay in the Cork area. This time, a quick flight across to Dublin's fair city, from whence local musician and singer Derek Day and I motored across to our hotel in charming little Westport. Just in time to dump our gear, freshen up and to nip back into Castlebar for the reception, and then indulge in gargantuan helpings of an abundant and delicious variety of food and wine. Throughout the week, hospitality was second to none, Derek and I commenting on the almost complete absence of any show of superiority or 'side' on the part of the many big names among writers and artists.

A few of those present were singers, Colin Anthony, Denis Lotis and Tony Stevens, the latter singing 'My Woman' written by Ray Davies of The Button Down Brass Band, carried off the first prize. (I met Tony again with the band, some four years later, when in Jersey.) Singer-composer Simon May, a friendly character, tagged along with us, and from EMI there was record producer Bob Barratt. And there were entries by composers who sadly had died prior to the festival date – Gordon Franks and Malcolm Lockyer. There was also an entry by Leslie Osborne with co-writer Henry Duke, from Brighton. Strange to relate, many of the big names did not make it to the televised Friday night finals, compèred by Terry Wogan.

The week was made that more memorable by the appearance on Tuesday night of George Seymour who sought me out, having spotted my name in the programmes. (I had first made the acquaintance of George in 1970 at Campbell Connelly Music when they published an album of Southern TV's *A Hymn for Children* which included my entry, 'Candlelight'.) Through his life-long connection with the music business, George was interested in the years I had spent with the Strauss-Miller Company, having known and worked with all the gang in the past. A sociable and well-respected person in the business, he kindly introduced me to Chairman of the Jury (and, at that time, also of the Songwriters' Guild) Jimmy Kennedy, who, in the thirties, had penned 'The Isle of Capri', 'Harbour Lights and 'South of the Border', to name but a few of a whole string of hits.

George put it to us: "Have you brought your survival kit?"

Puzzled, we countered, "No, what the heck is that?"

"Oh, you'll need it to get through the week. I should know; I come over to the Festival almost every year. Nip down to the local chemists for some aspirin, Alka-Seltzer and all that jazz!"

Getting back to our hotel at nearly four o'clock one morning, having joined in the social activities by helping to supply some of the music for dancing plus a session when we had with us a couple of lads from the RTE orchestra, and tenor saxist and jury member, Harry Gold, we soon learned the harsh truth and wisdom of George's recommendation! Where else could you roll in at such an unearthly hour, ring the bell, mutter some apologies for being so late, yet receive the cheerful response, "Oh, 'tis aul roight, sorr, dere's t'ree more still unaccounted for!" adding, "Can oi get yers somethin' to drink?"

And on a more serious note I would agree with the belief that we humans are far removed from the material and mundane world in the wee hours, spiritually rising above it all to another plane. In my experience, the music seems to unfold and float with inspired weightlessness, like a piece by Debussy, in those hours after midnight when (strangely) one feels neither mental nor physical weariness.

Coming down to earth again, what better way to round off the Irish connection than with two more anecdotes, typical of 'It could only happen in Ireland.'

The shop in Westport, with a notice in the window which read, 'We are open until closing time.' And something which appealed to my macabre sense of humour was the close proximity of the cemetery to the County Mayo Hospital which was conveniently situated on the other side of the road. At the cemetery entrance a large notice warned: 'NO DUMPING'!

I had entered two songs, having no doubt whatsoever in my own mind that 'But That Was Yesterday' would be selected. It was musically and lyrically superior (especially as it had been featured in a Gibraltar final) to the other entry, a last-minute idea, a country type of song. So what happened? Those responsible for choosing the qualifying tunes selected the country number, 'Concrete Jungle'. Hence, one more Certificate of Merit for my collection, signed by Jimmy Kennedy.

When in conversation with other writers, I discovered that there were some who shared my views about the panel's selection. They too often submitted more than one song, having a firm conviction as to the best of the bunch, yet it was always ignored in favour of another which, in the writer's opinion, hadn't a ghost of a chance. But very seldom do we know the make-up of selection panels, even less the reasoning behind its choice of finalists. I think they tend to get so weary, blasé and fed up with listening to so many songs that the edge of their judgement becomes dull and blunted. Here are the words to...

CONCRETE JUNGLE

Verse 1: City just like many others, with an atmosphere
                                    that smothers,
          Overgrown and overloaded with mankind,
          Where the rats just can't stop racin'.
          Might as well go rainbow chasin'
          For a crock of gold that they will never find.
          It's like livin' in a hive, and I know I won't survive.
          People all around me, yet I'm so alone.
          City life, I've grown to hate it,
          Might have known I'd never make it.
          There's no soul and just a man-made heart of stone.

Chorus: So it's Good-bye, concrete jungle, goodbye-ay-ay,
          Goodbye, concrete jungle, good-bye.
          I'm getting off the rack, the beaten track,
          Tell the pack I won't be back,
          Goodbye, concrete jungle, good-bye.

Verse 2: Wipe the slate, yes, wipe it clean,
          Look for pastures new and green.
          Where there's so much that the hand of God
                                    designed,
          Like the spirit deep inside, it won't rest while it's
                                    denied –
          Precious freedom that can bring me peace of mind.
          Countryside, how I adore you,
          Countrywide, let me explore you,
          Down the winding lanes that help me to unwind.
          City life, I've grown to hate it,
          Now I know I'll never make it,

Time to pack my gear and leave it all behind.

Repeat chorus: So it's good-bye etc., etc.
And, from an earlier entry, something in an entirely different vein:

THE EMERALD OF EMERALD ISLE

Sweet Killarney, you're the emerald of Emerald
                                        Isle,
Silver waters, easy-flowing, easy-going, ev'ry
                                        mile.
Streams in the mountainside, like tears upon your
                                        cheek.
Valleys where the hills divide, sunbeams playing
                                        hide and seek.
Sweet Killarney, like a jewel, in a setting,
                                        evergreen;
Seasons coming, seasons going, but you're always
                                        sweet sixteen.
Reflecting God's perfection with the heaven of your
                                        smile,
Sweet Killarney, you're the emerald of Emerald
                                        Isle.

And so we leave the blarney, Killarney, and the wearin' of the green, as a voice told us from the airport control tower, "Come in, number t'ree, your toime's up!"

In Shrewsbury, in 1979, the First British International Song Festival and Orchestral Competition was born. It came unstuck, financially, becoming unique in that it achieved the sad distinction of being not only the first, but also the last! My orchestral entry, 'Shopping Spree', made it to the final, and, to my great satisfaction, pushed out Tony Hatch's, 'Isabella's Theme'.

You may be rightly inclined to ask why so many big names in the business muscle in on competitions surely intended for lesser-known writers, all mixed up with amateurs, or, at best, semi-pros. I have quoted but a few, and the answer surely lies in the fact that the number of festivals and competitions has increased dramatically world-wide in recent years. Many, like Castlebar, began in modest, even austere fashion, strictly for the likes of me, but soon became truly international, with entertainment, tourist and holiday attractions thrown in for good measure. Growth too in the prizes offered, reflecting the relentless march of inflation. Also, sponsorship has more and more attracted the big names with whom unknowns have to compete.

Personally, I am at a loss to understand their participation. When you compare the kind of fees they command for their services, the prize money to them is mere chicken feed. They have some indisputable advantages from the word go. Probably their own first-class studio; if not, then unlimited sources for the production of a singer or group, or both, to present the song. You may think it all very unfair. But there it is – a fact of life – all in the game.

Save for 'Shopping Spree', of which I had an orchestral recording, *all* the items which qualified for the final were submitted, as the rules then allowed, *without* a demo disc or tape – simply a piano manuscript with melody and words. The same applied to the Southern TV competitions covered in 'Religioso'.

The trend has gone towards looking for *sounds* rather than a good song, one which tells a story, paints a picture. It was ex-secretary of the Guild, Victor Knight, who expressed his dislike of the demo system, many years ago. Initially, the demo was born out of sheer necessity – for the *musically illiterate*. Not overlooking the fact that during the past thirty-odd years, a great deal of pop has stemmed from such individuals and groups, even though much of it is here today, gone tomorrow. Nevertheless, a trend was created to which we *all* had to conform, irrespective of musical ability and status. Ironically, it is those with sound musical training, the arrangers (again!), session musicians and producers who have been vital to the creation of a viable end-product over the decades when the financial benefits have lined the pockets of the seemingly endless invasion of the music biz by an army of musical illiterates.

I can recall many occasions from publishing days when songs were accepted or at least considered on the spot. A manuscript and demonstration at the piano (vocally, sometimes leaving much to be desired!) did not deter the publisher, who often was also a musician/arranger, from his prime task of assessing the song's commercial merit. But I didn't sit and lament the passing of the craftsmanship of putting musical thoughts to manuscript. I earned money from the musical illiterates by setting up and advertising a service, one which transferred songs from tape to manuscript in coherent and playable form. I reckon there must be a songwriter in every street, as publishers and record companies are constantly deluged by demos. Still, it's good business for the recording studios and tape manufacturers...

It's a forlorn hope I express in that, just as the teaching profession has been forced to bring back the three Rs, the music profession equally, needs to bring back the three Ms - Music, Musicians and Manuscript!

CHAPTER THIRTY-TWO

RELIGIOSO

Screened by Southern Independent Television in the years 1968-76 was a series of competitions for new hymns, carols and songs in religious vein, on a given theme. It was a happy and successful era for me, the title of my entry for the 'Carols for Children' competition being most apt:

SOMETHING TO SING ABOUT

1. We've got something to sing about, something to sing
                        about –
    Christmas! Merry Christmas!
    Bells have something to ring about; listen, they're
                        ringing out
    Christmas! Merry Christmas!
    No other story has been told so many times before.
    It's simple glory may be old, but holds new hope in store.
    That's why there's something to sing about.
    Let's rejoice and sing about
    Christmas! Merry Christmas!

2. We've got something to sing about, something to sing
                        about –
    Christmas! Merry Christmas!
    It's worth singing a song about, what would we do
                        without
    Christmas! Merry Christmas!
    We hope that you will join us, spread the message of
                        good cheer,
    Maintain this perfect harmony throughout the coming
                        year.
    We'll all have something to sing about,
    Let's rejoice and sing about
    Christmas! Merry Christmas!

3.　We've got something to sing about, something to sing
about –
Christmas! Merry Christmas!
Bells have something to ring about, listen, they're
ringing out
Christmas! Merry Christmas!
The star that sped to Bethlehem and turned night into day
Is followed by all wise men who have learned it
lights their way.
The world needs something to sing about.
Let's all try to bring about
A very, merry Christmas! Merry Christmas!

'The Agony, the Ecstasy' – already detailed, featured in the final programme of the series – a very good arrangement and presentation by the Nigel Brook Singers. The Josef Weinberger Music Publishing offer of publication, however, was declined, as it was intended to include *every* entry in the music album, and there were no plans for commercial recording. It wasn't worth giving up a large slice of royalties just to have the satisfaction of seeing one's name in print. Furthermore, I was able to promote the piece myself, taking one hundred per cent royalties, still retaining the copyright.

I came to know Ronnie Bridges of Southern Music (also for many years lyricist at the famous Windmill Theatre) purely by chance when doing the routine circulation of songs around Tin Pan Alley. I sent him the music with the suggested title 'The Power and the Glory' and, shortly afterwards, with his lyrics added, our joint effort joined more than 6,000 others for consideration in Southern TV's search for 'A Hymn for Britain'. We made it through to the final six, the hymn being published in an album by Feldmans.

THE POWER AND THE GLORY

1. The Power and the Glory, since time on earth began,
   Have been of Thee, our Father, and not possessed by man.
   Though man may build his buildings, in steel and man-
   made stone,
   The Power and the Glory, God, are Thine and Thine alone.

2. The skill of man's invention, on land or under sea,
   Is still Divine, O Father, and surely comes from Thee.
   Mere man could do no great things, if he were on his
                                               own,
   The Power and the Glory, God, are Thine and Thine alone.

3. By land a man may travel. In space a man may fly.
   But man has made no mountain, no sea, no star, no sky
   In all our human progress. Thy wonders still are shown.
   The Power and the Glory, God, are Thine and Thine
                                               alone,

4. Thy Power, and Thy Glory, O God, will always last
   Until Thy Kingdom cometh, until our lives are past.
   To Thee we give our praises, that as our world has grown,
   The Power and the Glory, are still Thine and Thine
                                               alone.

Another visit to the Southampton studios in 1970. This time for the finals of the 'A Hymn for Children' competition. Local school choirs and percussion groups took part – what a magnificent job they did! Olive, Brian and I arrived early in the afternoon to be told that 'Candlelight' was the red-hot favourite amongst the staff – and the children loved it. The hymn was a classic example of how the human brain can store information for years, until the time is ripe to make use of it. The idea, in tune and title only, was inspired by a Christmas service, attended by many children, at St Peter's Church in Broadstairs, remaining dormant until the STV competition happened along. The melody was recalled, reborn, finally finding completion with the addition of words. Where writing to order is concerned, I shall be hard put indeed to ever equal, or better, the evocative simplicity of 'Candlelight' in a mere thirty-two bars.

CANDLELIGHT

While I kneel and pray by candlelight
I close my eyes, and day turns into night.
And often, I wonder what my life would be
If His Creation my eyes could not see.

The sea, the moon, the mountains capped with snow,
A tree in bloom, the sun that helped it grow.
O Lord! Hear the prayer I'm giving
For those in darkness living
Never to see candlelight.

'Candlelight' has since been used by a number of local radio stations and it was included in a beautifully produced music and record album which sold very well indeed, thanks to the prompt and efficient promotional vigour of George Seymour of Campbell Connelly.

My involvement in the long series prompted the question from some viewers, 'Are you very religious by nature?' It would be dishonest and hypocritical of me to deny the lure of prize money, albeit tiny in comparison with the international festivals, the publicity and the royalties. On the other hand, truthfully, I was unable to resist the challenge of writing for, what was for me, a hitherto totally unexplored dimension. But I had no visions of producing anything in which I did not believe, nor of producing anything profound, mind-bending or earthshaking. No, I am not a regular church-goer; nor a well-intentioned or misguided do-gooder. Simply conscious of the powers of good and evil, light and darkness. Preferring to seek and to appreciate the good, wholesome things in life; trying to balance them against the immense suffering of others, within my own circle and worldwide, but without overdoing the introspection. Despairing, when so often it doesn't add up – an imbalance of the scales. Beliefs, disbeliefs and doubts, meditating what it's all about. The involvement was, if anything, a kind of life-line helping to balance the turmoil, disappointments and sorrows encountered in my environment and the long, middle-of-the-road sojourn. An uphill crusade, every inch of the way.

'If at first you don't succeed, try, try, try again' and 'practice makes perfect' were the twin mottoes of Daisy's teachings when I was a kid. So one strives for that elusive quality – perfection (not always synonymous with success) – but, if it doesn't work out, well, have another go! So it's hard, having an inborn optimistic and philosophical outlook on life which doesn't always play fair, and in a world which is far from perfect. It's today and tomorrow which are important, even though as the song wistfully says, 'Tomorrow, tomorrow, you're always a day away.' But at least, when opportunity

knocks at my door, it finds me at home, eager to open the door.
Whether the miracles performed in Biblical times are truth or merely
legend, I don't know. But is not the universe itself a miracle?

So there is nothing special about my thoughts or religiously
orientated songs. Thoughts that must surely be shared by millions of
others with fond regard for the world in which we live. Perhaps the
final lyric in this happy, but somewhat reflective and philosophical
chapter sums up the situation. The problems are still with us, even
though the song was penned in 1971. Slightly pop-orientated, it made
a shortlist of entries, that's all, in the STV competition on a theme
dealing with current world problems. It was dismissed as being 'too
controversial'. Well, it's controversial subjects that make us think,
isn't it?

FACT OR FICTION?

Verse 1:   Most ev'rybody would agree
    The world, a better place could be,
    But what we preach we seldom teach or practise.
    How can we hope to find Perfection
    Without Supreme Direction?
    So I'm prompted just to ask you this:

Chorus: Have you read any good books lately,
    Fact or fiction?
    There is one I can recommend,
    Without contradiction.
    It's the greatest, oldest, yet the latest
    Book upon the shelf –
    Fact or fiction? Fact or fiction?"

Verse 2:   The world's a swiftly changing place.
    All systems go – a frightful pace.
    The human race, hell-bent on making progress,
    It worships things material,
    Neglecting those ethereal,
    Expecting to find instant happiness.

Repeat chorus: Have you... etc.

190

Verse 3:   Pollution and permissiveness,
             Drop-outs, drugs – say, what a mess.
             It seems the road to hell we are descending.
             But by grace of God man still survives
             All perils that the book describes.
             CAN HE FULFIL ITS DREAM OF HAPPY
                                        ENDING?

Last chorus: Have you read any good books lately,
             Fact or fiction?
             There is one I can recommend,
             Without contradiction.
             It's the greatest, oldest, yet the latest book upon the
                                        shelf.
             Fact or Fiction? Why not read it?
             Fact or fiction? You may need it.
             Fact or Fiction? Decide for yourself!'

'Written any more hymns lately?', 'When's the next competition?',
'Are you going on the telly again soon?'
    These are the sort of questions put to me by locals, the power and
publicity of the box creating the impression that I was uninterested in
or incapable of writing anything other than religious works. If only
my music broadcast in BBC Radio programmes had aroused as much
interest and publicity, instead of being confined to a few paragraphs in
the local press!
    Whether they felt sorry for me or whether they were being kind, I
didn't always know. But there was a solid consensus of opinion that
'Candlelight' was lovely and should have carried off first prize. Some
even said outright that the competition was 'rigged'. 'Candlelight'
really was a *hymn*, not a pop song like the rest. Not much use, post
mortems. But it was nice to know that Thanet people had viewed that
competition and others with great interest.

CHAPTER THIRTY-THREE

MOLTO JOCOSO

In the autumn of 1973 I did a gig with a four-piece band led by tenor saxophonist and vocalist Derek Day, who used to be with the Bert Hayes Band at Butlins. Rather than a 'one-off' gig, it turned out to be an association which lasted more than ten years. The band's repertoire was still set far too much in the thirties and forties era, but had the potential for change, and I subtly gave it some nudging into the seventies by constantly adding arrangements of new material, with an emphasis on vocal numbers, bringing it bang up-to-date. Drummer Roger Head, being the youngest, was enthusiastic: "I love the pop arrangements, Bill! I've been telling Derek for years to ditch that old pad [the repertoire, or library] of his."

A rather sweeping statement: one cannot afford to ditch *everything* old, willy-nilly, in favour of the new. Tried and trusted tunes would always be wanted, but the remark was timely and encouraging. Later, Roger was replaced by an even younger and very efficient beater-of-skins, yet with lots of professional experience under his belt, Kevin Cooke. And on string bass, another good companion, and fellow ex-Londoner (even if he is a Spurs supporter!) Ron Wheeler, with many years in the circuit, including a stint with jazz outfit, The Clem Vickery Stompers. Yes, football was often the subject during the interval, with Ron rooting for the Spurs, Derek for the Gunners and yours truly, faithful as ever, although a long way from the terraces of Upton Park, for the Hammers, whose mixed fortunes inspired Derek's fun-line in 'I'm Forever Blowing Bubbles', in the singalong waltzes – 'They fly so high. Nearly reach the sky. Then like West Ham, they fade and die!'

Mention of string bass always has me chuckling about gigs at the Grove Ferry Inn which overlooks the winding River Stour – a popular spot for fishing – and for those who, as the song has it, love 'Messing About on the River'. At the end of the building used for dancing was a tall platform at least eight feet above floor level. What it had originally been used for was anyone's guess, but, reached by several steps, it served as the stage. It was large enough to accommodate a grand piano and the four of us. But the bass player could only stand in one particular place. It was in the early sixties when many had not yet switched to bass guitar. The distance between the floor of the stage and the roof made it impossible for a bass to be held upright! But at one end, near the back, was a small trap-door. When opened, it took the scroll, the top part of the bass. That was the saving grace. But it was bloody draughty for the bass player!

Like bubbles and West Ham, fading and dying might be applied in a completely different context when in the eighties the realisation suddenly grabbed me. Overnight, it seemed, the situation had become reversed. For so long the youngest – the baby in the band – I was now the daddy of 'em all! So many musicians of my generation had given up playing – ceased or deceased! Yes, we were a dying race all right! I am reminded of Eric Bing's jest after attending the cremation service of prominent local musician, Leslie Wheeler. Looking back from the car park, we observed smoke puffing from the crematorium chimney.

Eric turned to us and said, "There he goes! Smoke gets in your eyes, Les. Three flats."

Shocking, irreverent, the straight-laced will say, but such black comedy, I'm sure, would have been appreciated by Leslie.

For seven years, the Derek Day Band held sway at the Hereward Hotel, Cliftonville, playing several nights a week for each summer season. They were mighty long summers, however, beginning at Easter and running through to the mini-breaks at the end of October. No other local residency could match such a lengthy season in the seventies and early eighties, when the decline in the number of venues and functions began to accelerate like crazy. (The Hereward lasted until the mid-eighties, when it was converted to flats.)

There are many incidents to relate from that time. One, in particular, was the chap who came up to the stage after we had played a couple of easy-going and innocuous pops – 'Sing, Sing A Song' and 'Amarillo' – protesting, "A lot of us don't know all that punk rock music! We like something we know!" (Make with the purple hair and the safety pins and chains, man!)

And the evening when entertainment had to be curtailed when, sadly, an elderly guest suffered a fatal heart attack. Relating the incident to a colleague the next day, the incident evoked the swift, witty rejoinder, "Christ! The music wasn't *that* bad, was it?"

The majority of holiday makers came from up north and we would mingle with them during the interval. In common with the beer, a great deal of wit also flowed in the lounge; on one occasion the subject was dialects.

It gave rise to a remark by an elderly Lancashire lady, "D'you know, lad, there are more than one hundred different 'darlecks' up north?"

Quick as a flash, one of the young bartenders replied, "Don't you worry, madam. Send for Doctor Who – he'll soon get rid of 'em!"

Depending on which part of the country you come from, the 'Slush' or 'Slosh' was a typically popular party dance. Non-dancers will probably ask, 'The *what*?' To the best of my knowledge, the dance originated in the Midlands about thirty years ago, holiday makers being largely responsible for its spread elsewhere. "Eee, lad! Tha's not lived if tha's not done t'Slosh!"

Not forgetting another musicians' pet hate, 'The Birdie Song'. Peculiar to this area is 'The Farmer's Wife'. How and where it originated, I haven't a clue. I don't suppose anyone else has, for that matter. Curiously, though, the eight bar chorus is the same as a tune of a South African Boer War song, which I picked up from members of a SAAF squadron during wartime (no, *not* the same war, cheeky!). Its title was 'We Are Marching To Pretoria'. Even 'curiouser and curiouser' (as Alice remarked), there are some folk who prance around in similar fashion, but to the music of 'Y Viva España'!

Probably the brainchild of the holiday camps is the 'Campus Eight' – usually to the tune of the 'Teddybears' Picnic' (though after that, any six-eight tune will do). But again, depending on location, it is also known as the 'Picnic Dance' or the 'Flying Ballet'. One becomes accustomed to requests like 'You Are The One' – deciphered as 'Night and Day' or 'With Someone Like You', meaning (as we should all know!) 'Let The Rest Of The World Go By'! Close also are 'Are The Stars Out Tonight?', viz., 'I Only Have Eyes For You'. Not much difference! Star prize to the holiday maker from Manchester who requested the 'Doggy Song'. Plainly surprised by the baffled look on our faces, we asked her to sing us the first few bars. She hadn't got beyond the first two before we all shook with laughter, exclaiming, "Oh, *that* one! You mean the 'St Bernard's Waltz'!"

During a long season, the type of clientele – ages, personalities, and tastes – can vary enormously from week to week, so inevitably there comes an evening when it needs every trick in the book, every ounce of expertise, to overcome the waves of apathy, usually due to a lack of dancers, or people for whom bingo has far more appeal. Since the days of the Master of Ceremonies are long since passed (except for civic, Masonic and similar functions), it is up to the band, and the front man in particular, to divine the tastes of the audience. There is a line in the song 'There Will Never Be Another You' which runs, 'There will be many other nights like this,' and on evenings such as these, with Derek doing the vocals, we were prompted to mutter, *sotto voce*, in unison, "My God! I hope not!"

We played the 1976 summer season at Madison's Holiday Camp – oops! Sorry, holiday *village*! It had been created on a former RAF wartime site. The very first time I clapped eyes on the place, I remarked with a grin, "It hasn't changed much, has it?"

The check-in at the gates was akin to a RAF guard room, many of the buildings reminiscent of ex-RAF dwellings, and the gigantic structure housing a gymnasium, a swimming pool, lounge, ballroom and bars bore a striking resemblance to that which I had encountered at St Athan in 1940. All that was missing was the square-bashing area!

In busy July and August, cabaret acts were a feature, but in the early weeks, redcoats had an irritating insistence on filling (wasting was more apt) the spot by calling for acts from the audience. One evening in particular, when finding out who was going to do what and how, a bluff and hefty character with plenty of chat handed me a list as long as your arm, declaring, "I'm going ter do a Maxie Bygraves sing-a-long, starting wiv 'Oo's Sorry Nah'."

"I reckon we'll just about have time for the last waltz and 'Goodnight Campers' after this lot," I said humorously to Derek.

It fell on stony ground.

'Oo's Sorry Nah' hadn't got beyond the first four bars before the tone-deaf, self-styled Maxie changed key and got himself out of tempo too. It went on, agonisingly, like that until just past the middle of the song when I could stand no more. He was impossible to accompany. I gave it up as a bad job and let him get on with it. There were four other members of the band standing in the wings. They almost choked on their beer, then howled with helpless laughter, as did I, as Maxie, suddenly realising that he was on his tod, stopped, turned, looked up at the stage and snapped indignantly, "Wotsammarrer? Dontcher know it!"

(A fellow pianist now refuses to accompany such suspect acts. Having been involved in a similar incident, he had to demand an apology from the organiser of the function who, in his announcement, made it appear that it was the pianist who was at fault, not the so-called singer! It doesn't matter how well the accompanist knows the song, for lumbered with a tone-deaf, unable to keep time, non-musical singer, it is all to easy for people to get the woefully wrong impression.)

Coincidentally, Frank had undertaken a sentimental journey the same summer, so when he and Margaret visited us later in the year swapping stories gave rise to a great deal of merriment. He related to us the visit, during Battle of Britain Week, to RAF St Athan. There on cine-film, was the pill-box fortification, deserted, but still intact, the hedges – the unofficial way in, way out gaps no more. A tall, forbidding steel mesh fence now enclosed the camp perimeter. The village hall where we had played Saturday nights, was a victim of the spread of sophisticated clubs and discos, rarely used now. Frank managed to root out the verger and persuade him to open up the hall so that he could wallow in nostalgia.

"I literally stepped back into 1940," exclaimed Frank, somewhat dramatically. "Nothing had changed. Dusty wooden chairs lined each side of the walls; the same old clock over the door; the well-worn floorboards; the same old revolving crystal ball in the centre of the ceiling, and... guess what?"

I was way ahead of him.

"Don't tell me," I laughed. *"The same old piano, too!"*

(In 1989, Frank pulled up roots in Sussex, and for Margaret it was a return to her native land. They sold up at the right time – the property market having reached its peak, soon to fall to an all-time low – and bought a bungalow at a ridiculously low price about five miles from Cork. Frank took up playing again, doing gigs with the Cork City Jazz Band.)

The decade threw up a batch of oddities in the charts. Suddenly, the pop world discovered eighteenth-century genius, Mozart. I am indebted to *The Daily Mail* for its kind permission to reproduce 'Dark thoughts in G minor', a humorous gem which filled the Comment space one Saturday back in 1971.

There has been only one topic of conversation on the pop scene this week – the arrival of the mysterious Mozart 40 in the Top Twenty. Those two seasoned Tin Pan Alley operators Morrie and Rube are still knotting their brows over it!

'This Mozart – we never had a demo disc from this boy. Who manages him?'

'I keep telling you, Rube, this is an old number. 1788. I looked it up already.'

'It's number twelve in the charts and you're telling me it's been there for the asking, since 1788. Morrie, what have you been doing for 183 years?'

'Rube, this number never got into the gravy till now. Lots of classy combos tried recording it – Royal Philharmonic, London Symphony... but I ask you, are those boys smoking Corona Coronas like you and me?'

'So what's changed? They got a new arranger to schmaltz it up?'

'That's the funny thing. They haven't. Given it a bit of groove in the rhythm section, true. But otherwise they're just sight-reading the score. Your actual Mozart.'

'Mozart, schmozart, you mean to tell me that kind of stuff can outsell Frankie Sinatra's 'My Way'? It must be the lyrics.'

'No lyrics. It looks like making number one without so much as a Vodeo-do. And it's out of copyright.'

'Out of copyright! You mean everybody's making bread except Mozart?'

'Except poor old Wolfgang Amadeus Mozart.'

'Well, what are we waiting for? What else did he write?'

'Do me a favour. Haven't I looked through the catalogue already? There's a number here we could adapt – how does this grab you? Marry me Figaro?'

'I like it. A girl's number.'

'Then there's 'Eine Kleine Nachtmusick...'

'Not so fast. What did you say his first name was?'

'Amadeus.'

'I've got it! We form our own group to wax this stuff and we call it – The Amadeus.'

'Too late, Rube. There's a group called that already; playing gigs at the Festival Hall. Been at it for years but never made the charts.

'But have they ever cut a *single*? There's your answer. It's the r.p.m. that makes the difference between a hit and a miss.'

'You mean forty-five instead of thirty-three?'

'Listen! This Mozart wrote Allegro Molto on the sheet music. If he could have got forty-five r.p.m., would he have settled for thirty-three? 'Course not. That's what Allegro Molto means.'

'You means, Rube, if Mozart had only written his stuff in singles for the Top Ten he might not have died in poverty?'

'Mark my words, Morrie, he'd have made eine kleine halfa dollar. That's pop business. The least we can do is to make it for him.'

Oh, the tragi-comic irony of it all!

There were other invasions of the Top Ten, a hitherto unknown Joe Dolce becoming temporarily primo del pops with his fun number 'Shutuppa Ya Face'. 'Two Little Boys', 'Grandad', 'Amazing Grace', 'Day Trip To Bangor' were all an entirely different kettle of fish, but, classical or not, loved or loathed, they helped to inject a degree of originality into the fairly dreary and predictable charts, albeit short-lived. I have my own oddities on file at home, written out of sheer contempt and cussedness for conformity. I would hazard a guess that there are many other writers of my ilk with comparable songs which, given studied consideration, and recorded by the right artistes or groups, could also shoot holes through the blanket uniformity of the charts. Another quirk is the application of oddities for dancing purposes, which tends to prolong their life, although departed from the Top Ten, to the extent that they become a 'standard'. 'Yellow Submarine', uncharacteristic of The Beatles' norm, and corny into the bargain, was soon seized upon as an additional tune, along with others, for use with the 'March of the Mods' craze. Had it been written forty years earlier, it would have become a ballroom natural for the Palais Glide.

At this point I must recall 'Hooked On The Classics' – the then latest in musical atrocities – a 'Classical Muddly' by the Portsmouth Sinfonia, its conductor, John Farly, reported as saying, "It's great. It could put kids off classical music for life." Later came something quite the reverse – a record by the Royal Philharmonic Orchestra of popular classics, but welded on was a monotonous, sickening, relentless disco beat. Well, as we all know, the Sinfonia's offering was made in fun, and treated accordingly, whereas the RPO's record was an intentional commercially aimed intrusion into the pop world. To the classical lovers who take it all too seriously, it could put *them* off for life too! As for converts from the disco world – they are likely to be as ephemeral as their kind of music. Who is alienating whom?

CHAPTER THIRTY-FOUR

MOLTO ACCELLERANDO

And so to this year of grace, 1993. Sadly, perhaps *dis*grace would be more fitting as so many years have sped by for, although the map of Europe has dramatically changed and officially the Cold War is over, there remains uncertainty, vandalism, stress, disease, famine, pollution and now, massive soul-destroying unemployment. The gloomy reprise of Twentieth-Century Blues continues.

Despite all the undreamed of advances, we, the human clever-clogs, have created far more complexities than simplicities. Regretfully, I have to share the views of many of my generation: it is a much harder and harsher world than before. Even taking into account the hardships of the dark days of the forties, at least there was unity of purpose.

When I began writing, spring was just around the corner, abundant life pushing up through the good earth. The vernal equinox, the *real* new year, not the first of January, as dictated by our calendar. Spring, summer, autumn and winter – the recurring earthly cycles have always been firm favourites in descriptive music, Vivaldi's 'The Four Seasons' being perhaps the best-known and best-loved. But I would guess that spring is foremost in inspired music, more than all the other seasons put together. Even my own piece of light music, 'It's Spring Again', performed just a couple of times at the Broadstairs Pavilion, otherwise unsung, unpublished and unwanted! Mendelssohn's 'Spring Song' is capricious, light and airy, while 'Rustle of Spring' by Sinding expresses joy in a rather more boisterous and dramatic fashion. There are none of the preceding qualities in my favourite, Grieg's 'To the Spring'; a plaintive, sensitive theme, tinged with an air of expectancy and mystery of the annual miracle, bursting into fulfilment in the theme's restatement in broader and more flowing form. Along with the C minor piano concerto by Rachmaninov, parts of Tchaikovsky's 'Romeo and Juliet', Beethoven's 'Pathétique' sonata, and some Debussy 'Arabesques' and so many others of the Romantic period, Greig's opening melody can move me to tears, cut me down to size. I become acutely aware – painfully aware – of my personal musical inadequacy. Were I ever to be invited to be exiled to a desert island (which, as Roy Plomley admits in his book, should be a 'deserted' island) with just eight records, I would find the task of final selection a monumental one in the face of the vast store of beautiful music which is available to us all. If you are thinking that because of my birthplace I should rightly select 'Knocked 'Em In The Old Kent Road' well, yes, it has been considered. But my favourite London number – in fact, one probably shared by millions – is 'A Nightingale Sang In Berkeley Square', even if it is a posh part of the capital compared to the Old Kent Road!

The long summer seasons, musically speaking, have vanished. Just memories of the patrons (bless them) who insist, 'I know what I like', which really means 'I like what I know'. Our endeavours were to please everyone, a mixture of music bridging eight decades, with hard-earned expertise. Tuneful waltzes, quicksteps and fox-trots; the occasional tango and rumba vying with jazz, old time, the 'slosh', and pop like 'YMCA', 'The Hustle', 'Love Is In The Air, and 'Knock Three Times', plus the new oddities encountered, learned or laughed at, at the end of each season.

Speaking of forever learning and expertise brings to mind a social gathering long ago when the conversation veered round to my musical activities. A middle-aged woman made the curt comment, "Sitting playing the piano for three or four hours, I don't call that hard work – it's easy."

Sarcastically, I'm afraid, I defended myself with the reply, "Yes, it's easy. It only takes a lifetime to learn how to do it, and do it well."

Compare the ignorance of that remark with the far more perceptive and factual utterance of my Dad's brother, Albert, when we visited his Gants Hill, Ilford home, together with the children in the mid-fifties.

During an impromptu musical evening he observed, "It must be easy money for young Bill when he goes out playing. He enjoys it so much."

Of course! Enjoying one's work is surely what life is all about, And the secret of all professional art is making something difficult appear deceptively easy.

In my younger days, I was often asked, "Was your father or mother musical?" or "Do you come from a musical family?" Resisting the old chestnut about playing on the linoleum when I was three, I can merely say that my father's ability was limited to a few tunes which he busked at the piano, *always* in extreme keys (on the black notes, to you) and *always* in the same broken octave style in the right hand, the left defying description or classification! Apart from that, brother Albert gave reasonable and resonant vocal performances of Gilbert and Sullivan pieces and popular Victorian ballads. (Sad ballads which were known in music biz as 'bad salads!') Youngest brother, Henry, once played similar music at the piano and harmonium. Indeed, Olive and I spent many an enjoyable weekend in Colchester where Henry and his wife, Grace, were steward and stewardess at the local Liberal Club. Henry's wife died soon after the war, so father and daughter (also called Grace) moved out and took over The King's Head (complete with Roman dungeons!) in the town. After 'Time, gents' was called, many locals would stay on and join in the family musical parties.

Recalling his younger days, my father would tell of the harmonium being taken with them on outings, along with the beer, out to the wilds of Epping! They would join in choruses of favourites such as 'Will You Love Me In December As You Do In May?' Oh, the simple, inexpensive pleasures in which they indulged, in a much more leisurely age! So one could say that musical appreciation was not lacking, but hardly that my forebears were exceptionally gifted in the arts, their main contribution, for which I am forever grateful, being that of selfless encouragement.

Returning from the brief excursion into Victorian and Edwardian days and ways, we come to the slow-slow, quick-quick-slow dictum of the Sylvester strict tempo school of thought which dominated the ballroom scene for several decades. While it may be very convenient for dancers to follow inflexible rules that the waltz, fox-trot, quickstep or whatever shall be played at a fixed number of bars per minute, regardless of the tune, there are a host of contradictions from a strictly musical and aesthetic point of view. Fox-trots, for example: meeting the Sylvester requirements are tunes like, 'On The Sunny Side Of The Street', 'Louise', 'Small Hotel', 'Raindrops Keep Fallin' On My Head' – all up-beat numbers. But the following are also listed as fox-trots – 'Laura', 'Stardust', 'Misty', 'Dream', 'People', 'What Are You Doing The Rest Of Your Life?' and to play them to suit Mr Sylvester is to destroy their beauty. They are best interpreted at a slower pace. They are the kind of numbers we love playing usually in the last hour or so of a dance, when the lights are low, everyone is well lubricated and couples cuddle and shuffle, rather than dance, known as the 'smooch'. Ruder definitions abound, the best two I recall being 'womb-trembling' ballads and 'groping, bum-clutching' music! There are many more 'anti-Sylvester' examples. Even with quicksteps, there are those which can be best described as 'in between' – too slow for classification as a quickstep, too fast to be a fox-trot, and some are best for use in jive numbers. Had the purists completely taken over in the ballroom, many beautiful tunes might have been excluded simply because their best tempo, musically, did not conform to the rigid rules of those dancers hooked on 'strict tempo'.

Here we have the extremes again. The admittedly skilful, attractive and delightful, but artificially contrived, disciplined niceties of *Come Dancing* couples on one side. On the other, the uninhibited, do-as-you-please, do-your-own-thing cavorting of the disco devotees. Fortunately, by far the larger group comprises the less critical masses, of all ages, good, bad and indifferent dancers, with no inhibitions, appreciative of tunes and the standard of entertainment rather than education, who simply want to enjoy themselves. The real middle-of-the-roaders, one might say. Long may they live!

In the fifties, we would play, in exaggerated corny style, Victor's signature tune, taking the mickey; then follow with an extemporised chorus by Don on alto sax, Len, the drummer, with a smile saying, "Don, you know Victor wouldn't like it!"

Decades later, Terry Wogan loves to make the Eurovision Song Contest the butt of much light-hearted ridicule and banter. It wasn't my cup of tea either until the Beeb threw it open to singers and groups in general, rather than inviting entries written to suit one well-known selected artist.

I decided to experiment; to find out just how far an old 'un like me could get. My ad in *The Stage* yielded thirty-odd replies. I chose a young girl singer, Penny Gold (appearing at 'Warners' in the Isle of Wight), with a two-piece harmony group, to do the demo. Ringing each day to check progress, out of over four hundred entries, I was told that it had survived as far as the last forty. Not quite good enough to make the final eight, but good enough to prove my ability to write in 1991 pop style. The Beeb has since returned to its old formula which, to me, is restrictive, so I didn't have another go. Here's the lyric to my disco-type entry:

STAY OUT OF MY DREAMS

Verse 1:   In dreams so much you give to me,
And say that you just live for me,
Every night ev'rything's right.
But there's somebody new, I guess,
Who makes my dreams seem meaningless.
I wish I knew, and if it's true, won't you

Chorus: Stay out of my dreams, stay out of my dreams,
They only make me blue.
Stay out of my dreams, stay out of my dreams,
Till make-believe is through.
Hey! Don't give me a mean time,
Love me the way you do in dream time,
Make it for real – keep it that way,
But if you feel you're gonna stray,
Out of my arms – stay out of my dreams.

Verse 2:   When will I hold you in my arms
The way I hold you in my dreams,
Every night, ever so tight.
If dreams foretell what's gonna be
Stop teasing me, start pleasing me.
Make them come true and till you do

Repeat Chorus: Won't you stay out of my dreams etc.

I would submit that more music has been bequeathed to the piano than any other individual instrument, unequalled in fact, and embracing a wide and varied musical spectrum, much of which is tuneful, melodic light music. So much so that even my substantial collection is but a fraction of the total output. We pianists are terribly spoilt by such a vast repertoire. Testimony to the earlier-expressed cliché 'it'll never die out' is the popularity of the piano bar, which has become the focal point in many establishments. Certainly far more musically acceptable than the latest electronic craze, karaoke, used by many who should confine their vocal efforts to the bathroom!

Just as we thought we had hit the pits, along came RAP...!

Muzak – that canned monotone, bereft of all dynamics – is often difficult to hear above all the rhubarb, rhubarb at large gatherings, but nevertheless it is insidious, irritating and superfluous. At the risk of arousing the fury of fellow composers who derive some income from this source, I would venture the opinion that there is, in fact, a surfeit of canned 'wallpaper' music. In no way can one compare the proliferation of today's noise epidemic to that of the thirties, so I wonder what a critic of those times would write were he alive today. I quote from Constant Lambert's *Music Ho! A Study of Music in Decline*:

> The appalling popularity of music in the present age
> is one of overproduction – so much food and so much
> starvation. So much music-making and so little
> experience of a vital order...

He maintained that the widespread use of the loudspeaker was little short of a public menace. How fascinating that his observation 'the more people use the wireless, the less they listen to it' is so true of today's public and public places!

The strident beat, the ear-splitting din made by outfits playing for peanuts in clubs and pubs today isn't far short of being lethal! (And that's just listening on the *outside*!) Which reminds me of the Ramsgate seafront pub's notice board I saw recently, which raised a chuckle. It read: 'Live Music every Thursday – Tonite – Ronnie Scott's Rejects'!

I was delighted in the early eighties to once again provide the alternative to muzak for a few years when live piano music was restored at my old haunt, the San Clu Hotel (which, upon John Robson's demise was bequeathed to his son, Simon). He sold up, and the place just was not the same. Nothing, it seemed, could ever again equal the countless enjoyable functions of the past. During the interval one evening, a resident complimented me on my music, adding, "Especially the humour of those last two pieces." For the moment, I didn't know what he meant then, recalling the titles, I was also amused – Bob Farnon's 'Westminster Waltz' followed by Sondheim's 'Send in the Clowns'!

In the same decade, the ten year association with the Derek Day Band terminated, Derek's death being an untimely and unexpected tragic end for someone aged a mere fifty. Derek had also held the post of secretary of our local branch of the MU. Eric Bing paid tribute in a moving article, 'Étude in Dedication' published in the Union's journal *Musician*. Later, I recalled that during the summer season, Derek had not responded to requests for 'My Way' – unusual and out of character for someone who I believe enjoyed singing more than he did playing tenor sax – '...and now the end is near, I face the final curtain'. Premonition... or simply coincidence? His Scots-born wife, Margaret, gave me a list of outstanding dates to honour up to about one year ahead. I took over, but with a heavy heart, having psychologically been knocked for six. So many tunes, especially Derek's vocal items, were happy memories tinged with sadness.

The succeeding years brought about a *molto accellerando* of the demise of live bands and groups and many of the premises which had once employed them. Disastrous for many instrumentalists, but, for the versatile pianist, no problem. In fact, it was the catalyst for the restoration of the variety I yearned for, albeit for only two or three years. I played for classes, exams and rehearsals plus shows at the Winter Gardens and Granville theatres of two local stage-cum-dance schools. That well-worn adage 'never appear with children or animals' is totally out of place; the enthusiasm and energy of pupils aged from five to eighteen was joyous and heart-warming, and the music and dances, mostly from shows ranging from ballet to rock, spanning some eight decades, far more satisfying than yer average gig.

Returning to composing and orchestration, the content of this book dealing with the subjects will bring either inspiration or desperation to aspiring songsmiths and composers, depending on the amount of tenacity, determination and reality present in their make-up. I wish them well in their endeavours, knowing full well that thousands will not get very far. Immortality in music is for the gifted, precious few, frustration for the many – me included! *The Daily Mail* (29th November, 1980) contained a few paragraphs – 'Thank Heavens' – devoted to the revivals in the West End and elsewhere: *Gigi*, *Oklahoma!*, *My Fair Lady* and *Pal Joey*, all giving more pleasure to more people than all the contemporary dramas which soon lose their colour, flowering for a day, then vanishing. Sadness is expressed in that no one at the moment seems capable of writing such joyous, unforgettable shows. It pays tribute to the talents of Rodgers and Hammerstein, Lorenz Hart, Lerner and Loewe, Jerome Kern, Cole Porter, the Gershwin brothers – how much bleaker the twentieth century would have been without them, grateful to them while waiting for somebody new who *can* write the sort of shows and songs described above.

In the decade following 'Thank Heavens', the West End had its flops and successes, some in the latter category having made millions since for the writers. Yet they have a common denominator – they contain one or, at best, two memorable tunes, whereas the writers listed in 'Thank Heavens' (plus some more I can readily call to mind) gave us musicals absolutely *overflowing* with easily and long-remembered hit songs, not just one or two. Songs which I believe will prove to be imperishable.

So there you have it, Mister Would-be Songsmith; who better to emulate than such eminent writers – craftsmen all. Even assuming that you do have real talent, the chances of making it on a part-time basis are a million-to-one against. To make any impact one needs to make frequent personal contacts with those who matter – contacts which occur through the natural circulation and movement in a working musician's life. Had I been aware back in 1946, of the Gulliver-like strides I would take, then my story might have been a vastly different one. All too easy, of course, to be wise after the event. An awareness and realisation that came too late. The newly-sown perennials in the English country garden of musical colour became uprooted while in bud, replaced by the fashion flowers – standards and a proliferation of hybrid *musicale vulgaris* – also destined to bloom and fade quickly.

Here, it is fitting to recall an old clip from a national daily. A picture of would-be songwriter, one Geoff O'Neill (about my age, I would guess) holding an armful of manuscripts, just a few of more than five hundred songs and three musical plays he had written over a period of twenty years. Unhappily, *none* was ever printed, published or played! Until that moment I had reckoned myself to be well in the running for the MOST UNSUCCESSFUL WRITER AWARD! Now, looking back at my track record and the fifty-odd songs and a couple of dozen orchestral items which represent twenty-five years' output, my achievement, albeit modest, when compared to that luckless writer reads like a super success story.

Hope of getting commercial recordings and establishing some of the new light music works ended when the doors closed irrevocably on the Repertoire Rehearsal Scheme in 1973. Through my evaluation of the variation and diversity which light music offers, that which was intended to be a pleasantly conducted musical journey became, in common with other writers, a fight for survival, caught up in a dedicated and enthusiastic crusade. Remembering that there were several hundred items used or promoted through the scheme, their abandonment in favour of pop constituted rejection of *all* composers, regardless of status – pros and semipros, known and unknown, veterans and beginners. For the record, nevertheless, I find that my works clocked up well over one hundred broadcasts despite the constant withdrawal of suitable programmes. Additionally, about half as much again were broadcast through the medium of TV and local radio. Nowadays, royalties emanate from an entirely different source. Amazingly, pieces written in the late fifties are being chosen for use in two recent films, some TV commercials and for a double audio cassette of Enid Blyton's *The Famous Five* series. And the royalties far outstrip those paid for BBC radio spots – far less hassle too! I also did an hour long chat programme on Radio Kent which included fourteen pieces of mine – a mixture of orchestral items and songs.

I believe my criticisms of Auntie Beeb comprise a fair, accurate and valid assessment, confined as they are to the preponderance of pop, lack of new light music by the living composer and of local radio. Like a nephew being invited so many times to afternoon tea, I only got the cucumber sandwiches, never being offered the strawberries and cream! (All say 'Aaaaah' and cue violins!)

Obviously, listeners' requests are limited to the music dispensed by the Beeb and commercial radio stations, principally through commercial recordings. So there's a mighty lot of music denied the listener which, as the old song has it, will not be going 'around and around and coming out here' simply because it hasn't been commercially recorded, much of it still-born or not heard enough to be considered for survival. Pop and nostalgia, cheaper to produce, easier to sell, equals profitability.

The Radio Times, July 1992 contained a special report on the future of Radio 3. 'Going downmarket' was the expression used to describe programmes which would have a "broader, lighter appeal – shorter pieces, crisply presented". Not the right expression, I fear. One doesn't necessarily go downmarket in order to gain broader appeal.

I wrote, enclosed a cassette, admitting my scepticism. I was right. Adrian Thomas replied: 'You are right in your general assessment. I have very much enjoyed your cassette, but regret our brief does not at the moment cover the lighter side of the repertoire as represented by your own music.' So much for all the hype! The Beeb's attitude towards light music is as uncompromising and rigid as ever.

Add to this the contemporary music publishers who are nothing more than accountants and bookkeepers with no sense for genuine talent and you have a rapidly diminishing supply of standard music. We are left with just a record business overwhelmingly biased in favour of the teenage market, a huge proportion being cacophonous, illiterate rubbish.

CHAPTER THIRTY-FIVE

CODA

Four years ago I began devoting my musical services almost exclusively to charitable events and causes. Much of this stemmed from TARA (Thanet Active Retirement Association), after Olive and I took up membership. Not unusually there were differences, cliques, sniping, petty jealousies and splinter groups within; too many people who, despite their age, still had not learned that life is too short to go on nursing past grievances, forever 'a-fussin', a-fightin' and a-feudin'.

Nevertheless, I managed to unite half a dozen ladies, who until then had operated independently as The Cameos, with a similar number of men, separately known as The Loose Ends, the end-product being a fifty-minute show (which we changed each year) providing entertainment at residential homes, day centres and church halls for various clubs and organisations, the elderly, the infirm and the blind. Not a pretty sight – the Zimmer frames, the walking sticks, wheelchairs and hearing aids. A sober reminder of how fortunate we are to still be reasonably healthy and, above all, mobile. There but for the grace of God...

Arriving at one such venue and finding it deserted save for the matron and a few staff, I was reminded of the forces' jibe about ENSA – 'Every Night Something Atrocious'. I turned to George (a colleague and ex-journalist, who shared my zest for writing and interest in all forms of music) and said, "Hey, someone must have told them we were coming!"

The largest sums raised emanated from the annual performances of a full-length show at the Broadstairs Pavilion. Since The Grand Ballroom closed, the Pavilion has had to 'double' for dancing too, but as it was built sixty years ago, intended for just concerts, its capacity is limited. Two annual functions which I have done for many years now are the Dickens Ball at the end of the Festival, and New Year's Eve for the Dickens Fellowship, when we dig out from the archives polkas, a couple of Strauss waltzes and the 'Sir Roger de Coverley'. After all those years playing at West End hotels for functions with an ambience that reeked of elegance and style – such swish venues – it was a harkening back not only to wartime RAF concert party days,

210

but also to humble beginnings: 1936, memorial halls, church halls –
all unglamorous local places. Déjà vu!

My musical training began at the age of eight, strictly classical for
several years, then moved on to all other forms of music – invaluable
training which had bred versatility, a broad-based appreciation and
provided a safeguard against elitism. No, I'm not too proud to
rehearse, encourage and accompany the less talented but enthusiastic
performers. Indeed, subtle nudging and suggestion brought results; a
lively and dedicated company. Yes, the wheel has turned full circle
and so much has happened in the intervening years, years which seem
to get shorter and shorter as one grows older. Years of the
razzmatazz twenties; swing; jitterbug; rock and roll and the twist.
Years when ringing the changes, moving with the times, albeit very
selectively, came easy. Years of revolution in popular music with the
appearance of electronics, synthesisers, digital recording. Years
which coincided with a take-over by the affluent, teenaged population
with full employment, the vote at eighteen, the permissive society,
hippies, drop-outs and flower power, and pirate radio...

Rubberlips Jagger was violently protesting 'I Can't Get No
Satisfaction'. He should have joined the Dave Clark Five, that filthy,
lecherous, lucky lot who undoubtedly were deriving great satisfaction
from 'Feeling Glad All Over'. And we were constantly assured by
the gabblers of trivia, the DJs, that it was all FAB! *Their* good old
days? Looking back, it's amusing to find that the sixties and seventies
doggerel now sounds melodic when compared to the atavistic,
diabolical rubbish of the last decade or so, which seemed to worsen
with the advent of the equally trashy video. *Top of the Pops*?
Financially yes. Musically no! The pits!

Going back even further there are, for me, fondly remembered
song-associations, twisted tune titles and fun lines, mostly in the
'oldies' which, near the end of the evening, are bound to have people
singing as they dance. I love to hear that, and I so often did on so
many gigs. And, second only to light music, was the delight and
pleasure derived from music in the Latin American idiom –
'Fascinatin' Rhythms' indeed.

That sixties hit (in which the writers, David and Bacharach, threw
out every rule in the songwriting book by constantly changing the time
signatures), 'Anyone Who Had A Heart', became topically twisted –
'Anyone For Purple Hearts?' as was 'The Bridges Of Paris'. The

first line, also typical of the days of the permissive society: 'How would you like to be, upstairs in bed with me?' In *Hello, Dolly!* 'You're looking swell, Dolly' (aside) 'Hello, what's she been up to?' and 'I hear the band playing and the room swaying', (aside) 'Brahms and Liszt again!' As for 'Save Your Kisses For Me', that was warped into 'Save Your Missus For Me!' Ideas for awarding spot prizes at dances produced light-hearted invitations like 'The first lady to reach me wearing a bingo dress' (eyes down, look in!).

'Happy Birthday' and 'The Anniversary Waltz' crop up most frequently, a request for the latter by a couple celebrating their fortieth year of marriage drawing the realistic comment that 'Help Me Make It Through The Night' would be more appropriate! Fond memories of how we at No.16 would tease Millie about boyfriend Jim, idolised in her favourite songs, 'My Wonderful One' and also from *The Chocolate Soldier*, the song 'My Hero'. And memories of Jim, who also played some nice piano, in his favourite waltz, 'Poem' – better known as 'Moonlight Madonna'.

I recall drummer Len Parrish saying, as we showed signs of flagging near the end of a typical long gig, six until perhaps one in the morning, "Last three over four, Auld Lang Syne, F'reezer, Head and Shoulders – pack up and go home!"

Translation: the last waltz, followed by 'Auld Lang Syne', then, 'For He's A Jolly Good Fellow; and the first six bars only of the national anthem.

A page in Queen Victoria's daily journal reads: 'I like to be employed. I hate being idle.' Had I kept a diary, it would have read: 'I hate being idle. I like to be *usefully* employed.' I like to gain some pleasure and satisfaction from my labours, A visible or audible end-product, as in gardening, painting, home decorating or music. So Father Time still hustles me, but the years of *sempre prestissimo* and *agitato* are more and more being replaced by *andante tranquillo*.

Memories were also revived when Olive and I recently attended a reunion of the WAAF at her old camp, Chicksands, down by the riverside, at Bedford. As expected, it had all changed beyond recognition, save for the ancient priory which Friends of Chicksands Priory were strenuously striving to preserve. An RAF unit was now dominated by the USAAF, and children were playing baseball in two fenced-off compounds!

Similar was our trip to Blackpool. The Tower and Ballroom complex was now a ghastly hotch-potch of post-war architecture; places of so-called entertainment blaring pop muzak; karaoke and George Formby ditties abounded amid the clanking of the familiar sea-front trams; and the Wolesley Road houses where we were billeted are now converted to tatty holiday flatlets.

Still razzmatazz but, as expected, 1993 style didn't appeal. Olive and I took refuge in Stanley Park and the Lake District.

And my 'Golden Mile' no doubt is doomed to obscurity even though 'I Do Like to be Beside the Seaside' with its 'brass band playing tiddly-om-pom-pom' is way out of touch with today's image.

Happy is the man whose hobby is his work! To quote Mister Irving Berlin, 'I don't know where I read it'; and the same applies to another quotation: 'All artistic occupations are financially hazardous.' But my experiences in the post-war years of publishing and playing and again since 1982 have proven the validity of the first quotation, but not the second. In-between years represented a long, dualistic sojourn, contrasting twin journeys, sometimes exhausting, yet exhilarating. Thanks to being blessed with robust health and an abundance of energy and stamina, I survived. Here it is apposite to quote the surprise element in a letter dated 3rd December, 1971 from the secretary of the Light Music Society, in reply to my membership application:

> ...it is unusual to have associate members who are so actively engaged in music and are members of the MU, the ACCS and the PRS, but, if at present, you also have income from another source, that puts you in the associate category. You will be hearing direct from the treasurer, who will send you your membership card, effective from 22.11.71.

An appropriate date, I thought, it being St Cecilia's Day – the patron saint of music. Abundant proof that one can attain professionalism in the fiercely competitive music world without always doing it full-time. Just as there are amateurs and semi-pros who excel, conversely there are not a few pros I have met who fall far short of professional standard and ability; plenty of semi-pros could run rings round them. Professionalism is therefore defined only by the standard, the dedication and approach to music-making. Many operatic societies long ago dropped the word 'amateur' because the term appears to cast some doubt on their standards of professionalism. Locally, the Margate Operatic Society has presented many splendid productions, this year's *Showtime* being the twenty-first anniversary of the series. From a current local rag:

> Amateur doesn't have to mean unprofessional, as Margate Operatic Society prove, year in year out, with their summer and autumn productions. The beauty of seeing one of their shows is that you get a first-class performance at second-class prices.

And one cannot always equate money with ability. There are those who have failed to make a 'pile' because of shyness or a retiring nature, even perhaps modesty. Yet there are others, no more gifted musically, who make (to use a phrase from the Mozart article,) much more than eine kleine dollar! In a lifetime of music-making, I am so very glad and happy that I was around in those earlier halcyon days (even if I too was sometimes guilty of fumbling four bars in!), contributing to popular music's heyday, with especial affection for the decades of the thirties, forties and fifties, never to be equalled.

It will soon be time for me too to 'pack up and go home'. But, before I do, it would be remiss of me to close without reference to the book about my idol, the Cole Porter biography, *The Life That Late He Led*, which I read a couple of years ago, discovering some intriguing song construction parallels. For example, the way he created the original melody of a song as if it were orchestrated; that's the way I hear it in my mind – something which no doubt rubbed off on me from arranger Art Strauss. Next, a similarity with 'Candlelight' which I had stashed away for years until an opportunity presented itself for full exploitation, even though in no way does it match 'Anything Goes', which Cole never entirely discarded, expanding it into a hit song and show, *twenty years on*! His biographer, George Ellis, writes that the lyrics troubled Cole more than the music. Me too! Finally, there is the conflict of wanting public acclaim, but sometimes just wishing to please oneself and the public be damned. Something which matches my mention of writing non-run-of-the-mill songs, just for the cussedness of it and the charts be damned! Even now, I still find Lerner and Loewe's transformation of Shaw's *Pygmalion* into the wonderful musical *My Fair Lady* an outstanding achievement. But if that presented a daunting challenge to the writers, what of Cole's *single-handed* treatment of Shakespeare's *The Taming Of The Shrew*, transforming it into the highly successful *Kiss Me, Kate*? For me, the way in which Shakespeare was merged, in words and music, with the sounds of Broadway was nothing short of magic, pure genius, not forgetting, of course, Cole's vast linguistic mastery, including his education in Latin and Greek. Yes, Mr Porter, head and shoulders above the rest; if I had written your biography, the title would have been *You're The Top*.

Not Verona or Padua, but to Venice, with the words to a love duet – the most recent song written (with a demo which would have been entered for Eurovision had the format, as I wrote earlier, not been changed). But, like 'Anything Goes' and 'Candlelight', it won't be discarded. It'll fit 'another op'ning, another show' some time, somewhere. Fittingly, in a twelve-eight barcarole fashion, complete with mandolins, this is romantic Venice as it used to be; before the smells, the pollution and the noisy petrol and diesel-powered craft threatening to outnumber the gondolas. And when you were most unlikely to have just one cornetto snatched from your hand! A love duet with a happy ending.

MANDOLINS MAKING MUSIC

Boy: Venice in June, romantic dangers.
Girl: Calling the tune, making lovers of strangers.
Both: Gondolas gliding by, the moon was riding high
                               above,
        Mandolins making music while we were making
                               love.

Boy: We said farewell, fate closed the door on us.
Girl: How could we tell this date was in store for us?
Both: Never dreaming our paths would meet,
        Hearts skip a beat once more for us.
        Mandolins making music while we were making
                               love.

Boy: Drifting and dreaming, time had no meaning.
           Soft were the nights, the lights, your eyes,
           Your lips – Venetian wine.
Girl: Midsummer madness, carnival magic,
Both: Two lonely people playing Harlequin and
                           Columbine.

Boy: Venice in June, choosing our parts again.
Girl: Recalling the tune, losing our hearts again.
Both: For ever the scene is set, where first we met.
           How could we forget?
           Mandolins making music while we were making
                       love,
           Mandolins making music while we were making
                       love.

Whatever one's personal taste in music – the greatest and often immortal at the top or, at the bottom of the heap, that designed to make the fast buck – it must be apparent that, in between, there is so much music which is pleasing to its composer, aspiring not to profound heights, nor stooping to satisfy the lowest common denominator. Accepted and likeable, yet capable of becoming established and even making respectable sales over the years. My training and ability has not fitted me for the higher plane; nor do I seek to insult the intelligence of others or affront my own musical sensibilities with a load of rubbish. My melodies may have fallen constantly on deaf ears, even *tin* ears sometimes!

I have no regrets about my self-imposed MOR role, even if 'Melodies of Mine' becomes my epitaph. A folk song or a symphony; from Bach to Bacharach; Schubert to Sondheim; Farnon to Franck *et al* – they all have their particular appeal. That I have trodden on a few toes, I do not doubt. Tough! By the same token, hopefully, my heartfelt expressions may have broadened the musical appreciation of others who do not listen with their feet.

A REPRISE OF 'LIFE' ending...

And so the final curtain falls – for you there are no
                                    curtain calls,
The greatest show goes on, but you are 'resting' now.
And then they rate you 'great' but it's too late – and
                                    how!
But then, that's life, I guess. Yes, that's life, I guess.
Yes, that's life, that's life –
The greatest show on earth!

Leopold Stokowski has the last word:
'Music comes from the heart and returns to the heart.'

I hope you enjoyed it, Dee.
Love,
Bill.

INDEX